THE SHIPYARD AGENT

THE SHIPYARD AGENT

AUGUSTA CLAWSON
AND THE WOMEN WELDERS OF WORLD WAR II

BEVERLY LIONBERGER HODGINS

Essex, Connecticut

An imprint of The Globe Pequot Publishing Group, Inc.
64 South Main St.
Essex, CT 06426
www.GlobePequot.com

Copyright © 2026 by Beverly Lionberger Hodgins
Cover image of shipyard at night © *The Oregonian*. All rights reserved. Used with permission.

All rights reserved. No part of this book may be reproduced in any form or by any electronic or mechanical means, including information storage and retrieval systems, without written permission from the publisher, except by a reviewer who may quote passages in a review.

British Library Cataloguing in Publication Information available

Library of Congress Cataloging-in-Publication Data available
ISBN 9781493087631 (paperback) | ISBN 9781493087648 (epub)

To Augusta and all the shipyard gals . . . who wore boots on their feet, leather on their backs, soot on their faces, and burns on their skin, with pride in their hearts because they helped save—and change—the world.

CONTENTS

Author's Note ix
Introduction 1

CHAPTER 1: A Nation's Call for Help 5
CHAPTER 2: Augusta Clawson—Until War's End 21
CHAPTER 3: Henry's Pacific Shipyards 37
CHAPTER 4: Who Was Henry John Kaiser? 55
CHAPTER 5: Housing Shipyard Workers 65
CHAPTER 6: Celebrated Childcare Center 75
CHAPTER 7: Training Women to Weld 81
CHAPTER 8: Hazards in the Hulls 91
CHAPTER 9: X-Ray and Asbestos Perils Exposed 107
CHAPTER 10: Medical Care for All 115
CHAPTER 11: Men vs. Women Welders 123
CHAPTER 12: A Tight Seam of Support 131
CHAPTER 13: Racism in the Yards 141
CHAPTER 14: A Fractured Failure and a Comeback 153
CHAPTER 15: Best Woman Welder in the World 161
CHAPTER 16: Augusta Clawson—Beyond War's End 169

Notes 189
Bibliography 205
Acknowledgments 217
Index 221
About the Author 233

AUTHOR'S NOTE

Several years ago, while conducting research at the Oregon Historical Society Research Library in Portland, Oregon, I entered the name "Lionberger" in the general search bar. One name appeared: that of Mabel Lionberger, my grandaunt by marriage. Up popped a photograph showing her decked out in a complete welder's outfit, soot smeared across her face. Having been removed from her by generations and later geographically, I'd not heard about her war production contribution. I was hooked. I wanted to know more about her experience of working as a woman welder in a shipyard during World War II. The result of that discovery, along with the subsequent discovery of a woman named Augusta Clawson, is this book.

While researching Augusta Clawson—and after sending an email questionnaire to my extended family—I discovered several female family members who were involved in the war effort in various ways, including in the same way as Augusta was, as a welder in a shipyard.

The following effort lists five women from my extended family who were engaged during World War II in work connected directly to shipbuilding in the Portland, Oregon, and Vancouver, Washington, area.

Mabel Beatrice (Shriver) Lionberger, my grandaunt, was forty-two years old when she was employed as a welder at Henry J. Kaiser's Oregon Shipbuilding Corporation (OSC) located in Portland's St. John's district. Sharp as a tack and an excellent welder, she received accolades for her work. I doubt that Mabel expected to become a bit of a celebrity when she entered shipyard work. But she was featured in the *Oregon Journal* newspaper in January 1942, where a photograph captured Mabel and another woman welder reading a telegram at the desk of their supervisor. The telegram, and he, were inviting the women to compete in the Best Woman Welder in the World competition. Mabel agreed to compete and placed well at the OSC level. That was important enough that her family-written obituary proudly announces she placed second in the competition.

Jean Marsolie (Neil) Johnson, my first cousin once removed, was twenty-two when she worked as a welder at Commercial Iron Works (CIW) on Ross Island, situated in the Willamette River south of Portland's city center. Her mother, Clara, who worked as a burner at the same shipyard, had convinced her to try shipyard work.

"And so, I went down, and I liked welding," said Jean. "I got the hang of it pretty quick. I loved it" [working at the shipyard], Jean added, "busy, busy, busy." When I asked her if she participated in the contest held to find the best woman welder, she stated—as frank and to the point as ever—"We didn't have time for contests!"

A cousin of my mother, Elaine, I knew her as *Aunt* Jean. Shortly before her death at the age of ninety-three, she told the story of meeting her leadman at the shipyard, Rudolph Johnson. Jean brightly described how—after becoming acquainted through their work—they one day commiserated over being stood up by their respective dates and decided to go out with each other instead. Soon, sweet Jean and Rudy fell in love and quietly married. Jean continued to work at the shipyard until pregnant with their first child. She would use her welding skills often on the farm in Bonners Ferry, Idaho, where they settled after the war.

Clara Mae (Witcraft) Neil Gadot Palmer, my grandaunt, worked as a burner. At forty-five, Clara was an attractive and cheerful woman with a twinkle in her eye, and one of my favorite people from childhood. It was during general research that I discovered a document upon which Clara listed her occupation as "burner at shipyards." She likely wielded an acetylene torch in her job to cut and shape the steel that would be welded aboard during the construction of a ship. Her welder daughter, Jean, could have easily been handed some of her mother Clara's work.

E. Louise (Hooton) Lionberger Emmons Reed, my grandmother, was a widow who married her second husband during the war and who would outlive one more. In late September 1945, when she was forty-eight years old, she wrote to my father, Dean. President Harry S. Truman, serving since the April death of President Roosevelt, had announced the end of World War II, following the surrender of Japan. To say the United States was struggling economically is probably a most gross of understatements. Dean was still away serving in the Merchant Marine, sending money home. "I'm taking care of a little neighbor girl," Louise wrote to her son, "whose mother works at the shipyard. She pays me $1.00 per day. Said she didn't know how long it would be before she would be laid off—as a great many are losing their jobs now at the shipyards."

Betty May Lionberger, my first cousin once removed, was a friendly and fun older cousin whom I remember visiting on her family's ranch in White Salmon, Washington. I discovered that at the age of twenty-two, she'd been listed in the 1943 Portland city directory with her occupation described as "machine operator." Her employer was listed only as "IFMCo," undoubtedly the Iron Fireman Manufacturing Company (IFMC), a company that in 1943 was "instrumental in building engines and parts for the Liberty Ships produced at the Kaiser Shipyard."

During this time, Betty lived with my grandaunt, Eva Ruth (Landis) Lionberger, whose husband Harold was away serving in the military. This arrangement between my father's cousin and our aunt reflected the situation of many war wives as well as single women who decided to live with other women and their children during the war years, thereby reducing each woman's individual cost of living. And, I imagine, offering additional benefits such as the support and comfort of a family-like environment.

Augusta's life as revealed over the course of my research provided an intimate look into the experiences these women in my family would have likely had during World War II. In the end, our family was fortunate—everyone came home.

INTRODUCTION

Despite experiencing great personal loss not once but twice before reaching school age, and again at the age of thirteen, stoic Augusta Holmes Clawson would mature—perhaps in part because of those experiences—into an intelligent, discerning, and enterprising woman. She seemed determined to contribute to society during her lifetime—especially to the society of women working in vocational positions outside of the traditional home.

Fiercely independent, she never married and once wrote when asked the name of her spouse that she "never found one." Surrounded by great friends and mentors, and by fulfilling that role for others, she must have felt immense satisfaction from all that she accomplished before she died in her ninety-third year.

A well-educated—some would declare intellectual genius—graduate of Vassar College, Augusta H. Clawson added a master's degree in personnel administration from New York University to her curriculum vitae a decade later. In the interim, still a young woman, she co-owned a bookstore in her hometown of Plainfield, New Jersey.

As the world was being overwhelmed nation by nation with news of the ever-growing conflict that became World War II—having already spent thirteen years in teaching and supervisory roles at a girls' vocational school—Augusta had gained skills that she felt prepared her to be of service. At the end of 1941 came a harsh awakening for American citizens hoping to cling to neutrality. After the catastrophe that descended on battleship row in Hawaii's Pearl Harbor, they would be needed in the fight, and millions wanted to defend their free country.

The Shipyard Agent

Two days after the shocking ambush, President Franklin Delano Roosevelt gravely addressed America's citizens using his familiar *fireside chat* approach, which included this statement as his voice broadcast across the nation's radio waves: "We must share together the bad news and the good news, the defeats and the victories—the changing fortunes of war."

Surely Augusta listened to the president's radio address along with the rest of the country. "We are all in it . . ." How appropriate then that she, unafraid but with measured conviction, would agree to be "in it" by becoming a spy. Not a spy in the usual sense of the word, but as an agent of change in the world of women working in vocations.

Ever active in her community through various social, service, and literary clubs, in 1943, with a watchful eye, she immersed herself into the pool of shipyard workers in the Pacific Northwest. After undergoing shipyard training, she worked as a welder beside other women welders at Swan Island Shipyard in Portland, Oregon, for nearly two months.

During her brief but significant mission, Augusta kept a detailed accounting of her experiences. At the end of every shift, she sat in front of a typewriter in her room. Probably with aching hands, she recorded her experiences, documenting her routine *before* work—breakfast at the counter of the Park Avenue Grill—*during*—hot, demanding work alongside her friend called Missouri—and *after*—starting with her shipyard bus ride back to the city center and her room. Augusta wrote about everything concerning the training and work environment as well as the recurring departure of women welders from the shipyard, plinking word after word onto a sheet of paper. Her accumulation of frank and honest story about her experience as a welder—the truth as only a woman welder could tell it—was published by Penguin Books in 1944 under the title *Shipyard Diary of a Woman Welder*.

Little did women welders and women in other war production jobs know that not only did this new and strangely enticing work provide support to the war effort, but it would also immediately, albeit begrudgingly to some, raise the perceived value of women working outside of the home. The results of the experiences of these women welders—along with those experiences of women in myriad other war-production-related

Introduction

jobs—proved a woman could do a man's job. The evidence of the work of women in industry in World War II would later bolster the efforts of women not yet born in their struggle for equality in the workplace.

Yet many women employees inside the Yard at Swan Island were quitting shortly after training, unable or unwilling to cope with the work of a shipyard, especially welding. Enter Agent Clawson. As a special agent from the Training Women for War Production Vocational Division of the US Office of Education in Washington, DC, Augusta would observe firsthand the shipyard work to determine why the women were quitting and make recommendations for improvements. She would witness these emboldened, vigorous women playing an invaluable role in the victories achieved by the United States during World War II. Not only in the Pacific Northwest, but also across the nation to the Gulf Coast and up the Eastern seaboard, women welders worked hard, often at a fever pitch, proving their stamina inside the nation's shipyards. They and their male cohorts assembled a record number of ships—behemoths that were sent with confidence, and perhaps a wish and a prayer, to carry American men to war.

Some dubbed these women *Winnie the Welder*, and *Wanda* or *Wendy the Welder*—or referred to them as *welderettes*—as though the work they did was somehow a smaller, more feminine version, an imitation, or lessening of the work done by men. But there was nothing feminine about the work that women welders performed, which was identical to the exacting, difficult, and exhausting work performed by men who were welders. Women of all ages left their jobs as waitresses, grocery clerks, secretaries, and domestic laborers to work in the shipyards. As did stay-at-home mothers, who delivered their babes-in-arms to day-care centers or to helpful, willing neighbors or relatives so they could report to work building ships to get the men-at-arms to sea and on to distant shores.

Women welders endured great discomfort from the welding hood, nerve-racking noise, burns from hot slag and sparks, and respiratory problems from fumes inside the hulls where they worked. They suffered debilitating muscle and joint pain from repetitive motion and the awkward overhead welding position. Plus, some were demeaned by the sometimes-resentful male instructor as they trained, and some were harassed sexually. Despite that, and as is often common within workplaces, camaraderie developed among those working closely together in the shipyards, and for Augusta, especially woman-to-woman.

Although the work was dirty and wearying, most of these women prevailed. Employing women in the shipyards kept the yards viable and productive. These women worked in lieu of the men who left to serve in the military and alongside those who remained. Some men chose to work in the shipyards if unable to join the military. Others served in the armed forces abroad, returned home, and then as veterans who had completed their service also entered shipyard production work.

Those brave women who reported from home to sign up for shipyard work, walking into the shipyards in civilian clothes, quickly became accustomed to a different wardrobe and a different mindset. They likely did not realize how important an impact their sacrifices at work would make on women of coming generations. These patriotic, determined women planted seeds during the war by simply doing what the country needed done to remain a free country, accepting the work of men and discovering they could, indeed, handle the work. Yet two decades would pass before the nation would begin to witness growth that would lead to extraordinary and powerful, decades-long social movements aimed at opening the eyes and minds of the nation to discrimination against women in the jobs market, and in society in general.

During those decades, Augusta Holmes Clawson would continue to make extraordinary contributions to the betterment of women, especially in the vocational workforce.

NOTE: To keep true to this story and the voices of the storytellers of World War II, the term *Negro* has been used as well as the terms *African American* or *Black*, and the term *Indian* has been used as well as the term *Native American*.

NOTE: The title of the shipyard in-house publication, *Bos'n's Whistle*, may also be spelled as *Bosn's Whistle*, or as *Bo's'n's Whistle*, depending upon the issue being cited, because the spelling alternated throughout the duration of publication.

Chapter One

A NATION'S CALL FOR HELP

"We are now in this war. We are all in it all the way. Every single man, woman and child is a partner in the most tremendous undertaking of our American history. We must share together the bad news and the good news, the defeats and the victories—the changing fortunes of war."
President Franklin D. Roosevelt
Fireside Address to the Nation
December 9, 1941

Admiral Chester W. Nimitz, US Navy, also addressed the country's civilian citizens, "My fellow Americans: I ask your help. On behalf of all your fighting sons, brothers, and husbands whom I command in the Pacific. I ask that every skilled man and woman in America who can work in a shipyard volunteer immediately."[1]

Not to be outdone, General Dwight D. Eisenhower queried, "Who are the women who will help retain the needed manpower for the production battle at home? Who are the women who will help fight our country's war?" Who are they, he asked. Soon he would know who they were. Every willing woman from every demographic in America.[2]

"The colonel's lady and Judy O'Grady are sisters under the welder's hood," remarked Mrs. Jane Martin, a personnel expert at Portland, Oregon's shipyards, to reporter Fred Hampson. Quoted in the August 1943 *Statesman Journal* of Salem, Oregon, Martin believed the women in the shipyards were "good workers, willing, deft and, usually, with a fair complement of ingenuity." She described the various prewar positions of women who she knew were employed at the shipyards: "There is a woman truck driver who used to be an x-ray technician. A girl in one of the warehouses speaks seven languages, which she didn't learn hanging around the car barns. There is an assembly checker with a Ph.D. and a scaler who used to sing in light operas. A former lawyer is in the yard."

Martin added that she "doesn't know of any real colonel's wives in local shipyards, although she wouldn't be surprised. (You never know who they turn out to be.)" Might this have been a reference to the secret presence of a government agent inside the Swan Island Shipyard a few months earlier? Martin would have been one of the few people who knew the truth about Augusta Clawson's identity.[3]

On June 13, 1942, the Office of War Information (OWI) was created by executive order. Its purpose was to guide the "press, radio, motion picture, and other . . . information programs . . . to facilitate the development of an informed and intelligent understanding, at home and abroad of the status and progress of the war effort."

That same year, the OWI addressed the subject of women working in industry by publishing a booklet titled, "War Jobs for Women." Again, the subject matter in the booklet addressed the war effort by stating: "Every American woman wants to help win the war." General Eisenhower had been concerned about how to "retain the needed manpower." The OWI believed, "The problem is how and where to fit into that big word which is daily growing bigger—womanpower." The report surmised that it was the experience of being able to produce "some physical thing which will help win the war" that was enticing well-educated women to enter war production. The report further stated: "They argue that they can work with their heads later on, and that while their country needs such service in order that freedom can go on in the world, they will earn a living with their hands and consider it a worthwhile part of their life experience." This was followed by a description of war industries employing women:

> Aircraft and Parts; Small Arms and Artillery Ammunition; Agriculture and Canning; Communications; Chemicals (industrial); Chemical Products; Electrical Machinery; Firearms, Guns, Gas

Masks, Parachutes; Machinery; Machine Tool and Machine Shops; Radio Parts and Equipment; Rubber Goods (industrial); Scientific and Professional Instruments, Photographic Apparatus and Optical Goods; Surgical, Medical, and Dental Instruments and Supplies; Ship and Boat Building and Repairing; Sighting and Fire Control Equipment; Tank and Auto Parts and Equipment; Transportation; Utilities; Oil Refineries; Mines; Lumber and Saw Mills.[4]

Portland, Oregon, and Vancouver, Washington, concentrated on the ship and boat building and repair industry. These two northwest cities, divided by the powerful Columbia River roiling beneath the Interstate Bridge, focused on recruiting large numbers of women from all walks of life to the shipyards industrialist Henry J. Kaiser built there. These were the Oregon Shipbuilding Corporation (known locally as Oregonship) located at the confluence of the Columbia and Willamette rivers in the St. John's neighborhood, the Swan Island Shipyard in Portland situated on its island in the Willamette River, and the Kaiser Vancouver Shipyard in Vancouver, Washington, on the banks of the Columbia River.

The Portland–Vancouver area became known as having surpassed all other shipbuilding regions in the country in answering the call of leaders such as President Roosevelt, Admiral Nimitz, and General Eisenhower. But before that could have happened, the campaign to bring workers to the shipyards in the Pacific Northwest needed to succeed for several reasons. History would prove that the results of this campaign were far-reaching and would permanently change the literal, racial, and economic landscape of the area.

It was said that "nowhere in the Northwest, other than Seattle, did it [the war] so completely restructure community as in the Vancouver-Portland area."[5]

OWI's push to inform citizens of the war effort and to send a persuasive call to women across the country included the use of a familiar visual device. For there were shoes left standing by men gone to war. Women were desperately needed to fill them.

Because it was the age of pinup girls, when most believed a woman's place was in the home, the government employed a pinup-girl-glamorous approach in their recruitment drive to ramp up stateside war production work. These attempts in the form of boldly designed posters could be seen embellishing walls throughout America's cities.

One such poster presents a woman with lovely auburn hair, rosy cheeks, and full lips. Her shining hair rests on the lapel of her coat. With her nails polished red, a wedding band encircles her finger. Her hands clutch to her heart several V-mail from her serviceman husband. V-mail was the short name for Army Micro Photographic Mail Service. Created to move mail as quickly as possible from servicemen and women overseas back to the states, and vice versa, V-mail was "a special form . . . which permits the letter to be photographed in microfilm." Much easier to transport, the small microfilm images were reproduced upon arrival and then delivered.[6]

Beneath the poster's attractive image are the words "Longing won't bring him back sooner . . . Get a War Job! See Your U.S. Employment Service." It was a straightforward message for the women of America, which could have been interpreted, "Snap out of it! Get to work!" Their help was needed to win the war.

It soon became apparent to anyone working inside a shipyard that a war job would not be an attractive job and the women who accepted war work would spend their days, and possibly their nights, looking nothing like the woman on the poster.

La Verne Bradley, in her *National Geographic Magazine* article, "Women at Work," agreed: "These aren't the glamour jobs—but they're collateral to victory."[7]

Join Us in a Victory Job beckons another poster, its words framing an image of six women standing in a line. Four women are dressed in uniforms of the various branches of the armed forces, one is wearing a nurse's uniform, and at the front of the line stands a woman wearing bib overalls over a yellow blouse, her dark hair tied up in a scarf. Is it a telling message that the woman representing the home front war work is at the front of the line? Other poster slogans read: *Do the job he left behind. We Can Do It; Soldiers without Guns; Good Work, Sister—We Never Figured You Could*

A Nation's Call for Help

Poster designed to persuade women to join the war effort through war work. "Longing won't bring him back sooner . . . Get a War Job!" Lawrence Nelson Wilbur, artist. United States War Manpower Commission, ca. 1944. ENOCH PRATT FREE LIBRARY, MARYLAND'S STATE LIBRARY RESOURCE CENTER.

Do a Man-Size Job! America's Women Have Met the Test; and *Help Bring Them Back to You! Find time for war work!*

These well-honed messages were aimed at America's able women.

Other posters, dramatic in every way, urged support for the soldiers and sailors fighting to keep the world free. A feeling of urgency came in the form of slogans under graphic images such as, *Think* (in bold print across Uncle Sam's top hat) *Production Means Life or Death* . . . (under which in very small red type . . . *'To Your Brother American Who May be*

Facing Death This Minute for You') . . . *Don't Lose One Minute—Work;* and *Must Win! Speed Up Production.* Some posters applied stark words and images that could certainly be interpreted as motivating in a guilt-inducing manner. One such motivator, positioned below one arm of a fat white cross supporting a soldier's empty helmet above a devastated battlefield, bore the words *Marks the* Extra *Day You Took Off.*

Various print publications were also engaged in the public campaign overseen by the OWI to urge women to work in war production. One example was a US Army weekly titled *Yank*. In 1945, photographer Private David Conover was sent on assignment by his captain, one Ronald Reagan, to photograph workers inside the Radioplane munitions factory in Burbank, California. His presence in the factory that day could be said to be responsible for changing the life of a young bride named Mrs. Norma Jeane Dougherty. Norma Jeane became Marilyn Monroe, famous model and legendary actress. The photographs taken of her at the factory were never used inside the rag called *Yank*. Yet taken as he was by her fresh-faced look, it was at Conover's suggestion she ought to try modeling that set Norma Jeane upon her path to stardom.[8]

Famous illustrator Norman Rockwell joined the cause of inspiring women to seek employment in war production work, creating an original image titled *Rosie the Riveter* as the cover art for the May 29, 1943, issue of *Saturday Evening Post*. Rockwell's image is not the Rosie the Riveter image most people associate with the name. That "We Can Do It" fist-raised image by illustrator J. Howard Miller was created, also in 1943, as a Westinghouse Company in-house campaign poster with the aim of boosting the number and the spirit of women recruited to work in the plant for the defense industry.

Instead, Rockwell used Mary Doyle Keefe, nineteen, as the model for his *Rosie*. He painted her image as a strong young woman in blue dungarees perched upon what appears to be a tree stump (stumps were used as seats in the shipyards by welders), holding a ham sandwich. Her lunchpail, labeled *Rosie*, supports her arm. Protective goggles rest upon her forehead against her drawn-up red hair, a face shield thrown back. A rivet gun lies across her lap with its air hose strung across, while she rests her feet in their dark penny loafers upon a disregarded book. Clearly the book is *Mein Kampf,* complete with a swastika. A large American flag is the background of this cover illustration of Rockwell's.

Mary Keefe was never a riveter—nor a welder—but a phone operator, nor was she as muscular as Rockwell depicted her, for which he later reportedly personally apologized. Keefe was said to remark after seeing the finished painting that she never actually saw a copy of *Mein Kampf* during the sitting. *Mein Kampf* beneath her feet ... the not-so-subtle message Norman Rockwell inserted in this painting.[9]

Women of the Pacific Northwest were no different than those across the rest of the nation. They took these messages seriously, eager to help stamp out the Axis powers however they might.

La Verne Bradley said it best in her concise article: "The balance of power rests in women's hands. Literally. Behind the whine of sawmills and roar of blast furnaces, the hammer of arsenals and thunder of machine shops—in shipyards, factories, foundries, slaughterhouses, and laboratories—women are manipulating the machinery of war."[10]

Some women reported to factories and became *Rosies* who riveted together fighter planes. Others sat at sewing machines stitching together parachutes or myriad other accessories for the armed forces. Such was the case at Jantzen Knitting Mills in Portland, Oregon, who were no exception when it came to a long-established profit-making business switching to war work. During those war years, Jantzen—internationally known manufacturer of swimsuits—developed an additional line of product: military items "to support the war effort, including sweaters, parachute bags, sleeping bags, [and] gas mask carriers," as well as a military version of swimsuits.

Bradley reported that some women swept up their hair in the red and white bandanas that identified them as Women Ordnance Workers (WOW), daily facing the dangers of working surrounded by ammunition and weapons. Still others enrolled in President Franklin D. Roosevelt's Works Progress Administration (WPA) classes in welding. Many women went directly to shipyard training centers, or to independent shops or schools employed for the cause by the US government.

Throughout industries and communities, various informal monikers were applied to women war production workers. Welders were tagged

The Shipyard Agent

The US Army poster "Soldiers Without Guns" illustrates women filling war jobs as office worker, welder, and factory worker. ADOLPH TREIDLER, ARTIST. UNITED STATES, 1944. PHOTOGRAPH. HTTPS://WWW.LOC.GOV/ITEM/2002719121/.

Winnies, *Wandas*, and *Wendys* or even *Rosies* (who were *not* welders), while in allied Great Britain, welders were simply called "fusion engineers."

Women might be called *Government Girls* if they worked in administration, *Betsy the Burner* if their skill was burning through steel with an oxy-acetylene torch. And there were the *Rocket Girls* working secretly in Pasadena, California, to help develop and build rocket-fuel-propelled weapons.[11]

Even these many and varied roles already taken up by women could not fill the great need for shipyard laborers, craftsmen, and craftswomen. Still more hands were necessary on deck, so a nationwide search was

Unidentified woman burner using an acetylene torch to cut steel plates down to size outside the Oregon Shipbuilding Corporation plate shop, 1943. © *THE OREGONIAN*. ALL RIGHTS RESERVED. USED WITH PERMISSION. PHOTO FILE #2209.

conducted for individuals in need of work to come to the shipyards of Portland and Vancouver. There, Edgar Kaiser, Henry's son and shipyard manager, immediately conceived a program of recruitment, and he expected it to succeed.

The younger Kaiser implied as much in an issue of the *Medford Mail Tribune* in February of 1942: "Portland needs 10,000 new houses within walking distance of the shipyards, Edgar F. Kaiser, general manager of the Oregon Shipbuilding corporation, said yesterday." Then, during the spring, Edgar initiated his national recruitment campaign to raise the number of employees at the Kaisers' Swan Island, Oregonship, and Vancouver shipyards, "sending up to seventy-four recruiters across the nation to talk up Portland shipyard employment opportunities and to arrange for immediate train travel to Portland-Vancouver." The

Kaisers provided advance train fare to anyone willing to come, with the agreement that the amount of the fare would be deducted from employees' paychecks over time.[12]

In April, the *Medford Mail Tribune* highlighted the story of one woman who came to work on the machinery of war, and why. "Mrs. Mary C. Carroll," it was reported, "who has one son in the Philippines and supports three other children at home, put on her helmet today and entered the shipyards. It was a welder's helmet, and she is among the first women to enter production work at the Oregon Shipbuilding Corporation."

In the *Bo's'n's Whistle* dated May 26, 1944, a small article titled "First Woman Welder Finally Identified" appeared. Her name was Clara Furnold, another woman who had been encouraged by her husband to try welding at the shipyard. Clara had injured her foot early in her employment and was away when the reporter was searching for the first woman welder. Betty Olsen came with Clara and was the second woman welder to enter work at Swan Island's yard.[13]

Bradley believed she understood what drove women like Mary Carroll, Clara Furnold, and Betty Olsen to work in war production: "Mainly ... they are there because there *is* some man in service.... And they are fighting to keep the country running, to keep the world supplied, to get their man the stuff he needs so he can get through and get back."

During the World War II years, a woman's place would have been in the home if not for the nation's call for help. "I find it rather hard to work and keep up a home," wrote the author's grandaunt, Edith Lionberger Alkire, "but not too difficult. And I don't feel right about quitting my job until Germany is licked."[14]

In the Northwest at Swan Island, welder Lois Housman explained, "I felt like that was the only way I could help with the war." This was a sentiment that would be repeated many thousands of times by women working in a variety of defense industry jobs.[15]

Two months later, the *La Grande Observer* noted that many thousands of women were responding to the same call to war production work across the nation. The article began by declaring that war work "has dealt the sewing circle a severe blow." Describing the current work of women as "an inventory of industry itself," the article went on to say that women were "winding coils, assembling airplane engines, inspecting parts and instruments, operating milling machines, radial drills, turret lathes and drill presses . . . . [And were] crane operators, women welders, women flame cutters, women toolmakers—women everything."[16]

When autumn fell, the Kaiser Company was still gathering employees for all three shipyards. The *Herald and News* of Klamath Falls, Oregon, stated that women were needed to fill welding and sheet metal jobs, with women welders to be paid one dollar and twenty cents per hour while sheet metal helpers would receive ninety-five cents per hour. The article also declared that the housing situation for shipyard workers had eased with the construction of five hundred houses for families and a dormitory for single women.

"Within a year women made up 26.8 percent of the employees at the three Kaiser yards." During the week of October 16, 1943, that percentage would translate to 24,105 women, according to Robert R. La Du in his book, *Her Finest Hour: Shipbuilding in the Portland Area During World War II*. Nearly one quarter of that count were women welders.[17]

La Verne Bradley states in "Women at Work" that by August 1944, 16,500,000 women were working outside the home, one quarter of whom had not even considered such jobs in 1940, and that in 1939 there had been only thirty-six women employed by the nation's shipyards. "At war's end," she declared, "the country will emerge with a vast pool of skilled, semiskilled, and professional women."[18]

While dispensing the nightly news, evening radio broadcasts could claim some responsibility for soliciting workers—men and women—to West Coast shipyard work. Just such an experience happened to a family from the state of Idaho, according to their daughter, Dora. "My Dad called us in to listen to the 'Philco' radio, that the Japanese had attacked Pearl Harbor. That very night my uncle in Seattle called my dad that there was a call out for workers in the shipyard. Dad, my brother, and a boyfriend left the next week to go out. When school got out, my sisters, brother and mother went out [to the shipyard in Seattle] and I went to the union office where there was a need for women electricians."

Many women came because others in their family had already answered the nation's call for help. Young Jean Neil, working as a clerk in a grocery store, considered enrolling in President Roosevelt's WPA electrician classes. Then Jean's mother, Clara, who was working as a shipyard burner, approached her. "'Come on, why don't you come down and go to welding school,' she'd said. And so, I went down, and I liked welding," Jean reminisced. "I got the hang of it pretty quick. They had most of them [women students] in the school for two weeks. I was there nine days. Just to go to the school, they gave me ninety-seven cents an hour." (This she would express with awe still, decades on.) Jean would spend her wartime career as a welder at Commercial Iron Works on Ross Island in the Portland vicinity.

Like Clara and Jean, many women were already living in the greater Portland area when they heeded the call to join the ranks in the shipyards. At other times, women joined at the urging of friends. In the book

Builder's progress photo of LCS (Landing Craft Support) at Commercial Iron Works Shipyard in Portland, Oregon. July 21, 1944. NAVSOURSE ONLINE–U.S. NATIONAL ARCHIVES PHOTO BS69622.

Don't Call Me Rosie: The Women Who Welded the LSTs and the Men Who Sailed on Them, by Kathleen Thomas, one young woman named Blossom Ann is reported to have heard that the shipyard offered better pay than she was receiving at a downtown department store, Meier and Frank. "There were three of us that grew up on 48th Street. Margaret was the cute redhead. Betty was my girlfriend and then me. And so, Marg was talking to my mother and said I should come down to the shipyards.... Better money. So that's where I ended up," she said.

She was hired by the Swan Island Shipyard, riding the bus to work. "I wanted to work on the line. That's where they put everything together. On the line. A boat was built every three months. We had three shipyards going 24 hours a day for these ships. Every three months, they would send a boat down [a way]. That's when I got to see one."[19]

La Du, in his preface for *Her Finest Hour*, offers a brief but wonderfully detailed description of the city and its shipyards during the war years, as follows:

> During the World War II years, the shipyards and shipbuilding dominated everyday life in the Portland area. Stores advertised leather jackets and elbow length gloves for welders while shipyard buses filled with workers traversed Portland streets day and night. The Willamette River was filled with ships recently launched as well as merchant vessels loading lend-lease materials for Russia and elsewhere. The night was filled with lights from the shipyards as the swing and graveyard shifts followed the day shift in producing Liberty ships, tankers, and other vessels. Streams of sparks from welders and burners cascaded down the 30' sides of ships as finishing touches were applied to hulls in the river awaiting delivery to the Maritime Commission.

A shipyard lit at night was becoming a common sight across the nation to facilitate meeting the emergency shipbuilding quotas brought by the need to defend against the enemy in conflict. Inside *LIFE* magazine's January 1950 issue, a night scene photograph from the Terminal Island shipyard in Los Angeles with lights ablaze carries the caption "lights illuminated it at night like a happy entertainment park."[20]

The Shipyard Agent

Lights illuminate victory ship hulls under construction on the ways at Oregon Shipbuilding Corporation, where work continued around the clock, 1945.
© THE OREGONIAN. ALL RIGHTS RESERVED. USED WITH PERMISSION. PHOTO FILE #2209.

At Swan Island in 1943 over 40 percent of the welders were women, according to *Good Work, Sister!*, an oral history of women shipyard workers.

One of those women was Lois Housman, whose husband Joe went to work in the shipyard first and then encouraged his wife to try to learn to weld. "So, I went down," Lois recalled, "and joined the union and signed up. Then I went through school, but Joe told me to stay until I could weld overhead." It was during training that Lois would meet Augusta Clawson. They "got to be pretty good pals," she said. Lois, like Augusta, had come to work.

There were a great many war production workers who were determined to see the job through to the end, including women welders. One woman's path to the shipyard was circuitous and difficult during the last years of the Depression in her small hometown. This is a shortened version of her story:

> *Now is when my secret life started. I was 13, maybe almost 14, I met [him] . . . and [he] wrote a letter to the county marriage department and stated I was pregnant (which I wasn't) and had permission to marry and [he] signed daddy's name. We traveled all over doing odd jobs, hitch hiking from location to location for six months to a year. [Then] I never saw him again.*
>
> *At sixteen when I got out of school, I went to chef school for nine months. I went to work for a family cooking and housekeeping for a year. [Next] I went to electricians' school for four or five months in Portland. I quit that and learned about welding in the shipyards, so I applied for welding training and passed the course . . . and was out tacking [attaching two pieces of metal by small temporary welds] when others were still trying to complete the course.*

This was only one woman's story, with a positive conclusion. And yet, something was going wrong by spring of 1943. Other women were quitting the shipyards, with some walking out not long after entering employment. Agencies in Washington, DC, decided they needed to determine with certainty the cause of this exodus of trained workers at such a critical time. The price of these defections was too high. The War Production Board and the Training Women for War Production office needed answers.

CHAPTER TWO

AUGUSTA CLAWSON— UNTIL WAR'S END

"I wonder how someone in Ohio decided to do a doctoral thesis on me. In fact, I wonder how she stumbled on my existence at all."
—AUGUSTA H. CLAWSON, OCTOBER 1987

According to the US Federal Census in the year 1900, the Clawson household on West Seventh Street in Plainfield, New Jersey, consisted of Frank Titsworth Clawson, a dentist; Ellen Augusta Holmes Clawson, his wife; and their two-year-old son, Augustus Holmes Clawson. On June 23, 1903, also in Plainfield, twin daughters were added to the accounting: Augusta Holmes Clawson, named for her mother, and Frances Myra Clawson. It seemed the family could not bestow the names Augustus, Augusta, and Holmes often enough, these names having originated with Mrs. Clawson's father, Augustus Dole Holmes, an early sea captain.

Tragically, only three days after the birth of Augusta and her twin, Frances, their mother died. Her cause of death was reported as "acute Bright's Disease," an early term for nephritis. Then, three years after the death of their mother, Frances died at the tender age of four. Augusta was so young to endure such a great loss, yet years later she would say that she "distinctly" remembered her twin sister. Not only did she remember her, according to her niece, Ann, but she "talked about her twin often."

When Ann visited the family home many years later as a child, she passed by the bedroom that had been shared by Augusta and Frances. Upon each bed sat identical baby dolls. Young Ann felt there was an unspoken rule in the household: no one was allowed to play with the dolls. On the walls of the room hung photographs of two little girls, the twin Clawson sisters.[1]

The death of Frances left Augusta and her older brother, who answered to the name of Holmes, to be raised by their grieving father. It appears, according to the 1905 New Jersey State Census record of the occupants of the home at 672 W. Seventh Street, Dr. Clawson had in-home help in the years following the deaths of his wife and daughter. Listed as members of the household were an Irish cook named Nellie and a woman named Eleanor Demarest, along with his parents, James and Henrietta.

The Clawson family's neighbors were the Woodcock family, according to that census report. Three years later, Frank Clawson married his neighbor's daughter, Marion—fourteen years his junior—with whom he fathered four more children. Petite Marion became a loving stepmother to five-year-old Augusta, who grew very fond of her younger half-siblings as they arrived. The family took to calling her Gug or Gusta, nicknames used with affection throughout her life.

As the eldest daughter in the family, Augusta seemed destined to set an example for her younger half-sisters and half-brother as she matured. Years later, on a page of the Lewinsville Presbyterian Church newsletter called *In the Spotlight*, a piece written by Bettie Vodra honoring Augusta

Clawson family home in Plainfield, New Jersey. Birthplace of Augusta Clawson and twin sister, Frances, in 1903. The splendid house no longer stands. COURTESY OF ANN HENDERSON KRAMER.

Augusta H. Clawson poses with her four half-siblings (*left to right*): sisters Barbara "Bobbie," Jeanette "J.," Margaret "Margie," and brother Franklin W. "Wells" Clawson. Photograph circa 1922 by Luckey Studio, Plainfield, New Jersey.
COURTESY OF ANN HENDERSON KRAMER.

stated: "She was a second mother to five [*sic*] children. Her undisguised love for children was nurtured at this time and stays with her today." Evidence of the close relationship between Augusta and her half-sisters is also found on the Vassar reunion forms. Over the years she included each of her sisters when providing information to answer: "names and addresses of three people likely to know your whereabouts."

With the goal of attending college, which had certainly been an intention of Augusta's, she enrolled at Plainfield Seminary—a school in her hometown offering "primary, academic, and college preparatory

Vintage postcard. "Plainfield Seminary, Plainfield, N. J.," where Augusta enrolled as a preparatory student. New Jersey Postcard Co. Inc., Newark, NJ. Date unknown. Postage one cent. AUTHOR'S COLLECTION.

departments." Located within walking distance on the same street as the family home, at the seminary she could enroll as a day student rather than boarding at the school, especially preferable since the offer of boarding consisted of two or three rooms at most in the home of the school's administrator.

At its opening in 1855, the Plainfield Seminary, better known as "The Chestnuts" (likely for the surrounding old chestnut trees), housed the Opheleton Female Seminary. In 1867, Miss E. E. (Eliza Elvira) Kenyon, "a prominent society lady and founder of the Monday Afternoon Club" (of which Augusta would become a member), along with Kenyon's sister, Mrs. Maxson, took charge of the leadership of the seminary. At the end of Augusta's final year at the seminary, its doors closed permanently, leaving only a faithful alumni group to remember the institution.[2]

It seems certain that Augusta remembered her experiences at Plainfield Seminary, as evidenced by her life of service. In her fourteenth year, the seminary formed an auxiliary "for knitting," where the students also learned to "make scrapbooks and trench candles, send books to the soldiers [of World War I], and contribute regularly to the work of a hospital in Normandy." Augusta, along with the rest of humanity, could not know that World War I would *not* be the war to end war, as predicted by British author, H. G. Wells. Nor could she know how significant a role she would play over twenty-five years later in the world of working women, especially when World War II and its dangerous instigator slithered into the scene.

In 1920, Augusta's brother Holmes died of pneumonia at the age of eighteen. Surely saddened by this loss of her only remaining sibling who shared their mother, Augusta nevertheless was a dedicated student, probably aware how vital it was to continue her schooling as the building block to support a future career. She had, after all, been under the tutelage of Eliza Kenyon, an independent, unmarried businesswoman and educator. This experience likely informed many of Augusta's decisions as she became her own fiercely independent woman. Graduating from Plainfield Seminary on June 10, 1919, at the fifty-first and final commencement ceremony of the school, she strode onward, enrolling at Vassar College in Poughkeepsie, New York. Before her freshman year began in September 1920, she traveled to Puerto Rico and to Nova Scotia, where she would later establish a summer home in Barrington. She graduated in 1924 with a Bachelor of Arts in English.

Her years at the private liberal arts college were foundational. During her first two years, she studied many of the standard subjects of English, chemistry, French, history, Latin, and mathematics. During this time there was much talk within society of the "modern college girl," not all of it complimentary. An English professor at Vassar, one Burgess Johnson, expressed his opinion on the matter:

> *Grandma has no right to criticize the modern college girl. She probably has a few Cain-raising times tucked away in her memory. I don't think bare knees are any more immodest than the stately hoopskirt of half a century ago.*

Augusta Holmes Clawson's senior portrait, Vassar College, Poughkeepsie, New York, 1924. *THE 1924 VASSARION*, VOL. 35, VASSAR COLLEGE YEARBOOK. AUTHOR'S COLLECTION.

> *The worldly wisdom of the college girl does not erase the blush of youth and innocence. The college girl is as much a marrying girl as ever but postpones it. She will help decrease divorces because she can make the more intelligent selection of a mate. Besides, the majority of men no longer seek butterfly wives. They have discovered an educated girl can be a business partner as well as a charming wife.*[3]

During her junior year Augusta continued English and mathematics and added philosophy, physiology, and psychology. Music was a new course for her in the second half of her junior term; she added art studies during her senior year. Bible, botany, economics, geology, German, Greek, Italian, and other subjects were offered but not selected by Augusta during her four years at Vassar College. Between 1924 and 1930 Augusta completed graduate studies she described as "Part Time Educ." and "Adv. Educ. Psych." at Rutgers University, and "Problems in Second. Educ."

at New York University, abbreviating course names to fit onto a Vassar reunion form.

When asked decades later to describe what she "took away from Vassar," Augusta wrote: "A much needed maturity, independent thinking, new fields of interest, e.g., music which became a lifetime interest, 'a taste for excellence' and a sense of debt to Vassar." She placed the term *a taste for excellence* in quotation marks because she was borrowing a phrase from a commencement speech made by future famous actress, Meryl Streep, another Vassar College alumna, although of course, Streep graduated in 1971, forty-seven years after Augusta had, and twenty-six years before Augusta's death.[4]

Shortly after walking out the doors of Vassar College into the broader world beyond, Augusta began teaching at a continuation school, which she explained was "set up for young people who must start working before they have finished school—[fourteen] and [sixteen] year olds who are forced by economic strains to begin earning their keep early. The law requires them to attend school one day a week after they begin work ... the continuation school offers that one day."[5]

So it was that Augusta became employed as a teacher of courses in trade and industry at Girls' Vocational School in Elizabeth, New Jersey, where she also served as a placement and guidance coordinator. During this period of 1924–1941, music and art were added to the curriculum of vocational schools across the state of New Jersey "largely through her efforts."[6]

In the Plainfield city directory of 1931, Augusta H. Clawson's residence address was given as 672 W. Seventh, indicating she was still living in the house where she was born. A notation followed her name and address: "See the Plainfield Book Shop, Inc.," which is further listed as located at 321 Park Ave. This association with the Plainfield Book Shop, Inc. apparently began in 1926, when Augusta is reported to have purchased an interest in the shop. She listed 1924 as the year she became "half-owner, vice-president, and director" of the shop, where she would be "associated with Miss Cornelia E. Lyle in the conduct of the business." The bookshop also offered a lending library to the public. One can imagine Augusta as being partly responsible for the idea to develop a lending library as a service to the community.

In July 1931, the *Vassar Quarterly* published a report of a reunion for the class of 1924, recording that at a supper on that Friday night, sixty-two alumni had reelected alumni council officers, including Augusta Clawson as class agent. She attended many, perhaps all, of her Vassar College reunions throughout her lifetime and a description of activities clearly explains why fun-loving Augusta would choose to attend. The *Quarterly* reported: "On Saturday morning, '24 was especially proud of winning the cup of daisies tied with pink ribbon which was awarded at the Alumnae meeting to the class which carried off honors in the Alumnae Parade. We still don't know whether it was the yellow pajamas and hats, the marching, the singing, or our mascot, Calvin, but we were duly thrilled."[7]

A shocking event occurred in October 1933. As Augusta was driving her car along Route 28 between Plainfield and Lebanon, New Jersey, it was struck by another vehicle. According to the *Courier-News* of Bridgewater, New Jersey, a Mrs. Gladys Doane "was riding as an invitee in the Clawson automobile." Mrs. Doane and her husband, F. Clyde Doane—concert and live radio singers and performers—oddly sued Augusta as well as the driver of the offending automobile, according to the newspaper. Reportedly Gladys had been seriously injured. She may have been unable to perform for a time as the professional "dramatic-lyric soprano" she was, likely leading to lost income.[8]

"The following year, a newspaper article in March 1934 reported a suit asking "damages of $25,000 [with] her husband, F. Clyde Doane, seek[ing] $10,000 for loss of her services." Today's value of the amounts sought would be over $580,000 and $234,000, respectively. Augusta was a teacher. Surely this suit would have presented a great financial burden for her to carry.

The original newspaper report of the accident had not mentioned where the two women had been destined; they may have been returning home from an outing, perhaps one of Gladys' frequent vocal performances in surrounding churches. She was "well-known in music circles in New Jersey" performing as a soloist at "several of the churches and at Temple Shalom."⁹ The two women had been only thirty minutes from Plainfield, where Augusta lived in the family home and Gladys lived with her husband and professional partner.

Despite this reported contention in the court, the suit against Augusta—who was about nine years younger than Gladys—was dismissed. It appears that a friendship existed between the two women, or perhaps bloomed after the shared accident, that would last throughout their lives.

As would Augusta's propensity for risky driving, according to family members. She was declared, with a chuckle, to be a "horrible driver" by those who knew her personally. Apparently, Augusta would unfailingly prop a book upon the steering wheel so that she might multitask and read as she drove while at the same time snacking from a bag of candy she invariably kept stashed between the driver's seat and the door of her car.

Once the dust from the accident and threatened litigation had cleared, in June 1935, Augusta had graduated at the age of thirty-two with a master's degree in personnel administration from New York University, where she had enrolled two years before.

The Girls' Vocational School where Augusta was employed was renamed the Thomas A. Edison Vocational School in 1937, Augusta's thirteenth and final year there. On an "Associate Alumnae of Vassar College 1938 Biographical Register Questionnaire," she described that position as "Supervisor: Placement, Guidance, and Apprentice Coordinator" and the nature of her work as "Enrollment of pupils, assignment to courses, organization of new courses, supervision of student government and alumnae organization, coordinator contacting industry and school to build 'market' for students trained, to place in jobs for which trained, and to follow up. This includes organization of advisory board for every trade department comprising outstanding members active in these trades." Her responsibilities were a mouthful to describe and a handful to assume.[10]

Augusta could not have known that many of her diligently honed skills, often a result of her experiential learning, would significantly impact women in defense industry factories and shipyards during World War II.

The Shipyard Agent

Unsurprisingly, by now Augusta could be described as an industrious and engaged woman, intelligent, positive-minded, and driven—a description that remained accurate through her life. She was active in associations of various kinds. For example, she held memberships in the Plainfield Musical Club, the Monday Afternoon Club, the College Club of Plainfield, the Alumnae of Plainfield Seminary, and Vassar College. Some years later, Augusta would also join Altrusa International Service Club, described as "the first national business and professional women's organization in the United States." It's not surprising that Augusta would become a member of an organization whose "program ... cover[s] women not only in their working roles but also as citizens, taxpayers, consumers, and participants in a world community."

As a member of the YWCA, she described her volunteer work there as serving on the "Industrial Committee (because of correlation with placement work)." She was an active member of the Presbyterian Crescent Avenue Church in Plainfield.

Several professional organizations saw Augusta as a member, such as the American Vocational Association, the New Jersey Vocational and Arts Association, and the National Education Association. She served as first vice president of the Elizabeth (New Jersey) Teachers Association.

"[A]bout 1939 or '40" according to her recollection, Augusta served as president of the Secondary Teacher's Club. It was during her term as president that poet Carl Sandburg accepted an invitation to speak at a program for the eight-hundred-member organization. At the close of the program, it was Augusta's responsibility to see that Sandburg was delivered to the train station on time to catch his train. Once they were bundled inside her car, she drove off, bringing the three-time Pulitzer Prize winner to the station. But then, she suddenly realized that since she also was going into New York City, she could offer him another option: ride with her all the way to his destination. Sandburg happily accepted, according to Augusta, so happily that he "bounced" around her car before returning to his seat.

"After I speak, I always put a wool scarf around my throat, and I forgot to bring it. I also like to save my voice after I have spoken," Sandburg advised Augusta as they set out, likely warning her he would be silent and not to take it personally.

"There's a wool scarf in the glove compartment," she assured him, "and you may ride silently all the way, but please do exactly what you want to." She wrote that after he adjusted the scarf around his throat, he talked all the way into New York City.

The two hungry travelers stopped after following the directions of Sandburg to "a red and white-checked tablecloth place on Canal Street." Amid strains of music and the aroma of food, the two found and occupied a booth. Following is a portion of Augusta's description of Sandburg's personality during the hours they spent together on a brisk evening in New York City:

> *He talked constantly. One minute he was the poet explaining that people would think his Abraham Lincoln was his best creative writing. "It isn't, it was just hard work. Now my Rutabaga Stories, they're creative." The next minute he was a father chuckling about his daughter and the V-8 Ford. In the middle of the conversation he stopped dead, looked at me with a twinkle, and said, "I have to."*
>
> *I said, "Then do."*
> *He said, "I can't do it alone."*
> *I said, "Then don't do it alone."*
> *He stood up. The familiar shock of white hair hung down to his eyes. He said, "I have to waltz." So, we joined the gay group of dancers, and I waltzed with Carl Sandburg.*[11]

Augusta described how, back at the table about two a.m., she announced they should leave soon, as she "was staying with a friend in Knickerbocker Village and didn't want her to wonder what had happened to [her]." This friend was probably Gladys Doane, whom she called Glad, and who, according to the 1940 federal census, now lived in Knickerbocker Village in New York City with her husband Clyde.[12]

According to Augusta, when she finally brought Sandburg to his hotel in the wee hours, he said upon leaving her, "Goddess of youth and laughter, I thank you. Goodnight."

By 1941, Augusta was the talk of the town, literally, inside the *Courier-News* of Bridgewater, New Jersey, with the headline, "Augusta Clawson Goes to Capital." The article explained that "Miss Clawson" had left for Washington, DC, to take a position as a special agent, working as the assistant to Miss Louise Moore, the agent for Trade and Industrial Education for Girls and Women under the Federal Security Agency (FSA). Starting in 1939, the FSA oversaw food and drug safety, education funding, and administration of public health programs, all functions which seemed a perfect training ground for the future that was beckoning young Augusta. She had been asked to come to Washington while on leave from her previous employment at the Thomas A. Edison Vocational and Technical High School in Elizabeth, New Jersey.

As the years unfolded, Augusta spoke regularly and particularly regarding the training of women for vocational work. Indeed, in April 1942, she was in Los Angeles to meet with industrial-related agencies, assuring them that the fact that thousands of women were being called to fill labor positions would not "be the cause of women forcing men out of their jobs."

Back in New Jersey, it appears Augusta wrote anonymously as "Plainfield High School Alumnus," penning an editorial to the *Courier-News* in November 1942, and creating fodder for her dentist father to show the article around his clinic. The many opinions she possessed regarding youth and their future, as well as the future of working women, especially in vocational industries, needed to be expressed. Augusta wrote about a national high school program that promoted the subject, "War Shifts the Emphasis." With praise for the orators, she shared some of the presentation's key thoughts: "Yesterday we demanded the privileges, the carefree play and the security which our democracy offered in peace times. Today democracy demands of us responsibility, service and sacrifice. . . . If democracy today means going from security to sacrifice, from peace to war, we choose democracy." The youth of the nation were ready and willing also to serve the war effort.

Augusta was especially ready. Early in 1943 her title was Special Agent, Training Women for War Production, Federal Security Agency, US Office of Education, Washington, DC. The country was in need of yet more war production workers. Vassar College's Vocational Bureau (described as being formed to give vocational guidance) had invited Augusta to speak. Its director, Zita L. Thornbury, issued a memorandum to staff, writing that Augusta had accepted the invitation. Thornbury described Augusta further: "Since 1941 Miss Clawson has worked in 30 or more states visiting the west coast three times. She has the most demanding and pressing of tasks. Few have had her opportunities to see the production program in full swing from coast to coast and few women are playing such a vital part in the speed-up in industry."

Augusta had, Thornbury wrote, "arranged a stop-over on her way to the west coast. There she will get in to working clothes and plunge into a job in a war industry for the purpose of gaining more first-hand knowledge of conditions. . . . The induction of women on a vast scale," she added, "has made it necessary for educational leaders of the country to develop a program adapted to the urgent needs of industry and in the interest of the women who need help in making their adjustments."[13]

Also mentioned by Thornbury were two articles written by Augusta and published in journals: "Safety Clothing for Women in War Production Industries" in the *Journal of Home Economics*, volume 34, number 10, in December 1942, and "It's Up to You!" in a publication titled *New Jersey Club Woman*, volume xvii, number 5, in January 1943.

The month following Augusta's visit to Vassar at Thornbury's invitation, her training division in DC pondered why it was that women welders were quitting the shipyards soon after training. The staff considered whether training was where the fault lay. The training was not administered by the Office of Education in Washington, DC; most was overseen by boards of education at the state and local levels throughout the country.

Many years later, Augusta would reveal another reason: "They all gave sick babies as their excuse for resigning. If there had been that many sick babies in the Portland, Ore., area, we would have established an all-time record for epidemics."[14]

Meanwhile, Layton S. Hawkins, the director of the Vocational Division of the US Office of Education, asked a trained supervisor to "be the guinea pig" to discover the problems and find a solution. So, Agent Clawson was assigned to meld into the ranks of America's women welders incognito.[15]

Swan Island shipyard in Portland, Oregon, was chosen for the operation as it was relatively new and not completely organized. April 1943 saw Augusta arrive for welder training, which seemed appropriate, since only a month before, she had spoken at a "Women in Action" rally in her hometown of Plainfield, New Jersey, stating that women had a "threefold task" ahead of them upon entering industrial work:

1. Proving women's worth, showing whether she can work side by side with men in the plant.

2. Speeding production.

3. Releasing a man to fight.

Simultaneously the *Vassar Alumnae Magazine* published Augusta's article "The Time is Now!" which began with a clever and compelling poem:

> "The time has come," a woman said
> "To enter fields quite new,
> For building planes and welding ships
> Are jobs that we must do.
> How dare we send our men to fight
> Unless we pitch in too?"

"Time is bringing about strange things," wrote Augusta. "It is shattering outworn traditions, opening new horizons, shifting our sense of values. It is showing us that we must change our use of pronouns. Now is no time to say, '*someone* ought to speed up production,' '*they* ought to build more planes.' The only solution today is to say, '*I* must help with production.' Say it and follow your statement with action." She addresses readers, asking if they knew of Bataan, Wake Island, or Corregidor and what happened in each place. "Then do something about it," she intoned. "Join the production line and join it now."[16]

Emphasizing how millions of men had been lost from the job force to join the armed forces and millions of women were needed to replace them in the industrial jobs of the nation, she reported: "4,500,000 women are so employed now, and this year must see 3,000,000 more enter." After announcing such astonishing numbers, Augusta went on to assure women readers that the factories had changed from the days of the sweat shop. Promising that attitudes toward the acceptance of women in war production factories had also changed, she reminded readers "industry dreaded the entrance of women . . . Let them sew or knit," they'd said. "Let them nurse. Let them type or teach. But keep them out of the shipyards."

Augusta added, "Like most bugaboos, all these prejudices melted away." She explained how things had changed as instructors found that when it came to working in war production facilities women only lacked *familiarity* with the tasks and tools, not the ability to do the job. "Every day reveals a new way in which women can render service," Augusta admitted. "Encased in protective garments of leather, in a world of their own inside of welders' helmets, women are welding ships."

Positing that a woman perseveres because "she derives such a genuine satisfaction in being part of the fight," Augusta adds, "Those with small children should be the last to come." She believed childless women and older women whose children are grown should come to the war production jobs first. Augusta continued by providing many details and instructions for women about how to join the war production line. She closed her article with this: "The call to arms has sounded. 'American women, report for duty.' Choose what you will do. But do something and do it NOW!"[17]

Two months before her fortieth birthday Augusta accepted the assignment to help sort out the foibles of Swan Island Shipyard's welder training program and environment for women, which had been described by others as "chaotic." She shot off to Portland, Oregon, aiming to discover how to help those she would work alongside, hoping to enable them to persevere in their important shipbuilding roles.

The Shipyard Agent

While recording her observations into what she titled "Report on Welding Training and Shipyard Employment," Augusta would begin by stating, "Through the cooperation of the United States Office of Education, the State Division of Vocational Education and the Personnel Department of the Kaiser Company, I was privileged to train as a welder and to take employment in the Swan Island Shipyard. My purpose has been, through first-hand experience, to ascertain in what ways we can do a better job of training women for shipyard employment."[18]

Augusta found Swan Island surrounded by the Willamette River, save a road built two decades before—though not to reach a shipyard but an airstrip that had been the island's first public modernization.

In daily notations for her office of education report, Augusta adopted the shipyard's nickname, calling it simply The Yard. Her friendly female co-welders soon nicknamed her Jersey Gus, or often simply Gus.

"In April 1943 I made a strange bargain," she later wrote, "and because of it I have four ships at sea."[19]

"Dignified Augusta Clawson of the U.S. Office of Education went to work in a Kaiser shipyard, promptly was nicknamed JERSEY GUS by fellow welders."
"WOMEN AT WAR!," FEBRUARY 13, 1944, AKRON BEACON JOURNAL, PRIVATE LIVES SECTION, HTTPS://WWW.NEWSPAPERS.COM/IMAGE/148830981.

CHAPTER THREE

HENRY'S PACIFIC SHIPYARDS

"The ships that now lie at the bottom of the seven seas must be replaced not in kind, but with swifter, faster, surer craft, in quantity to serve every need."

—HENRY J. KAISER

"Will someone lend me a housetop, please? I want to shriek my news to the countryside. I am a full-fledged employee of The Shipyard; not a trainee any longer."

—AUGUSTA H. CLAWSON[1]

Rising to the occasion to fulfill perhaps the greatest need he had ever encountered as a builder—assembling ships to carry supplies to the fighting forces, troops to distant shores, and weapons to aid in ongoing battles—Henry J. Kaiser began by constructing a shipyard in Richmond, California, across the bay from San Francisco, the first of six along the Pacific Coast constructed by the Kaiser Co. It was in these shipyards that he developed a new idea: to apply assembly line production to the building of ships, those colossi of the seas.

Kaiser also rose to the occasion by relatively quickly bringing women into shipyard jobs beginning in 1942. According to a Bureau of Labor Statistics report on the "Percentage of Women in Maritime Shipyards" as of March 1943, the national average was 6.48 percent. Kaiser's Swan Island shipyard topped the list at 17.8 percent women, followed by Oregon Shipbuilding Corporation at 15.5 percent. Kaiser Co. Vancouver ranked at 14.1 percent with Kaiser's Richmond Shipyard at 11.9 percent.[2]

From the Kaiser Richmond shipyard, Henry moved to the Northwest and there built some of the most widely remembered shipyards: the Kaiser Company, Inc.—Portland Swan Island shipyard, Oregon Shipbuilding Corporation (Oregonship), and Kaiser Company, Inc. Vancouver shipyard. Swan Island and Oregonship were not the only yards located within the state of Oregon, however. The Oregon Historical Society Research Library lists several others of varying size and capabilities in the state that were also responding to the Emergency Shipbuilding Program for the duration of the war. These included yards in the cities and towns of Toledo on the Yaquina River, Astoria at the mouth of the Columbia River, Saint Helens on the Columbia River, North Bend situated on the edge of the Coos Bay, Columbia City on the Columbia River, Tillamook on Tillamook Bay—a two-mile-wide inlet of the Pacific Ocean—and Marshfield (now known as the city of Coos Bay) on the body of water from which its current name emerged, less than ten miles from the Pacific coastline.

Kaiser-owned shipyards became well-known and an example for shipyards across the nation for a number of reasons: the vast size of some shipyards; the before-mentioned assembly line production method, which contributed to the overall increase in production speed; the rapid development of housing projects and dormitories for employees; the early enlistment of women to work in the shipyards; the provision of child-care centers, along with the provision of nearly everything a worker needed for daily living, such as dry goods stores, medical clinics, entertainment and recreation facilities, and transportation to and from work, to name a few.

Similarly, in Washington State, several shipyards were engaged in the production and repair of war-bound vessels. This included the Seattle-Tacoma Shipbuilding Corporation in Elliott Bay, the Bremerton Naval Shipyard, the Everett-Pacific Shipbuilding and Dry Dock Company in Port Gardner Bay, the Tacoma Boatbuilding Company located in Commencement Bay, the Moran Brothers Shipyard in Seattle, and the Lake Washington Shipyard near Houghton, for example.[3]

In Portland proper, not far from the big three Kaiser shipyards, Commercial Iron Works (CIW), which entered the ship repair and building business seven months *before* the Kaiser yards were built, contributed to the Emergency Shipbuilding Program from their site on Ross Island. Built on old World War I shipyards located in the Willamette River in Portland, CIW "launched the first World War II naval vessel in the area on February 22, 1941 . . . the U.S.S. *Catalpa*, a YN 5 type net tender." Employees at CIW built nine or more different types of ships, such as Landing Craft Infantry (LCI) and Landing Craft Support (LCS) ships, gunboats, submarine chasers, net layers and net tenders, minelayers and minesweepers, and ammunition tenders. Commercial Iron Works also created parts that were used by the crews at Kaiser's shipyards and was called "the most versatile shipyard in the area." Not only that, but by the end of the war, CIW could claim the honor of launching the five hundredth ship built in the Portland area.[4]

As early as September 27, 1941, Oregon Shipbuilding Corporation had launched its first Liberty ship of the Emergency Shipbuilding Program—the "greatest emergency bulk cargo carrier ever devised."[5]

Christened the *Star of Oregon* by then Oregon governor Sprague's wife, Blanche, it was named after the first sailing ship built in the Oregon Territory by early settlers. The launching in 1941 was part of a nationwide coordinated and simultaneous launch of twelve ships. Kudos were also forthcoming at Oregonship for becoming the first yard to build more than a million gross tons of freighters—delivering more than one-eighth of the quota of merchant ship tonnage set by President Roosevelt for 1942. Oregonship set other records, as follows:

- "The first yard to achieve a schedule of 1.18 ships per way in one month. [A way is the structure of wood and concrete that supported each ship hull during construction.]
- The first yard to stage an all-feminine launching. Not only did Mrs. Fred Lingenfelder, wife of a shipyard worker, wield the christening bottle, but two women welders cut the metal props holding the hull in position."[6]

Oregonship launched its one hundredth Liberty freighter, becoming the first yard to build one hundred freighters on November 22,

1942, the same day the "all-feminine launching" had been held, the first of its kind in the region.

And the accolades kept coming, as Oregonship was declared to be "the first recipient of the gold wreath production award for delivering liberty ships from all its ways in less than 105 days from keel laying for [twenty-two] consecutive times." The Kaiser yard in Vancouver would earn a star as well. Swan Island shipyard would earn two. This accomplishment by Oregon Shipbuilding Corporation shipyard was significant enough to receive an article in the *New York Times* in October 1943: "Gold Wreath to Shipyard; Oregon Company Wins First Such Award After Other Honors."[7]

Continuing the streak, the Oregonship yard received two US Maritime Commission Awards at the launching of the yard's three hundredth Liberty ship.

Kaiser Company, Inc.'s Vancouver yard received kudos from as far away as the director of Merchant Shipbuilding in the United Kingdom. The praise arrived, however, while Sir Amos Ayre was on American soil, touring North American shipyards in 1942. He was looking for answers to the question of how to improve British shipbuilding procedures and production. These were crucial years; the war had escalated, and Britain was still lagging in building vessels of war. After he visited the Vancouver, Washington, yard, he remarked that he had observed a "revolution taking place in American shipbuilding. The use of welding was extensive." He also said, pertaining to his just completed tour, "Having regard to what I had already seen, this yard excels everything; it is impossible to exaggerate in describing this establishment."

The British director of Naval Construction also stated that "it is the DNC's policy to increase welding as much as possible . . . [and] firms should be encouraged to weld rather than rivet." Following these observations by British shipbuilding leaders, females in the United Kingdom would increasingly join in war production work as welders.[8]

In the echo of the praise for Vancouver's yard, Oregon's Swan Island shipyard would win its own awards. The yard filled every square foot of the island with its eight shipways, with housing and childcare facilities, parking spaces for workers' cars and buses, a cafeteria, an office building,

Launching of SS *Star of Oregon*, the first Liberty ship launched from the ways at Henry J. Kaiser's Oregon Shipbuilding Corporation, September 27, 1941. © *THE OREGONIAN*. ALL RIGHTS RESERVED. USED WITH PERMISSION. PHOTO FILE #2209. NEG. NO. ORHI_68779.

a first aid station, cranes, docks, and all the pieces and parts needed to create ships, along with storage buildings.

First mentioned in early documents of 1844 as Willow Island, the island began public life as the Swan Island Municipal Airport. The Port of Portland was allowed to connect the island to the mainland by way of a causeway built by placing fill in the river. This was completed in 1927 and allowed Charles Lindbergh to cross when he visited the airstrip in September of that year. The entrance road served its purpose for those seeking travel by air until 1940. But when the US Maritime Commission launched its Emergency Shipbuilding Program late in 1940, the Port of Portland leased the island to the federal government. The island would never return to use as an airport.

The Swan Island shipyard would produce 153 tankers during the war production period between 1942 and 1945. In fact, in 1943, Admiral Howard L. Vickery boasted, "Swan Island is the fastest tanker yard in the country." Surely, that was a pride-generating statement when received by the shipyard workers.

Vintage postcard. "Swan Island Airport Looking South from a Skyliner, Portland, Ore." © Brubaker Aerial Surveys. Mailed October 12, 1944. AUTHOR'S COLLECTION.

Aerial photograph of Swan Island Shipyard with its eight ways, showing seven supporting hulls of ships in varying stages of production. OREGON HISTORICAL SOCIETY RESEARCH LIBRARY, OHS.ORG. NEG. NO. ORHI49686.

The Shipyard Agent

In December 1942, Kaiser's Richmond shipyard was in the news for a nefarious reason. In the *Santa Cruz Sentinel* newspaper, a column announced, "Alleged Nazi Is Tried for Firing Oakum Warehouse." One Heinrich Roedel, identified as an "alleged Nazi," had set fire to over $500,000 worth of oakum at the Kaiser shipyard in Richmond, California. Oakum is described as "a preparation of tarred fibers used to seal gaps. Its traditional application was in shipbuilding for caulking or packing the joints of timbers in wooden vessels and the deck planking of iron and steel ships." This would have been a hefty financial loss for the Maritime Commission and the shipyard. Fortunately, there was no mention of loss of life in the fire. A shipyard burner who saw the culprit in the vicinity of the building the night of the fire testified against Roedel in federal court. This had been a grave attack against the war production effort.[9]

Fortunately, Richmond was not the only shipyard on the West Coast. Henry Kaiser's name was associated with "six new yards—three sponsored by Todd at Bath [Maine], Houston and Tacoma [Washington]; three more managed by Kaiser's men at Portland, Richmond and Los Angeles." Two more were in the Portland, Oregon–Vancouver, Washington area: the Kaiser Company, Inc. Vancouver shipyard and the Swan Island shipyard. *Saturday Evening Post* writer Frank J. Taylor penned a lengthy article about Henry Kaiser titled "Builder No. 1." In it he said, "The Kaiser staff tackled shipbuilding as a venture in moving great weights fast and efficiently."[10]

Henry Kaiser was not hesitant to share his sense of pride with the employees of the Swan Island yard regarding just that; they were bringing in impressive production numbers. One such example of Henry reaching out is a letter written by him on October 27, 1944, on Kaiser Company, Inc. letterhead praising the exemplary achievements of Swan Island Shipyard employees. "Men and Women of Swan Island," he began:

> *One hundred Tankers and six Navy fleet Oilers in two years—more than a million and seven hundred thousand tons of Tankers—is your service to the fighting fronts of the world.*

This pin you may wear with pride. It identifies you as a champion Tanker builder of the Swan Island Yard—champions of the world in Tanker production.

In the presence of your accomplishment, I stand in humble appreciation—grateful for your war effort and proud of the Swan Island organization.

This picture and this pin are material—which both you and I cherish—but the greatest award is the knowledge that your efforts are giving the boys at the front the fuel they need, when they need it.
Sincerely Yours,
Henry J. Kaiser[11]

"Award of Merit—Ships for Victory" pin given by the Maritime Commission to record-producing Swan Island Shipyard workers. This pin was earned and worn by Augusta Clawson. DIVISION OF WORK AND INDUSTRY, NATIONAL MUSEUM OF AMERICAN HISTORY, SMITHSONIAN INSTITUTION.

A letter from A. R. Nieman, a shipyard manager, was written on the same date as Kaiser's. Nieman wrote a detailed, praise-filled message to the Swan Island crews. And although he was a manager, he opened the letter with the words, "Fellow Workers:"

> *Long before the European invasion, you men and women here at Swan Island were called upon to produce tankers faster, better, and more efficiently than ever before. You responded with a vigor that emphasized your understanding of the vital part tankers perform for the allied war machine. The tankers you build make invasions and allied offensive warfare possible.*
>
> *Not only have you accepted the challenge of faster tanker production and responded magnificently, but you have also proved you are a champion by the bonds you buy, the blood you give, and the assistance you render all other war causes. Yes, you are truly a champion.*
>
> *In reviewing your past achievements, I know you are setting new records in production and workmanship. Our tankers, the lifeline of mechanized warfare, have proved that they are as good as the men and women who build them. And I know we all take justifiable pride in the knowledge that we are doing everything in our power to bring about victory!*
>
> *I personally consider it a great privilege to be associated with you Tanker Champs.*
>
> *Accept my warmest and most sincere congratulations.*
>
> *Sincerely yours,*
A. R. Nieman[12]

Champions or not, the process of construction-through-to-cruising of every seagoing craft meant all must follow the same routine. Each vessel would be constructed on the shipway, as stated by La Du, "from the keel plates to the superstructure, until the ship was launched." Once the hull was launched and moved to the dock, the interior was tackled, including "installation of ladders, doors, bunks, woodwork, . . . painted, and readied for her crew to take her on her shakedown cruise."[13]

Swan Island, with its evolving fleet of T2 tankers, was situated within a four-mile radius of Kaiser's other shipyards. And it was here to Swan Island shipyard that Augusta Clawson arrived to immerse herself into the hot and dirty world of welding together vessels of war.

President Franklin Roosevelt was interested in the production of his vessels of war, and he desired a better understanding of defense industry activities in the western United States. So, besides visiting the Puget Sound Naval Shipyard near Bremerton, Washington, he toured the military base at Ft. Lewis near Tacoma, Washington. Granted, this was a secret inspection tour the autumn of 1942. When he reached the West, he visited Kaiser shipyards, stopping at Swan Island to personally witness a Liberty ship launching of the *Joseph N. Teal*. The president's secret tour was so well-kept that no newspaper reported about the tour until the president had returned to Washington, DC.[14]

Well, almost no newspaper. Apparently, according to an essay by Duane Colt Denfeld, PhD, a small Seattle newspaper called *Aero Mechanic*, catering to the Boeing machinist's organization, published a story about Roosevelt's presence on the West Coast. The Secret Service soon discovered it and pulled the newspaper from "post offices and destroyed" them. Very few were distributed, with the editor claiming he was unaware of the decree of silence.[15]

The shipyards Roosevelt visited, as all shipyards, were critical to the war effort. Whether built by men or women, First Lady Eleanor Roosevelt paid tribute to shipbuilding in April 1943. President and Mrs. Roosevelt traveled to Henry Kaiser's Vancouver yard, managed by his son, Edgar, so Eleanor might christen the shipyard's first aircraft carrier—and the first *all-welded* carrier—the USS *Alazon Bay*. By doing so, she helped launch "the first of a new type of escort aircraft carriers to be built in this country," according to an article inside the April 8 issue of the *Bo's'n's Whistle*. "Eyewitnesses estimate around seventy-five thousand workers, residents and guests turned out to greet the first lady as she smashed a bottle of champagne across the bow of the USS *Alazon Bay*." Eleanor Roosevelt addressed the wave of humanity that swept out below her across the Vancouver yard, saying in part: "Building ships is an absolute necessity . . . You are doing it! You are doing it magnificently and I congratulate you today and wish for you good health and good luck so that as you look back over these years of hard work you will feel that you have done your part." Later, she would say, "It was a thrill to see the *Alazon Bay* go down the ways, because I realized it was one more fighting ship to help our men in distant places."[16]

First Lady Eleanor Roosevelt takes aim with a bottle of champagne preparing to christen USS *Alazon Bay* at Kaiser Co., Inc. Vancouver Shipyard, April 1943. Photographer: Louis Lee, 1943. OREGON HISTORICAL SOCIETY RESEARCH LIBRARY, OHS.ORG. ORGLOT1059.

Eleanor Roosevelt congratulates Edgar Kaiser on the *Alazon Bay* launching while his father, Henry, offers his handkerchief to wipe away champagne foam. Notice Edgar holds a second handkerchief at the ready. OREGON HISTORICAL SOCIETY RESEARCH LIBRARY, OHS.ORG. ORGLOT1059.

During brief stop-work events, gigantic vessels were often christened by diplomats, politicians, military officers' wives, and, as with the USS *Alazon Bay*, even the First Lady. Once launched with the breaking of a bottle of champagne, each ship's mammoth frame slid down rails, or ways, into the Columbia or the Willamette River, depending upon where its yard was located. Ships were then pushed and pulled by tugs and barges to the docks for fitting and finishing. Most welders welcomed any break-in-routine activities, for they often worked beyond a normal work week.

One of the most meaningful ships to be launched from Swan Island shipyard was the tanker *Oregon Trail*. This christening was in commemoration of the "100th anniversary of [the] arrival of wagon trains to Oregon territory."[17]

Once Augusta was actively welding, she began to theorize, noting the extreme conditions already present that spring. Perhaps whatever was the matter in the shipyard that affected women welders was occurring because of the summer season: "[T]heir leathers are so hot and heavy, they get more of the fumes, and their hoods become instruments of torture. There were times today when I'd have to stop in the middle of a tack and push my hood back just to get a breath of air." Perhaps this was the day she'd felt particularly haggard when she returned to her hotel room, sat down in front of her typewriter, and reported the ragged day she'd spent answering to the call, "Welder, tack here!" But Augusta persevered, continuing to work alongside other women welders and to observe the world of welding and shipbuilding that she had entered, gathering needed information.

While investigating, some of what she discovered was very basic, such as there was only cold water and a type of rough soap that was harsh on a woman's skin, so most never washed before leaving their shift. And there could be no argument that the work was dirty. Augusta confessed, "I never expected to catch myself eating lunch with my hands the color they are most noon hours lately."

Even before eating lunch, she and her group of cronies did not wash their hands. She explained that because the lunchroom was so far from their ways where they worked, "it's 'be clean and skip food' or 'be dirty and eat.' I eat. I compromise by insulating my sandwich from my filthy hands by gripping it daintily with a paper napkin."

Augusta had to catch a shipyard bus to her temporary home, the Multnomah Hotel, unable to find open housing through the shipyard. She also skipped cleaning up at the end of her shift in order to get to the bus on time to snag a seat.

Yet Augusta knew some improvements were already coming because of her report—such as orientation meetings and restrooms on the ways. Her friend Lois's husband, Joe Housman, had suggested adding restrooms to that level to reduce the use of ladders to get to a restroom after Augusta asked for a suggestion of what might improve working conditions.

A short time after she began reporting back to DC regarding her observations, there was talk among women welders about another new, good idea floating about the shipyard. Lois, nicknamed Missouri, was again especially glad to share what she knew. Now, Augusta's suggested orientation meetings were being held for all women when they first arrived at the shipyard. This was an improvement over simply submerging women with only basic training into the sometimes-turbulent environment of unfamiliar production work. Could there have existed a "sink or swim" attitude in some trainers?

Augusta must have practiced her poker face as she listened, wondering how her coworkers would react if they knew she was responsible for this much-welcomed work activity. Fortunately for women welders and others, the Kaiser staff were willing to listen and follow her recommendations, which came via the US Department of Education acknowledging Augusta's reports.

Everything was hard about the shipyard work, but the women carried on. "It's strange how suddenly one feels tired after the whistle... At night I'm so stiff and lame that I wonder how I'll navigate ladders next day. But next day I jaunt up and down and up and down and forget my aches."

She wondered, too, about the education level of the women welders building warships. There was no way for Augusta to decipher how much schooling a fellow woman welder had. She imagined no one thought she had a degree, let alone two. She also wondered if her shipyard friends believed she'd even earned a high school diploma. "I think we college graduates flatter ourselves when we think our academic degrees somehow set us apart from other people. I've honest respect for education that people have gained the hard way."

Earning the title *cover girl* was probably not as difficult for Augusta as welding could be and was surely not on her list of things to accomplish. Yet, in September 1943, after her mission on Swan Island was completed, Augusta became a cover girl of an industrial nature for the *American Vocational Association Inc. Journal and News Bulletin*. In the cover photo it appears at first glance as though Augusta is on a meal break at the

Swan Island shipyard. Captured leaning against a wall, she sits on the floor wearing her leather welding gear and her helmet emblazoned with the name Gus. Her welding hood rests beside her foot, a lunch pail and thermos bottle are open atop a box with the word *Hotel* written across. With a smile on her much too clean face, she's holding a piece of fruit in her also very clean hand, and a ring is visible on her left hand. Wearing jewelry on the job was strictly *verboten!* And upon close inspection, the wall appears to be covered in wallpaper and the floor is carpeted. For whatever reason, the photographer appears to have posed Augusta in her hotel, not in the shipyard.[18]

Welder Augusta "Gus" Clawson posed as if at a meal break at Swan Island Shipyard. Her hood rests beside her feet. Note the nickname "Gus" across her helmet.
DIVISION OF WORK AND INDUSTRY, NATIONAL MUSEUM OF AMERICAN HISTORY, SMITHSONIAN INSTITUTION.

Agent Augusta H. Clawson had been successful fitting into the shipbuilding industry as Gus. She must have felt a certain pride knowing she had learned how to weld, and how to do it well. Surely, there was great satisfaction in knowing also that she quite quickly had begun to provide help to the women who were showing up at the shipyard, increasing their chances at remaining in the essential, satisfying, and financially beneficial work.

Chapter Four

WHO WAS HENRY JOHN KAISER?

"I am certain that I was less than an average boy to everyone but my mother."

—Henry J. Kaiser[1]

Baptized as Heinrich, Henry John Kaiser was born on May 9, 1882, in Sprout Brook, New York, some sixty miles west of Albany, to Frank and Mary Kaiser (born Franz and Anna Marie), immigrants from Steinheim, Germany. The only son and youngest child, Henry seemed to have been imbued with ambition from an early age. The astounding and abundant fruits of his lifelong labor would suggest that the desire to achieve ran through his very blood and bones. According to *Pathfinder*, a booklet that was a forerunner of *TIME Magazine*, "Kaiser's specialty is the impossible." He found joy in discovering a need—no matter how incongruous with reality or past practices—and providing an idea for a solution to satisfy that need, while working and watching his vision take form.

Said to be the son of a farmer—who was elsewhere identified as a shoemaker—Henry began earning his way early. Young Henry was eventually successful in finding a job, although the search was hampered by the state of affairs in the nation at the time.[2]

It was 1893 and the country was suffering an economic crisis unlike any before: "a four-month spasm of financial hysteria known as the Panic of 1893," as described by historian John Caldbick. Several arguments exist as to the major cause of the Panic, including a preceding economic boom, failed banks, bankrupt railroad companies, and fear; specifically, fear for the future. Regardless of the cause, the resulting situation was shaping the world into which Henry Kaiser would grow to be a man.[3]

According to *White's Biographical Bulletin* of January 1946, "At the age of eleven he left school and went to work for a photographer." The *Spokane Daily Chronicle* later declared "Henry J. Kaiser got his first job when he was 13 as a helper in a Utica, N.Y., dry goods store."[4]

Following his mother's death when he was a teenager, he moved to the tourist town of Lake Placid, New York, to work in a photography studio, taking pictures of tourists. Eventually Henry purchased the studio from the man for whom he had worked. In 1906, Henry met and won the heart of a particular vacationer from Norfolk, Virginia, named Bessie H. Fosburgh. Kaiser Permanente historians merge these two pieces of information, informing readers that it was at the age of thirteen that he found "his first job as a salesclerk. His next job was in the photography business." One might conclude it was the photography business—and the meeting of a girl—that ultimately placed Henry J. Kaiser on a path that led to the building of roads, dams, and ships, to name only a few of his accomplishments.[5]

His photography business catering to those seeking pleasure and respite was very successful. He continued to expand the business by building other photography studios. During the summer, he catered to tourists such as Bess and her family in Lake Placid; by winter he shifted residences along with the tourists to Florida, operating out of another of his studios.[6]

Although Henry was doing quite well as a young man, he'd not yet won over the mind of Bess' father, Edgar, who felt the photography business wasn't stable enough to secure a solid future for his daughter. Fosburgh offered Kaiser a challenge, if not an ultimatum, that he "must close up his shop, go far away from summer resorts, preferably to the Northwest, get a job in a real business and arrive at a salary of at least $125 a month." He was to also establish a healthy savings account and build a home for Bess.[7]

Henry answered the challenge and went to the Northwest to explore "construction opportunities" as a means of laying a strong foundation—

in other words accumulating enough money to support a family before returning to present himself as suitable husband material.

Spokane, Washington, was where Henry decided to make his living. When he arrived in 1906, the population of the place was mushrooming. "By 1900, the population had reached 36,848, and by 1910 had more than tripled, to 104,402."[8]

Upon arriving in Spokane, he went to work for a long-established hardware firm, McGowan Bros., where he started by earning seven dollars per week. In six years, he was earning $250 per month as the "city salesman."[9]

Having achieved his goal of establishing himself in the business of construction, Henry traveled to Boston, Massachusetts, where Bess awaited, and the two were married on April 8, 1907, in the Hotel Touraine. It was reported to be an intimate affair, exactly as they wanted. Although not intimate enough, perhaps, as the *Spokesman-Review* caught wind of it six days later and broadcast the news.

After bringing Bess back to Spokane, Henry moved them into a home on Fourth Avenue near the center of the city. A few minutes away up the South Hill along Grand Boulevard stood, and still stands, Spokane's lovely Manito Park with its lilac, rose, and English gardens along with a sparkling glass conservatory. They left the house on Fourth Avenue after building a custom home near the corner of Sumner Avenue and Grand Boulevard. From the only photo found of the house in library archives, it appears it could have been constructed of brick beneath its attractive terra cotta round roof tiles. A quaint window peeks from under a dormer roof framed on either side by decorative wooden shutters.

The photo was taken in the winter season, but it must have been glorious in the springtime when all the dormant plants burst forth in bloom. A trellis ready to support what were likely climbing roses surrounds what may have been the leaded dining room window. On each side of the steps rising from the street garden beds appear filled with pruned rose bushes—or perhaps lilac bushes, which thrive in Spokane. Climbing to a pergola across the front porch is what appears to be a woody wisteria vine, sleeping in preparation to produce its fragrant, hanging lavender clusters. It seems obvious that Bess loved this home, surrounding it with

"Kaiser home. South Grand and Sumner Ave." Built by Henry J. Kaiser for his wife, Bess, in Spokane, Washington. Concrete steps are all that remain. 1890–1910.
"SPOKANE HOMES — (#02)," SPOKANE PUBLIC LIBRARY, HTTPS://LANGE.SPOKANELIBRARY.ORG/ITEMS/SHOW/1686.

multitudinous flora and foliage. It was a handsome house designed by early Spokane architect, W.W. Hyslop. Sadly, the house is gone today, except for its concrete steps.[10]

Once settled into their new home, Henry went from hardware merchandising to selling fuel to managing a paving company, then to starting his own. As a newlywed, he was busy absorbing the whys and wherefores of marriage along with those of the world of construction, or as Henry was said to prefer . . . the world of "building."

And build he did. He built a family with Bess consisting of Edgar, born in 1908 and named after Bess' father; a daughter who died at birth; and Henry Jr., who was born in 1917. He helped to construct the streets of the city of Spokane, paving the way, literally, for his future enterprises.

In 1914, the family left Spokane to move to Vancouver, British Columbia, Canada, to follow a winning construction bid for a road project there, and where Kaiser further fortified his paving and road-building business, Henry J. Kaiser Co., Ltd. After paving the streets of Spokane and building roads in Canada, he moved his family and household to the city of Oakland, California.

In an interview for *Life Magazine*, Bess Kaiser notes that once they left Spokane while the paving company was growing, "We never had a home." This seems to have been the case for some years. According to the Federal Census report of 1920, she and Henry were listed as part of the household of her in-laws, Henry's parents in New Paltz, New York. Perhaps they had only been visiting when the census taker knocked, for their two sons were not listed.[11]

It was reported that "she and the boys always accompanied their paterfamilias on his 90,000-mile-a-year tours of construction sites." It's obvious from the 1930, 1940, and 1950 census reports that they were comfortably ensconced in a home in Oakland, California, where the households included a twenty-six-year-old white maid, a fifty-year-old Chinese "houseboy," and a nineteen-year-old Chinese "houseboy," respectively. From this home in Oakland, his last and most important road-building project would begin with a contract to build two hundred miles of highway plus three hundred bridges in the country of Cuba.[12]

After his enormous effort in Cuba, Kaiser "achieved national prominence in the construction industry as one of the organizers of the Six Companies, Inc., organized by a formidable team of seasoned [contractor] veterans," which in 1931 was awarded the contract for building Boulder Dam on the Colorado. Henry and his fellow Six Companies, Inc. members would accomplish much in the years ahead. These experiences would directly impact the construction and running of the Pacific Northwest shipyards.[13]

It was said the "Six Companies stood as a monolithic entity in the new American West . . . [because of the] construction of the Bonneville and Grand Coulee Dams, the foundations for the Golden Gate and Bay bridges, numerous canals, tunnels, factories, shipyards, pipelines and refineries in the U.S. and abroad." The company, with Kaiser prominent in the organization, would take on the massive project of constructing the Hoover Dam.[14]

Kaiser had developed a keen mind when it came to understanding what was needed for any construction project, and how best to acquire or create what was required to accomplish the task, whether small-scale or herculean. He had earned an understanding of how to gather people who could get the job done without much hesitation. In 1934, "he formed and became president of the Columbia Construction Co., which built the Bonneville Dam on the Columbia River, near Portland, Oregon. Five years later, he organized and became president of Consolidated Builders, Inc. which constructed Grand Coulee Dam, the world's largest concrete structure." Later, the Six Companies, Inc., with Henry Kaiser at the helm, built the Shasta Dam in California.

To aid in the production and financial success of completing the projects of building dams, Kaiser built a successful concrete manufacturing plant to meet the needs of material for road and dam building. With his outstanding record as an industrialist building throughout the West, Kaiser attracted numerous other construction contracts. For instance, he "supplied the concrete for and constructed naval defense works in Hawaii and on the islands of Wake and Guam." It seems ironic that it was not long after Kaiser did his work to strengthen structures at the naval base in Hawaii that Japan would attack, destroying a fleet of ships that Kaiser and his company had tried to help protect.[15]

Even before the attack on Pearl Harbor, Henry Kaiser had not been standing still but had been involved in the earliest war effort. The Kaiser Richmond shipyards had been running even while the shipyards in the Pacific Northwest were being constructed. In Richmond, the shipyards had been tasked with "building cargo ships for Great Britain."[16]

The Congress of the United States enacted the Lend-Lease Act in January 1941, which was created to provide war materials to Great Britain and other Allied nations. Armed conflict had existed for Britain since the fall of 1939, immediately after the attack on Poland by Hitler's forces. The United States had declared Neutrality Acts when the war began in Europe, making the lending or leasing of materials the only way to provide aid at the time.[17]

Who Was Henry John Kaiser?

Most importantly for Kaiser concerning his contribution to war materials was that he built his own shipyards and his workforce consequently built all types of military vessels during the war production years. Near the end of those years, Victory ships slid down the Kaiser ways—called "this country's No. 1 hope for postwar shipping business." His contribution to the US Maritime Commission's Emergency Shipbuilding Program would comprise a significant portion of his legacy, along with his approach to hiring workers.[18]

> *Henry J. Kaiser was not your typical industrialist ... and his hiring practices made it easier for women and Black people to join the workforce. In 1942 he didn't hire people through the unions, which were composed of white male workers. To support wartime production, he integrated the shipyards—hiring black men directly and hiring women from the United States Employment Service [like Augusta Clawson was hired]. Union leaders, of course, voiced their opposition to this strategy.*[19]

In 1942, while the world was changing and women were beginning to enter the shipyards to become welders and burners and more, Henry Kaiser was already talking about what the nation would experience when the war was done. Perhaps like many, he could not imagine the war lasting as long as it eventually did.

In San Francisco on September 29 at a testimonial dinner in Kaiser's honor for his massive contributions to war production, he said:

> *I wish I could raise my voice just once so that it would reach every man, woman and child in these United States and say that we not only do not need to have a post-war depression, but, on the contrary, the very day that peace is declared America can enter on the period of her most promising prosperity; her greatest agricultural and industrial expansion; her greatest individual and social opportunity, and last, but not least, her greatest chance to become the hope of the nations of the world which will set themselves to the gigantic task of rebuilding the devastated areas.*

Going on to say, "I shall be the very last to urge that there is any benefit in war," Kaiser suggested one benefit: "We are getting rid of a lot of junk. The obsolete, the outmoded, and the worn-out is being melted down and fashioned into fighting equipment. Perhaps never before in the whole industrial era has obsolescence operated as extensively as it does today. When peace comes, why not turn the obsolete, worn-out, and ruined armament into the materials of reconstruction."

In closing, he remarked: "I sometimes hear it said that America needs a baptism of fire. This came to us at Pearl Harbor and Bataan. What we need now is a new baptism of faith and confidence from which will spring the morale to carry us beyond victory into the years of our greatest achievements, when our hopes are fulfilled, the era of good will be devoted to building rather than to destruction."[20]

Kaiser believed this strongly. He lived an incredible life under the banner of his beliefs, which were not necessarily of a religious nature. Henry McLemore had something to say about him in the *San Francisco Examiner* of September 30, 1942. "Suggestion:" he wrote, "That the Government E-for-excellence pennant be awarded the parents of Henry J. Kaiser for producing such a son. The west coast genius has now built a ship in ten days. Before he gets through Mr. Kaiser will have every one of his critics standing in a corner wearing dunce caps of such a height that their sides can be used for ski runs."[21]

An article titled "Gold Eagle for Oregon" was printed in the April 8, 1943, issue of the *Bos'n's Whistle*, which described "the presentation of the Maritime Commission's 'Gold Eagle' Merit Award Flag, evidence of [eleven] consecutive merit awards—the first of its kind to be given to any Maritime yard in the country."[22] Think of it . . . the first of its kind.

In May 1943, Henry Kaiser spoke at a baccalaureate service before seven thousand people at Washington State College (later Washington State University) in Pullman, Washington, where he received a "doctor of laws degree." Interestingly, this event was reported in the *Sidney Daily News* of Sidney, Ohio, under the heading, "Kaiser Is Said to Outdo Ancient." The paper announced that the regents and faculty members of the college offered tribute to Kaiser, "the builder of Grand Coulee dam and hundreds of Liberty ships." The tribute read: "We cherish our

Gold Eagle Pennant. "Receiving award for excellent achievement in war time production. *From left:* Mark O'Dea, Edgar F. Kaiser, Al Bauer, Henry J. Kaiser, and Clinton E. Smith." © *THE OREGONIAN.* ALL RIGHTS RESERVED. USED WITH PERMISSION. NEG. NO. ORHI68829.

association with you, whose mighty dams have dwarfed the pyramids. Through these mighty dams you have become a creative force in American life, and through your answer to the call of the united nations you are now a power in the making of a good new world of peace."[23]

There must be some measure of irony in the knowledge that an American named Kaiser—whose parents were born in Germany—would through the consequence of his life's work come to be called "Axis Smasher," one of the sharpest thorns in the side of Hitler.

Chapter Five

HOUSING SHIPYARD WORKERS

"The greatest mass housing project of any shipyard in the nation is gradually nearing completion here."[1]
—*Bos'n's Whistle*, Portland, Oregon

"Industrial housing shows what can be done in the building of modern communities for the people who have a mind to work."
—Henry J. Kaiser[2]

A great need for housing came with the great need for workers that brought the influx of shipyard and related war production industry workers to the Portland–Vancouver area. A sudden and unfamiliar crisis for each of the prominent Pacific Northwest cities, it quickly became apparent that some kind of housing was needed for new recruits reporting to shipyards. Workers needed to arrive knowing there would be a place to stay while they made themselves familiar with a new city, a new job, and perhaps even a new culture.

Fortunately, Henry Kaiser had experience working with government agencies to acquire federal funding for projects—in this case housing, and specifically dormitories. He had helped lead the Six Companies, Inc. conglomerate in building massive dams to power the West, and constructed roads to improve cities and to connect or cross borders. Thus, he was able to move forward quickly to begin hiring subcontractors to build the suddenly necessary shelter. On Swan Island, the housing took the form of both barracks and apartment buildings capable of housing ten thousand shipyard workers.

Three smaller projects were built in Vancouver neighborhoods to house over three thousand more workers and their families. The Vancouver projects began with the Fourth Plain Village Housing Project, the Fruit Valley Homes project, and the Harney Hill project.[3]

According to writer Kit Oldham, "Six housing projects, accommodating 45,000 people, were constructed in the area during the war. There were only around 18,000 people in Vancouver in 1941." This is one example of the sudden explosion in the population as shipyard workers streamed into the area, arriving daily by whatever means possible.[4]

One can imagine the shock such a population explosion could give to those who had been born and raised in the neighborhoods of Portland and Vancouver. There is the possibility such a shock was relieved if the city dwellers had been aware of the Kaisers' published national plea for workers to come to the shipyards. Many would have noticed the increased train traffic bringing crowds of people to surge through the tall, wood-framed glass doors of Union Station, walk across the tiled floor that spread below the high, carved ceiling, to then exit the other side into an alien city. Perhaps those citizens initially disturbed by the realization that their city was to undergo massive change settled their minds by remembering FDR's fireside address to the nation when he proclaimed: "We are all in it all the way."

People at Portland's municipal government were surprised to find an over-six-hundred-acre construction project that had not been on their docket. The development arising there meant that Henry and Edgar Kaiser and their company had bypassed the city of Portland authorities, gone directly to the federal government for permission to proceed, and gone forward with their plans to build temporary wartime housing. Since the land purchased for the project was actually outside the jurisdiction of the city of Portland, the Kaisers were not required to get permission from the city.

Years later, recognized as "The largest project [in Portland–Vancouver]—in fact, the largest defense housing project in the United States—[it] was called *Vanport* (a portmanteau of Vancouver and Portland), and [was built] to house 40,000 people. Of those 40,000 people, forty percent were African American." This factor also would change the face of the area. Then, what began as a plan for a little over 6,000 two-story apartments built of wood in what was, essentially, a swampland, grew to just under 10,000 apartments by the end of the construction project.

Originally referred to as Kaiserville, and officially named Vanport in November 1942, it was soon pronounced the second largest city in Oregon. The Kaiser company had been desperate to reduce the strain put on housing in the region when the number of defense employment workers rose from a few thousand to about 140,000 from 1940 to 1943. The housing shortage was said to have made it "difficult to secure and hold skilled workers."

It seems that when Augusta arrived in the city of Portland in April 1943, it was after most of the dust had settled off the feet of the crowds of new arrivals. There is no mention in her report of a housing shortage as one of the possible causes of women welders leaving the shipyard soon after training and beginning to work.[5]

The site that Edgar Kaiser acquired for the housing project was 650 acres of "Columbia River flood plain ... roughly equidistant between Kaiser facilities at Swan Island, St. Johns, and Vancouver." Again, called the largest wartime housing development in the country, it was, according to the essay "Vanport" by Carl Abbott, "a lightning rod for racial prejudice."[6]

It could be argued that racial prejudice was evidenced in the unspoken way black families were directed together for housing in a particular section of the development, for one example. This pattern was repeated in other wartime housing developments in the cities of Portland and Vancouver; "in most cases Blacks and Whites lived in separate areas within the projects."[7]

Tragically, three years after war's end, on Memorial Day 1948, Vanport, which was located between the edge of the city of Portland and the Columbia River, faced a threat that could not be ignored.

Authorities had been watching the rising river situation and had soon after the break of day distributed flyers to everyone dwelling in Vanport informing that they were safe. Then, during that one long horrific afternoon into night and no more than one minute after the shriek of a warning siren, water began to seep into Vanport City streets, rapidly growing in depth. The entire housing project would be inundated by a twelve-foot wall of water caused by a break in a dike along the railroad tracks. The city that had once housed 42,000 shipyard workers was swiftly demolished by the force of nature. The homes and belongings of nearly 19,000 people were gone in a frighteningly short period of time. The city of Portland was instantly called upon to stand together and bear the burden of providing temporary housing, food, and clothing for the thousands of victims. The newspapers soon declared that only fifteen lives were lost. However, some would later claim the number of deaths in the Vanport flood was purposely and greatly underreported. Vanport was never rebuilt.

Fortunately, three years before the flood, a portion of the housing that had been built as Vanport City was moved after the end of the war to Bremerton, Washington, to house shipyard workers who were now repairing battle ships that had come home. An article in the *Daily Olympian* added, "Units of the world's No. 1 housing project to be moved are mostly 14-apartment buildings which are dismantled, catalogued for easy reassembly, placed on a truck, and sent on their way to the repair yard city."[8]

Flooding was not the only hazard that destroyed shipyard worker housing. A raging inferno burst on the scene one cold November night in 1942 at the shipyard dormitory in Vancouver, Washington. Someone had accidentally ignited a devastating fire. Seven died; three of them women who had traveled from their hometowns to Portland to work in the Kaiser shipyards, eager to help with the war effort. Newspapers identified the deceased women as Edna Schafer of Bend, Oregon; Mrs. Agnes Johnson, who was described as a "New York negress"; and Sadie Crawford, who had arrived from Fort Jones, California.

Fire struck again a little over a year later inside Kaiser's Richmond, California, shipyard, in January 1944. A men's dormitory housing around seventy-five men burned, killing at least eight men, who were not immediately named. Others were believed to be buried in the debris and were yet to be found at the time the news was reported.[9]

Besides dormitories, whole neighborhoods were built strictly to house shipyard workers and their families. The Housing Authority of Portland (HAP) was established to organize the construction of housing developments in "Portland, Oregon, and environs." At least sixteen projects sprouted across the city and around its outskirts. Each project was designed with a certain number of "dwelling units," from as few as seventy-two units at a project named "Fir Court," to nearly ten thousand at the doomed Vanport City. Other developments were christened Columbia Villa, Dekum Court, St. Johns Woods, Parkside Homes, Hudson Street Homes, Gartrell Project, University Homes, Fairview Homes, Slavin Courts, Fulton Homes, Fessenden Homes, East Vanport, and Guild's Lake Courts. Two dormitories, Bellaira Court and Powers Dormitory, were also built under the auspices of HAP.[10]

Those workers fortunate enough to purchase a home could depend on newspaper advertisements listing houses for sale to include phrases such as "walking distance to shipyards" or "near shipyards." Otherwise, "By December 1942, war workers moved into public housing at a rate of [two hundred-fifty] families per week."[11]

The same year that Augusta came to the Swan Island shipyard, 1943, it was determined that it was time to provide dormitories for women in the yard. Four dormitories were subsequently built with 256 rooms each to house a total of "512 girls, with two girls sharing each room." Women who came to the dormitories were assigned to rooms with workers from their same shift "in order that no inconveniences might result." The rooms were described as:

> *comfortably furnished with two beds, chiffonier [chest of drawers], two closets, two overstuffed chairs; towels and bedding are furnished. Maid service is also available just as in any first class hotel. A large room has been provided with wash basins, mirrors,*

and cosmetic shelf and showers. Each shower has its own curtained dressing room. Laundry trays, ironing boards, and telephone service are also available.[12]

To keep dormitory life orderly, a matron was assigned to live in and oversee housing arrangements. At Swan Island, that matron was Mrs. Ella Nora Key. A prudential hire, Mrs. Key previously spent seven years overseeing a women's dormitory at the Grand Coulee Dam site. Likewise, "among the girls already living in the new dormitories [were] many who previously lived in the Grand Coulee project."[13]

In January 1944, dormitories had opened in the Oregon Shipbuilding Corporation after an expenditure of $1,500,000 for the complete project, including the purchase of land. Like the dormitory on Swan Island, workers were to be housed with people who were working the same shift. One section of the dorms at Oregonship was reserved for women. The rest was designated for men and managed by a man named Clarence Codding. It was stated that the dormitories would house 2,088 single men and women.[14]

With the construction of dormitories on Swan Island, the original barracks that had been hastily built to meet the original flood of war workers were set to close in May 1945. The barracks had once housed four thousand male shipyard workers, but by 1945 was reduced for various reasons to four hundred, who would transfer to various dormitories as the barracks closed.

Not only were shipyard employees provided housing, but also grocery and dry goods stores for a convenient opportunity to purchase what the workers needed daily. Also, recreation halls appeared, where shipyard employees could relax while playing pool or shooting guns in an arcade.[15]

A trailer was another option for housing shipyard workers. One of Augusta's fellow women welders chose this living arrangement. "Then there was *Big Elmer*," began Augusta while describing a fellow welder friend. "He and his wife *Shorty* McGinnis lived in a trailer, and both

Housing Shipyard Workers

"A well-maintained park of trailers available as housing for shipyard workers in the Portland area." Photographer: Al Monner. September 8, 1942.
© *THE OREGONIAN*. ALL RIGHTS RESERVED. USED WITH PERMISSION. ORGLOT1284.

worked as welders. Elmer was slow and easy-going while Shorty was a regular firebrand."[16]

Temporary trailer camps were erected for war workers. Some sported neat gravel paths between orderly rows of trailers, with wooden walkways provided upon approach to each trailer. This alone must have been a welcome feature in the rainy, mud-prone Pacific Northwest.

More trailer parks, as they were also called, sprouted in various areas around the Portland–Vancouver region. For instance, Meadowlark Trailer Camp was an example of cabins built at the trailer camp where some shipyard workers chose to live. This camp was near Oregonship in the St. John's neighborhood of Portland. It appears that the camp was built on private property owned by one J. F. Gilmore. Gilmore was apparently "arrested multiple times in 1943 for running a camp without a certificate of inspection." However, some might suggest that in his

The Shipyard Agent

"A hastily constructed cabin at privately-owned Meadowlark Trailer Camp for shipyard workers near St. Johns, Portland, Oregon." Photographer: Al Monner. October 29, 1943. © THE OREGONIAN. ALL RIGHTS RESERVED. USED WITH PERMISSION. ORGLOT1284.

favor, he did construct a small wood frame building in the camp whose purpose was announced by a sign affixed to the front of the building reading "Church of God."[17]

Although Augusta Clawson had come to work on Swan Island for her government assignment, employee housing on the island was occupied when she arrived, as were many other areas. However, the Office of Education arranged for a room at the impressive Multnomah Hotel. The hotel, which rose in three stately towers, completely occupied the block bordered by Fourth Avenue and S.W. Pine Street in the city of Portland. One might imagine Augusta appreciated having a private room where she could sit and log her government reports without spying eyes.

Multnomah Hotel, where Augusta Clawson roomed during her shipyard assignment. The hotel, now known as Embassy Suites, still occupies the same city block in Portland. Circa 1920. PDX HISTORY. HTTP://WWW.PDXHISTORY.COM/HTML/MULTNOMAH HOTEL.HTML

Leaving her room in the grand hotel each morning decked out in her welding gear, her lunch pail swinging from one hand, she would return each night to enter the elevator bringing the smudge of the shipyard welding job with her. She must have been a sight inside "one of Portland's most prominent hotels." The building remains, and today, following restoration, it is the Embassy Suites by Hilton.[18]

Chapter Six

CELEBRATED CHILDCARE CENTER

"Even the problems of registering for fuel oil and for canned goods seem to provide less of an enigma than that of finding a nursery for a child left homeless while mother builds the instruments of victory."
—Oregon Daily Journal, February 21, 1943[1]

"Only their loyalty and patriotism enabled them to leave their homes to help in the war effort."
—Augusta H. Clawson

Henry J. Kaiser's Oregon organization was forward-thinking in providing what was a bit of an unorthodox service for its shipbuilding families at the time: childcare located where one worked, which must have at first seemed fantastical to some.

It was Eleanor Roosevelt, when she came in 1942 to visit the Vancouver shipyard, who "put the bug in his ear." She took the time to describe to Edgar and Henry the type of care she had seen firsthand provided for the children of mothers working for the war effort in embattled England. Roosevelt also "pressured the head of the US Maritime Commission, Admiral Land [with whom she was acquainted] to approve funding for this" which he ultimately did.

Naturally, a press conference was held for any ship launched by the First Lady. She came to launch the USS *Alazon Bay* in 1945. The *Columbian* newspaper's Lois Wilkie Snyder reported that while answering questions for the press, Roosevelt "commented with approval upon the provisions being made for the care of children, and recreation of teenagers, for those whose mothers are employed in the yards. 'No woman can do a good day's work when she is worrying about her children, either the little ones, or the older ones,' she said, with understanding."[2]

The War Manpower Commission published their advice regarding care for children of workers in the informative booklet *War Jobs for Women*. Under the subject of day care, the text reads, "The War Manpower Commission has given an opinion that employment by industry of mothers of young children should in general be deferred until all other sources of labor supply have been exhausted."[3]

The *Victory Fleet*, a publication of the US Maritime Commission, agreed, stating in the May 31, 1943, issue: "The mental welfare of women workers is as important as their physical welfare.... Provision of nurseries by plants, community, or government is one way to relieve mothers for war work without endangering the health or social development of their children."[4]

With federal funding approved, Edgar Kaiser at once engaged an architectural firm to design two centers—one for Oregon Shipbuilding Corporation and one for Swan Island Shipyard—each to be used solely to provide childcare for children of Kaiser employees.

Providing childcare services was at this time an innovative, even phenomenal idea, one about which the only comment mentioned was, "thankfulness to Kaiser for the boldness of the conception." One wonders if Kaiser mentioned the influence the First Lady had rendered. An article in the March 1944 issue of the *Architectural Record* presents an architectural drawing of the layout for what was referred to as Kaiser's Child Service Centers. Noting that they were designed for twenty-four-hour childcare, architects Wolff and Phillips stated that the centers "serving Portland Shipyards are a Community School facility of a new and important type."[5]

The childcare center was built within eyesight of the housing units of shipyard families. At both Oregonship and Swan Island, the child service centers were built within the confines of the shipyard. Working adults could deliver their children for childcare, go directly to the

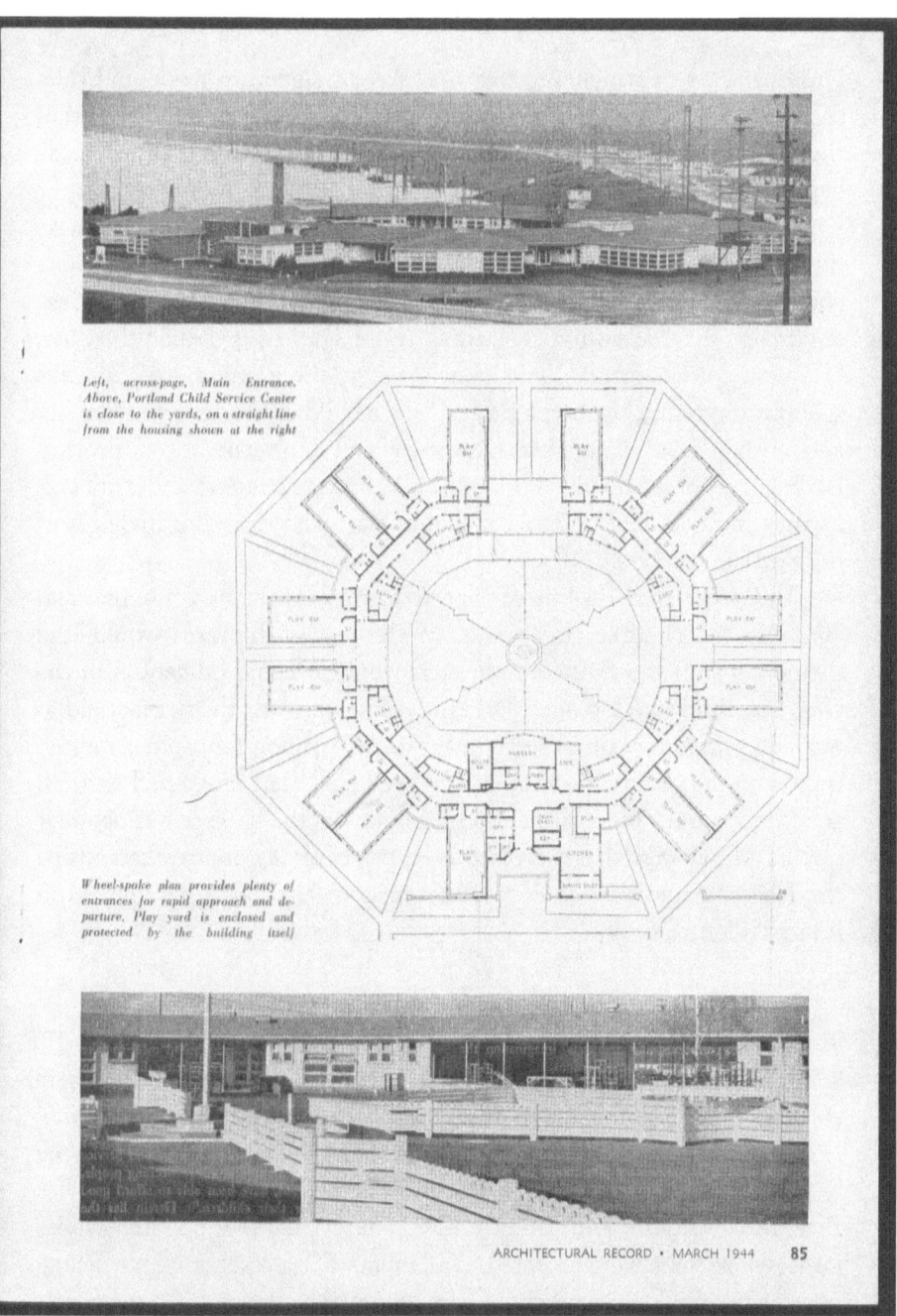

Architectural drawing of the proposed Child Service Centers, one each of which was built at Oregon Shipbuilding Corporation and Swan Island Shipyards. ©Architectural Record.

ARCHITECTURAL RECORD, MARCH 1944 ISSUE FROM THE ARCHIVES OF OREGON HISTORICAL SOCIETY COLLECTION 336. OHS.ORG.

building ways or whichever area they were assigned to work, and then easily return at the end of their shift to the child service center to gather their children, and perhaps pick up a preordered, prepared family meal, before returning home.

Henry Kaiser had invited the best in the business of childcare, education, and development to "set up ideal facilities and programs so workers could build ships without worrying about the safety and health of their children." The "best in the business" were Catherine Landreth, PhD, University of California, Berkeley, who set up the Richmond, California, schools program; Lois Meek Stolz, PhD, a child development researcher and author from Columbia University and University of California, Berkeley, who set up the Portland child service centers; and James L. Hymes Jr. (a student of Stolz at Columbia), who served as manager of the Portland centers.[6]

The experience that these experts gained organizing, running, and assessing the child service centers of the Kaiser shipyards would lead them well into the future where each would become influential in the world of child development. James Hymes, who was thirty years old at war's end, would go on to serve in President Lyndon Johnson's administration on the planning committee for the Head Start program. Landreth and Stolz would each write several books on the subject during their careers. What started as a project to help war production workers inside the Kaiser shipyards would expand across the nation to be applied in future childcare facilities.[7]

The Swan Island child service center had opened on November 18, 1943, where "only children whose mothers worked at Swan Island were enrolled." This is according to the November 17, 1944, issue of the *Bos'n's Whistle*, Swan Island edition. But the situation quickly changed for the better to be more inclusive as briefly described in the article, "Service Byword of Child Care Center": "On January 3, 1944, children whose fathers work here were accepted. On January 6, the kitchen began selling pre-cooked foods for workers to take home. Since January 17, the center has been open twenty-four hours a day."[8]

The centers allowed in children from eighteen months to six years old to a building described by its architects as a "radial wheel plan" design. That name is quickly understood when studying the architectural drawing, which shows how the design separated children by age for play and lessons while protecting them within the surrounding structure. All employees were eligible to use the child service centers no matter which shift they were assigned since the centers were now open twenty-four hours a day.

Children of graveyard shift workers became accustomed to arriving at the child service center at about bedtime, either already dressed for bed, or carrying their "night clothes in a bag." For the child's comfort, parents were instructed to bring each child to the center during the daytime for an introductory meeting with their teacher who would be with them each night, and to become familiar with the building where they would awaken each morning before breakfast.[9]

Mary Bryan Curd of the Oregon Historical Society also reported on the child service centers: "Older children could be enrolled for overnight care to accommodate parents who worked nightshifts. The facilities included a staffed kitchen and an infirmary, which cared for sick children and provided basic medical services. The centers also provided Home Food Service: any worker in the yard could buy prepared meals to take home at the end of a shift."

Curd also had this to say: "The childcare centers were integrated and open to the children of the growing African American workforce at the shipyards; but the racial prejudice by the white families was so severe, that most Black parents arranged for their own childcare. Very few African American children attended the schools."[10]

"The Kaiser Company employed 'Women Counsellors,'" wrote Sarah Stroman on the Oregon History website, "held open houses, and used their newsletter, the *Bos'n's Whistle*, to encourage workers to enroll their children in the centers." These counselors—something Augusta Clawson had certainly promoted—would sometimes meet women welders and other women at their work sites to discuss any concerns that might have arisen.

Besides the child service centers at Oregonship and Swan Island, nurseries, as they were described in the housing project, were the city of Vanport's answer to the need for twenty-four-hour childcare. It was astounding what Kaiser's teams had accomplished building Oregon's second largest city. Is it any wonder it was first called Kaiserville; the term *ville* originating from the French language meaning *town*? The infrastructure of the 650-acre site included not only housing and nurseries providing childcare, but also shopping centers, a movie theater, a small hospital, recreation centers, and schools. No doubt, those shipyard workers who chose to move into Vanport had felt fortunate for such a place to settle with their families while working to help win the war.[11]

By 1945, signs that production might be winding down—or at least was exiting the "emergency" stage—were appearing in the shipyards. A brief article in the *Bos'n's Whistle* announced, "Child Center Cuts Service to One Shift." In April 1945, as the war effort was slowing and a full two years after Augusta Clawson had suggested the benefits providing childcare services would bring, the Swan Island Child Service Center announced it would offer childcare only during day shift. Mothers who had been using the center during swing or graveyard shift would be allowed to transfer to a day shift position. The article stated that "Home service food, the infirmary, and immunization programs will be continued." The article also quoted General Manager Edgar Kaiser speaking of "the importance of human relationships in industry and [of citing] the Child Service Center as being a definite service to workers."[12]

Chapter Seven

TRAINING WOMEN TO WELD

"There seemed to be no system of selection beyond the single question: 'Are your eyes all right?'"

—Augusta H. Clawson[1]

Augusta's path to the Swan Island shipyard began on April 7, 1943, at an Oregon Employment Service office. There she applied for work as a welder and heard the obvious—that she must first take training. She was then handed a "certificate of availability." Directed next to talk with a counselor there, Augusta was told "training would take 40 to 60 hours, that I must cover my hair, wear overalls and high shoes or oxfords . . . [and I] would need goggles, helmet, and leathers."[2]

Because she needed a social security number to proceed with employment in the state, her next stop was the Portland Post Office. From there—since by 1943 shipyard employees were members of the International Brotherhood of Boiler Makers, Iron Ship Builders, and Helpers of America—Augusta reported to the union hiring hall.

At a table marked "Swan Island," her certificate of availability was accepted and her shift preference and starting date noted. "Be there at 7:00 tomorrow morning," the woman at the table instructed her. "Go now and have your fingerprints and photograph taken. Your dues are $30. You have 21 days to pay."

Augusta thought the union clearance routine was "very well ordered." She reported answering "rapid-fire questions: Maiden name? Home?

The Shipyard Agent

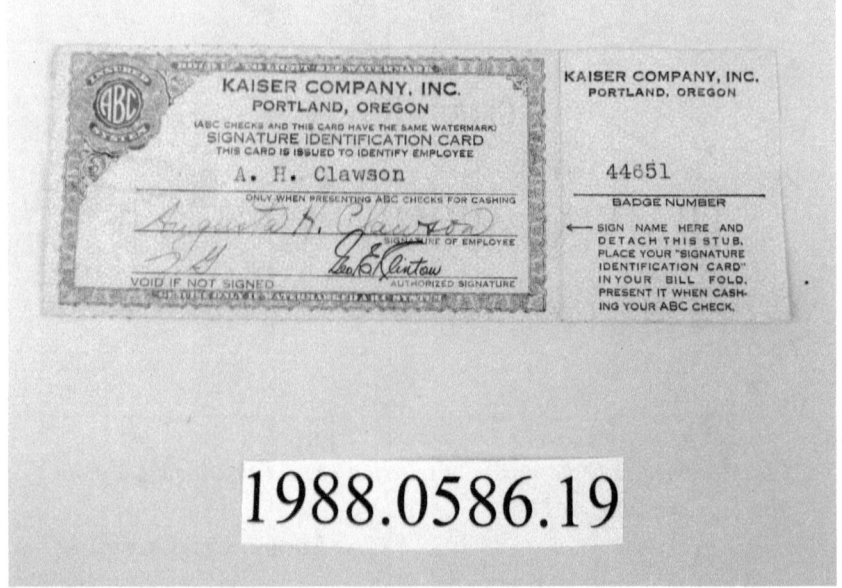

Kaiser Company, Inc., Portland, Oregon, employee signature identification card no. 44651 issued to A. H. Clawson, 1943. DIVISION OF WORK AND INDUSTRY, NATIONAL MUSEUM OF AMERICAN HISTORY, SMITHSONIAN INSTITUTION.

Where born? How long [a] resident of Portland? Previous employment in a shipyard?" and added, "I signed several forms, among them a promise not to attempt to overthrow the government." She received her Kaiser Company, Inc. employee signature identification card as A. H. Clawson, although she signed as Augusta.

After completing yet another form stating how many War Bonds she would buy, she was advised to take out "hospitalization and insurance." The counselor was thorough. "I was told to get slacks or overalls of some hard-surfaced material, to wear a man's shirt, to wear enough underneath it to keep warm. Heavy shoes would be needed and ski shoes from Lipman's [a fashionable Portland department store] were suggested. I'd need to buy leathers after a few pay days. I was told not to wear my watch for fear of ruining it." She was told that wearing a watch while welding would magnetize the workings of the watch.[3]

The Maidenform Company, too, had something to say about what women suddenly thrust into industrial work should wear. A full-page advertisement with a woman striding forward in coveralls, her hair drawn up in a scarf read, "Brassieres ... A Vital Necessity to Women at Work. Work in the war industries—for the most part—is much heavier than that to which a woman has hitherto been accustomed." This was likely a point well made for women entering shipyard work, such as welding.[4]

According to Augusta's official report, welders were required to purchase initial equipment. She found the whole experience confusing, which raised questions, for instance, concerning the purchase of the clothing she would need to wear as a welder in the shipyard.

Augusta Clawson poses outside her work environment wearing heavy welding gear and a smile. Hood and lunch pail are labeled with her initials. Date unknown.
COURTESY OF MARGARET "MEG" SONDEY.

"Should overalls fit snugly or be loose?" she wondered. "Should one purchase the kind with straps for tools? Should shoes have leather soles? Should one buy short or long socks, cotton or wool?" She concluded, "It is amazing how many decisions must be made without adequate information or knowledge."[5]

"My only regret," Augusta wrote, "was that [hiring] counseling came after all decisions were made."

Counseling provided before decision-making would make a world of difference in the realm of supporting new hires, according to Augusta's shipyard employment report. She detailed four areas where the women coming into the shipyard would benefit from advice:

1. "Selection of occupation based upon her adaptability and experience.

2. Obtaining her social security number, and birth certificate if under age 24.

3. Finances: She should know the approximate cost of equipment for her job before she obligates herself for other payments [such as purchasing War Bonds].

4. Preparation for the first day of training. She should buy the minimum amount of clothing for the job until she has reported for training.... The necessary items are welding gloves, slacks or overalls, and a jacket. She should wear her heaviest shoes and be sure her hair is covered."[6]

Comments recorded by Augusta regarding this day of preparation for entering welding school were detailed and revealing:

There is a very real nervous, emotional strain about a day like this.... Women without industrial experience have probably not encountered such impersonal and standardized handling before, and it gives one a helpless feeling. One feels cornered, as if one had signed over the power of free will and must report for this job without fail no matter what happens. It seems as inevitable and as bewildering as birth or death (or taxes). There are still so many unanswered questions that one is full of apprehension and a kind of dread of the unknown. Add to this the horror many women have of getting into a job for which they are unsuited and of being frozen there for the duration.

Other less important questions arose, according to Augusta's comments, regarding whether one must bring a lunch or use the cafeteria; where there would be secure storage available for any items such as an overcoat; if bringing money along is advisable; what the schedule of the shipyard buses is; how long it takes to travel to work each day, and so forth.[7]

―――

The office at Swan Island Welding School provided all newly hired employees with a badge. There, Augusta was also able to check out a hood and a steel brush for use during her training, which was to take place inside the welding building.

Once inside a welding booth, she was shown a "machine" and given the following explanations and demonstrations of the welding process:

black indicated high voltage, red low, and [he said] that I would probably use only the high. The amperage dial must be set in corresponding color range. Voltage is the push, amperage the heat. The latter differs with different size rod. Reverse polarity is used with white or grey rod, direct with all other. I was then shown a good working position resting [my] left elbow on [my] knee, steadying [my] right hand with [the] left. I was told how to detach the rod from the plate if it became stuck. I learned how to lessen the weight of the lead by looping it around the right arm. The instructor made one line of welding across the plate, guided my hand while I made one and told me to go ahead and practice.

"That's the only way to get it," the instructor had said. For the next two days, Augusta did just that; she practiced welding, and she got it. Oversight of the trainees by the welding instructors was inconsistent, she remarked, with some giving the women mid-session additional breaks of a few minutes besides the lunch break, some offering no break whatsoever. However, Augusta praised the "impersonal attitude of the instructors and the absence of any 'coddling' of the women trainees."[8]

Aside from the training issues, Augusta noted that there was only one toilet for all the women in the group, which she described as "inadequate" but added that she'd heard no one complain.

She received the standard training offered all women reporting to welding school on the Yard. According to Augusta, her training evolved in the following way:

- Third day—"changed to brown rod and was shown how to pad a plate"
- Fourth day (new instructor)—"learned to do a fillet weld with 3 passes of beads"
- Fifth day—"did a vertical weld on a flat plate and over this a vertical weave"
- Sixth day—"continued with vertical welds ... was shown 4 movies"
- Seventh day—"switched to work on the test plates"
- Eighth day—"took and passed my test" "did try overhead welding"[9]

Discussion among the women training at the school alongside Augusta led to agreement that there were still unanswered questions, and that the trainees "would have profited by access to printed material." Some women bought welding textbooks. "A number of us," reported Augusta, "wished we could see in print a lot of what was shown [in training films] rather than trust our memories to tell us which were the signs of too short an arc, too long, too hot, etc."

Believing the safety lectures were indeed helpful, Augusta nevertheless thought it would be better yet had the lectures offered safety information *specific* to welding, and not only general shipyard safety. "Many women have a fear of electricity because they have had no experience with it. Some even thought they might be electrocuted if they welded in the rain."

Welder Mabel (Shriver) Lionberger, author's grandaunt, wearing protective gear and supported by a welding cart, preparing to perform difficult overhead welding. Photographer: Al Monner. January 5, 1942.
© *THE OREGONIAN*. ALL RIGHTS RESERVED. USED WITH PERMISSION. ORGLOT1284.

Augusta was not convinced that women were dropping out of the shipyards because of the difficulty of the work—women were proving they could do the work of men—but because of inadequate training. And, of course, she had something to say: "I think the chief obstacles are six: 1) Strangeness, 2) Health, 3) Noise, 4) Height, 5) Climbing, 6) Inadequate skill and lack of confidence." Augusta believed that through improved training they could solve these "six causes of turnover among new workers" as she had identified them. She explained:

> *I was able to find a number of the defects in our training program and in the work plan which caused the women welders to quit. For one thing, in class each person worked in a little cubicle and could hear only the noise from his own work. Each one sat comfortably on a high*

stool made from the cross-section of a tree trunk. . . . It was easy and rather pleasant in class.

But when she described the first time she had entered the hold of a ship to work, surrounded by many other workers performing various tasks, all contributing to an incredible racket, she declared, "The noise was simply unbearable, maddening. It made me want to scream and scream I did just to see if I could be heard."[10]

Another reason workers were quitting, Augusta surmised, was because of "too little confidence in their skill, [leading to] dread [at] being asked to do work they think they cannot do." She developed a very detailed plan regarding the instruction of trainees. Following is a condensed version of her suggested plan:

A. Demonstration—instructors showing various welding methods

B. Practice—

    1. Overhead as well as flat welding

    2. Tacking with a curved rod

    3. Tacking from all sorts of positions

    4. Settings on different machines

    5. Tacking butterflies, "D's," saddles, clamps, dogs, etc.

    6. Burning off excess metal

C. Related Training—

    1. Safety: discuss any caution necessary in working with electricity . . . emphasize the use of goggles and hard hats . . . hold periodic inspections to be sure trainees are properly equipped . . . check carefully on shoes . . . caution kneeling on cold steel . . . information about hood lenses and air pipes for ventilation.

    2. Noise: Days differ. One day . . . below decks amid terrific noise, another day above with comparatively little noise . . . have cotton in one's pocket to plug the ears.

3. Height, climbing: Even those who are afraid . . . become accustomed. . . . Watch the men when they climb. There is a real technique. . . . There is always a safer way to reach the same spot.

4. Status of a Woman Worker: Each trainee might well be told the following—

   a. Go into the yard as a worker, not as a woman.

   b. You are on your own. The Yard offers excellent facilities, but no one has time to be your special guardian.

   c. You are assigned to work for . . . shipfitters and shipwrights. Do not resent this. This arrangement is simply to speed production.

   d. You may have to prove yourself the first few days before you are accepted as a partner in production. On you depends not only your own success but expanded opportunities for all women.

5. Morale: During training much can be done to build morale. . . . Some certificate of recognition might even be awarded to each trainee who furthers production by bringing in one more worker, by maintaining a perfect record of attendance, etc.

6. Nomenclature: Not a great deal is needed but some would be helpful. The new employee who is told to report to Port Tank 4 or Poop deck starboard will be glad she learned the difference.

7. Discussion of Trainee Difficulties: Question and answer sessions with either instructor or trainees asking questions aid in revealing trainee problems.

8. Upgrading: With the increasing numbers of women workers, there is every possibility some may be picked for jobs of increased responsibility. . . . Tell them about supplementary training and enlist their interest.

D. Visual Aids, Exhibits, and Printed Material—Instruction can be advantageously supplemented by the use of motion pictures, charts, exhibits, and printed matter.[11]

The Shipyard Agent

As a newly trained welder, Augusta was told where to report for work and to bring along her helmet. "There were no other instructions."

A memoir piece written in November 1943 by Anne Wallace, a fellow member of the American Association of University Women (AAUW), where Augusta had presented as guest speaker, describes what Augusta related about her feelings while anticipating her first day of work as a woman welder.

This feeling came following the long day of registering for employment in Oregon, joining the union, being assigned a location to work, and traversing a strange city to purchase unfamiliar work clothing. "By that time, she did not want to report at 7:00 a.m. as a welder. The first hurdle of courteous but impersonal treatment was almost too much."[12]

But Augusta kept her promise and on the next day began her government assignment, by rising from bed, dressing in her welding gear, and reporting for welding work at the great hull of a ship rising high above where its frame rested on the shipyard ways.

Chapter Eight

HAZARDS IN THE HULLS

"I certainly must buy one. If I'm to work down in a tank much more, it is asking for trouble not to wear a hard hat."
—Augusta H. Clawson[1]

During the year before Augusta entered shipyard work, she traveled to, studied, and worked in industrial environments while observing women employees. She was an adept observer.

As a skilled writer, Augusta published her findings regarding safety clothing for women in the December 1942 issue of the *Journal of Home Economics*. In the article "Safety Clothing for Women in War Production Industries," she included many details as to what to wear and why to wear each item. Some of the strongest points follow:

> *When before in history have women been urged to buy* safety *clothing? In fact, when before have they demanded garments that are* safe? . . . *More and more as men leave the jobs they have held, women are entering them.* . . . *All of this work is a far cry from the sewing machine or the office typewriter and entails far greater physical activity. The workers must be able to bend and reach and climb with comparative ease and safety.*

Augusta clearly describes each item a woman must consider:

No jewelry may be worn. Even the familiar wristwatch may catch on a rapidly moving lever and pull a hand in to be crushed. Jewelry may cause injury to its owner or may injure the material on which she is working....

There must be no freely flying hair. Not even bobbed hair is entirely safe....

Open-toed shoes are taboo.... Soles must be heavy enough to offer adequate protection from harsh materials....

Approved goggles are recommended or not as the job requires.

Gloves, too, depend upon the type of work.

Around machinery anything loose is a danger. There must be no loose sleeves, full skirts, rolled-up cuffs, or wide trouser legs.

It is vital that they follow safety procedures of dress from the opening day of training. If our women are to become a part of the working army, we must train them in the safest of work habits, give them the best techniques in the shortest time possible, and send them in to contribute their share in this all-out production for victory. They have a valuable contribution to make.[2]

With dangers ever present in the industrial welding environment, Augusta made many such discoveries. Electrical cords were being dragged through puddles of water upon the open deck, sparks and hot slag were spitting potential pain, debris was falling carelessly—the result sometimes crippling or fatal—from a deck above, fumes swirled toxins into the air. Because breathing toxic fumes often resulted in an employee contracting "Welder's Wheeze," as the condition was called, shipyard workers had the right to ask for air hoses when working where the ventilation was particularly restricted. Often, they were simply so busy they forgot to ask. Sometimes when they did ask, nothing was available.

Interestingly, within Augusta's report on her first week of work, she wrote, "I did not mind the fumes at all, but I had an outside booth. Both light and ventilation were far less satisfactory in the inside booths." And yet, at the end of her stint as a welder in the shipyard, she would state that she, too, had suffered from the overwhelming fumes in the welding work areas.[3]

She did not suffer alone, a fact which had been investigated, documented, and published as early as 1942. But had anyone been paying attention?

Nearly a year before Augusta became a welder, in the summer of 1942, following accusations and complaints against Oregon Shipbuilding Corporation, a study of "fume conditions" was "authorized by the Metal Trades Council of Portland and Vicinity," in other words, the Boilermakers, Steamfitters, Machinists, Electrical Workers, and Painters Unions. The study was conducted by four doctors from the University of Oregon Medical School listed as personnel: Drs. Frank R. Menne, a professor of pathology; Warren C. Hunter, a professor of pathology; Joseph Beeman, a toxicologist; and Norman A. David, a professor of pharmacology and toxicology. Following the distribution to and subsequent collection of questionnaires to forty randomly selected shipyard workers of all occupations from Oregonship, the forty were interviewed, as well. A following official "unbiased and neutral" report was published with the title: *Report of the Investigation of Fume Hazards at the Oregon Shipbuilding Company (Kaiser Company) at St. Johns, Portland, Oregon.*[4]

In the foreword of the report, the text very clearly states that the report is not *against* Oregonship but is intended to divulge conditions in all the Portland shipyards. And that Oregonship was selected for the study because it employed the largest number of persons.

Five thousand copies of the detailed report were eventually distributed. The report was neatly published and sent to all members of the Oregon Legislature, to every one of the state's physicians, to the Maritime Commission, to the Army and the Navy, to US Public Health, to Oregon's State Industrial Accident Commission, and to the State of Washington's Department of Labor and Industries. The results were also sent to all shipyards in the Portland–Vancouver area, and to all other yards along the Pacific Coast. Unions received copies as well. Henry Kaiser's

A QUESTIONNAIRE FOR THE INVESTIGATION OF WORKING CONDITIONS AT THE OREGON SHIPYARDS

(1) Name ....

(2) Age ....

(3) Previous occupations (duration of each) ....
....
....
....

(4) Nature of exposure ....
....
....

(5) Previous diseases ....
....

(6) Upper respiratory infections:
    (a) Paranasal sinus infections ....
    (b) Sore throat ....
    (c) Colds ....
    (d) Hoarseness ....
    (e) Cough ....
    (f) Pneumonia ....
    (g) Foreign bodies in lungs ....
    (h) Tuberculosis ....
    (i) Pleurisy ....
    (j) Asthma ....
    (k) Irregularities in breathing ....
    (l) Hay fever ....
    (m) Goiter ....
    (n) Adenoids ....
    (o) Use of inhalers ....
    (p) Use of sprays ....
    (q) Use of drugs ....
    (r) Tobacco smoking (extent) ....
    (s) Heart disease ....

(7) Shipyard occupation:
    (a) Date of employment ....
    (b) Type of work ....
    (c) Length of service ....
    (d) Number of hours ....
    (e) Shift ....
    (f) Exposure to fumes ....
    (g) Exposure to light ....
    (h) What protective measures exist for protection against fumes? ....
....
                            ....Were these measures used? ....
              Was there insistence upon their usage? ....

A medical questionnaire distributed to shipyard workers in Oregon to investigate working conditions. The focus was on the breathing of hazardous fumes while performing tasks, 1942. OREGON HEALTH AND SCIENCES UNIVERSITY HISTORICAL COLLECTIONS & ARCHIVES, HTTPS://WWW.OHSU.EDU/HISTORICAL-COLLECTIONS-ARCHIVES. COLLECTION 2007-007.

(i) What protective measures exist for the protection of the eyes against unusual light? ....
To what extent were these measures used? ....
To what extent was their use insisted upon? ....

(j) Effect of exposure to fumes while at work..................................
....
....

(k) Effect of exposure to fumes while away from work....................
....
....

(l) Symptoms:
    (1) Cough ....
    (2) Burning or irritation..
    (3) Hoarseness ....
    (4) Difficulty in sleeping..
    (5) Difficulty in breathing...
    (6) Pain ....
    (7) Night sweats ....
    (8) Loss of weight..

(m) Duration of exposure:
    Number of days..
    Number of hours..

(n) Treatment:
    At home ....
    At hospital ....
    Name of physician ....

(o) Date of last examination by physician.....................................
    Extent of examination..

(p) Condition of health previous to shipyard work........................

shipyard employees and industry practices were about to be scrutinized in a very big way.[5]

The closing statement from the foreword of the publication is thus: *The unsafe conditions, as shown in this report, can be corrected, and will be corrected.* If the conditions related to the exposure to hazardous fumes were corrected, why was Augusta facing the same reported conditions eight months later?

Some complaints against Oregonship became litigious. Within the introductory statement of the report is included the following tragic statement: "These complaints took form in the filing of certain suits for damages, either relating to the health of certain individuals, or accusations that certain deaths were due to exposure to hazardous conditions, notably welding and other fumes, by the survivors of a number of workmen who died while employed at the Oregon Shipyards."[6]

For lesser injuries, every shipyard built a first aid station providing "supervisors and medical service" for employees, which were overseen by the State Industrial Accident Commission. However, there was no help for welders and others suffering from breathing dangerous fumes, something for which there was no panacea. And apparently, the Workmen's Compensation Act "could only be held responsible for immediate, definitely traumatic injuries." Illnesses brought about by breathing toxic fumes were considered conditions that "developed insidiously," so they were not covered. Any help would have to come from their employer under the auspices of the Maritime Commission.

The injuries to many employees were not deemed "traumatic" and were not visible, falling under the categories of ill health or physical ailments. However, the *fumes* were visible, as reported on page seven of the fumes report. Under the heading, "Degree of Visible Fume Condition," the work areas examined by investigators were ranked by degree as to the severity of the condition:

a. Very bad—CO_2 Refrigerator Room, Ice Box Refrigerator Room.

b. Definitely bad—Production Welding in Fore Peak or After Peak Production Welding on Main Decks at Outfitting Docks, Void Spaces, Welding in Mop and Broom Closets, etc.

c. Bad—Magazines. [Ammunition storage area]

d. Possibly bad—Downstairs Pipe Shop.

e. Passable—Pipe Shop Loft, Engine Rooms with Production Welding.

Note item "b," where production welding ranks as "definitely bad" for visibility of fumes.[7]

Results of interviews with the forty participating employees were also published, with a heading that reads: "Medical Aspects of Shipyards Investigation in Study of the Disease Processes in Shipyard Workers Employed in So-Called Hazardous Positions." Is it revealing that the authors of the report chose to use the term "so-called hazardous" in the heading? Could the phrase have served as a linguistic tactic to avoid possible liability?

Skeptical or not, the report does record the honest, if not blunt, responses of employees of the shipyard. Often the subjects of the study are referred to as "individuals." At other times, as "men." Whether any women participated is not obvious on the charts, because initials of the workers were used in place of given names. However, it could be said that women who took on the work of men also took on the same exposure to hazardous conditions as men.

The group of forty were between nineteen and sixty-five years of age. The previous health of the workers was unknown, stated as thus: "No information was obtained as to the status of the vital capacity of the heart and lungs of these individuals prior to shipyard employment." They all received some degree of exposure to welding fumes. They had been employed in the shipyards for between three weeks to eighteen months, in the following positions: welders, welders' assistants, shipfitters, pipefitters, chippers, machinists, and painters. The majority, twenty-four individuals, were welders. All worked either day, swing, or graveyard shifts, and sometimes rotated through shifts.

Once the investigation began, interview participants were first asked for their opinions regarding the "availability and effectiveness" of any protective devices or practices at the shipyard. And while the interviewees answered the questionnaires individually and not in the vicinity of the others, their answers were consistently similar. Some examples follow:

"No blowers available at the time I became sick."

"Blowers and suckers available when you can find them."

"Ventilating fumes get bad in spots and close to the ceiling. Poor ventilation around vacuum cleaners. Escape of fine dust not controlled."

"Not enough blowers to go around. Complained of poor ventilation to foreman. No results. Some improvements lately."

"Air pump inadequate."

"Air hose of little or no value."

"Foreman indifferent to protective measures."

"Foreman told the man to work—'If others can stand it, so can you.'"

"Foreman and Safety Director are just about as useless as a 't_t' on a boar."

"Blowers were not available until 3 months ago."

One individual extended his comment with details of how he boldly demanded protection: "Told foreman I would not go down and work in the presence of fumes unless I had blowers and suckers. Condition very bad. Constant metallic taste in mouth. Foreman did not respond. [I] went directly to Safety Division. Representative was sent over, appeared, and asked about my complaint. He said he would remedy it, but I never saw him or the new devices again."

This compilation of responses was followed by a significant statement: "Not one single interviewed employee spoke of adequate ventilation."[8]

These experiences as reported and the corresponding complaints in the report occurred before Augusta arrived at the shipyard in the spring of 1943. Still, she was concerned with why some women were quitting relatively soon after being hired. One instance had been clearly explained in the shipyard fumes report: "A worker said that on the day previous when 3 women were welding in here the fumes got so bad that 1 woman had to 'knock off' at about 2:00 P. M. and go home, saying she was quitting."

Those interviewed were next asked to describe what effect they believed the exposure to fumes had on their health. Again, similarities can be observed, as follows:

"Had to go home. Chest hurt all the time."

"Drowsy. Mind all fogged. Disappears after leaving work. Nausea after breakfast. Raising of phlegm. Tightness in throat. Sweet taste in mouth. Pain in chest."

"Felt like I had a fever towards evening. Felt chilly at home. Sick to stomach."

"Pain in chest."

"Felt sick. Burning sensation."

"Soreness of lungs. Sickening metallic taste."

"Sleepy at first. Metallic taste in mouth."

"Burning in windpipe."

"Peculiar feeling in throat. Sweet taste in mouth."

"Burning in nose. Nausea. Vomiting. Severe headache."

"Stomach distress. Loss of appetite."

Investigators concluded this section by stating that "conditions represent comments made by the majority of welders" and that "the story of the effect of fumes experienced by the individual workmen is astoundingly uniform."

In discussing their findings regarding diagnosis and treatment for the shipyard workers, the study physicians wrote: "In a number of instances, the relation between the exposure and the immediate symptoms and the subsequent occurrence of certain respiratory infection was apparent. Some of these individuals recovered; a few of them have died."[9]

Despite the thoroughness of the thirty-one-page report from the four University of Oregon Medical School physicians in 1942, two years later Dr. Forrest E. Rieke, medical director of the Oregon Shipbuilding Corporation and the Kaiser Company, Inc.-Portland shipyards, issued numerous inter-office memorandums. In them he seemed to contradict the validity of every health concern previously mentioned. These memos were addressed to the medical staff in the shipyards.

In one memo written by Dr. Rieke, which he titled, "The Welding Process," he began by presenting a lengthy description of the practice of welding, the different types of welding, and how to avoid hazards of the occupation. He succinctly stated, "It is clear, then, that the *possible* health hazards of welding are of three types." The first type was "ultraviolet radiation injury to the eye (so-called 'Arc Flash') and exposed skin surfaces, complete protection from which is afforded through the use of proper welding shields, filter lenses, goggles, and leather garments." Either Rieke's opinion regarding the prevention of eye injury was naïve, or ill-informed.

The August 11, 1942, edition of the *Corvallis Gazette-Times* began with the heading, "Eye Specialist Needed to Aid at Shipyards." A determined group of employees had gathered to address the situation in front of the State Industrial Accident Commission, according to the article. The workers testified that eye injuries were so common "an eye specialist should be stationed at the yards."[10]

The second category of health hazards was "hot metal burns which are prevented through the wearing of the helmet, leather jacket, leather gloves, and long leather overalls covering all exposed surfaces." No matter how cautiously a welder worked or dressed, burns from sparks and hot slag (burning melted iron and steel) were indeed a hazard of the occupation. Augusta, even though fully clothed in protective gear as described above, could not avoid burns. In her report, she wrote, "We were given no advice on clothing and many of us had flash burns and slag burns on our necks. Our slacks were perforated with small burns and some caught fire and burned sizeable holes. Those who wore low shoes frequently had ankle burns. My glasses were well pitted by slag before the matron in the restroom told me to ask for goggles in the office."[11]

Welder Jean Neil Johnson at Commercial Iron Works on Ross Island also experienced burns while using protective gear. "You have a heavy screen over your face. But I'm paying for it [working as a welder] ... with skin cancer." When asked at age ninety-three if she believed that the skin cancer was caused by the work she performed in the shipyard, Neil Johnson answered, "Yeah, it's from sparks burning. Cause you can't help that. Sometimes one would go right down your neck."[12]

The third and final category was "systemic injury to the lungs and other organs through the breathing of harmful smoke and metal vapor, which can be avoided through the proper use of ventilation which removes the harmful materials before they are inhaled by the worker." Remember the statement from one of the interviewees for the report on fumes in which he complained that "Ventilating fumes get bad in spots and close to the ceiling. Poor ventilation around vacuum cleaners. Escape of fine dust not controlled." Apparently, there was no guarantee that even with ventilation, the devices would "remove the harmful materials before they are inhaled."

Rieke acknowledged that as far back as 1941, the shipyard, as well as the community beyond, were abuzz with rumors concerning the harmful effects of working while breathing welding fumes. He concluded by making the following revealing statement, which in his memorandum was set apart from other text and printed in capital letters:

"THE MAIN PROBLEM ASSOCIATED WITH WELDING FUMES AT OREGON SHIPBUILDING CORPORATION AND KAISER COMPANY, INC. HAS BEEN DAMAGE TO MORALE THROUGH RUMOR AND MIS-INFORMATION."[13]

Falling debris was another clear danger to welders. Augusta had observed careless work habits of the men working above her inside the hulls. She reported watching pieces of steel called "clips, dogs, or butterflies" dropping from above as the men welding in the heights of the hull didn't bother to look where a heavy piece might land once tossed aside.

Then, a terrible accident occurred when a toolbox somehow dropped from a crane (called a *whirley* in shipyard lingo), striking a man's head below, dealing a devastating blow. Additionally, Augusta reported another incident involving a woman who had slipped and hit her head, the blunt force rendering her unconscious.

The Shipyard Agent

According to Ann Wallace's essay reporting on a speech by Augusta, "Accidents created very little disturbance. The nearest workers stopped to see if they could help, and then work went on with no hysteria or fainting."[14]

Inside the hulls, Augusta believed that "the height was the main nightmare." She stated how at the top of one of the ways, the floor had suddenly disappeared but could be seen to reappear around a corner. "I was apparently expected to follow my shipfitter who swung under a guard rail, grabbed hold of a post and swung farther to reach the flooring. I did it but it was foolish, risky, and unnecessary. After I had done it three times, safety men ordered a catwalk with rails. This is part of what a woman feels she must do at first to prove she 'can take it.'" Augusta made it clear "women do not ask favors, but it is common sense to recognize [they] at first are not strong enough . . . to risk the climbing techniques men use."

Augusta's stature may have helped make it possible to keep up with the shipfitter. According to niece Ann, she was a "big lady, at least five feet ten inches . . . but with a weight problem." She remembered Augusta often drank Metrecal, a low-calorie, powdered diet food that was popular at the time.

Shorty, another woman in Augusta's close group of welder friends, told how a male welder had ignored the advice of his foreman to mend the leak in his hood, to not weld until it was done. Apparently, the welder thought he should keep working and planned to perform the repair after his shift. "By night," Shorty reported, "the man was blind."

Through her government report, an expansion of which became her *Shipyard Diary*, Augusta revealed the truth of the working world of women welders inside a shipyard.

Breathing toxic fumes was not the only issue in the bowels of the hulls for welders. Augusta wrote about the overwhelming racket surrounding her while working on the deck located immediately above the portion of the hull described as "double bottom." She began this portion of her report by stating,

The noise was so great all instructions were given by gesture. In a small room two welders, two shipfitters, a grinder and a chipper were at work. Two men swung heavy sledgehammers at opposite sides of a steel doorjamb. In the middle of it all the lights went out. The noise was excruciating, the air heavy and the whole scene bewildering; a rather stiff beginning after the systematic routine of training. . . . In terms of nervous strain, it was worse than a week of work at school.[15]

"Later I learned that all the men had cotton in their ears," revealed Augusta. "But no one had suggested that to me."[16]

Despite all this, she did state within her lengthy report: "I found later that the Kaiser Company has an excellent safety record."

Fortunately for Augusta, she was gone from the yard before the end of the year when, even though the Company had "an excellent *safety* record," they could not affect the spread of a flu of "epidemic proportions" reaching the shipyard workers, ergo the whole state of Oregon.[17]

An Interview With Frank Johnson, Safety Engineer

SAFETY PAYS...AND THE THREE KAISER YARDS

YOU can't build ships with dead men . . . with crippled men. And the job for 1943 is to build more ships. To build ships, you need healthy men—sound men. So you *protect* your manpower with safety programs. You point out the hazards. You get cooperation. And you keep everlastingly at the safety job, because 1943 calls for a stepped-up production program.

Workers at the three Kaiser yards made a splendid safety record in 1942.

At Oregon Ship alone the decrease in accidental frequency and severity in 1942 over 1941 has actually saved enough man hours to build an extra Liberty freighter.

But, enough *more* man hours could have been saved by

THE CAUSES OF

HANDLING TOOLS OR MATERIALS
'41 40%   '42 36%

EYE INJURIES
'41 21%   '42 28%

FALLS
'41 18%   '42 15%

STRIKING STEPPING OBJECTS
'41 10%

"Safety Pays." An informative article spread across two pages of the employee newsletter boasting good safety records for 1942. February 4, 1943. THE BO'S'N'S WHISTLE, VOL. 3, NO. 3. COLLECTION–BW-OSC–THE BO'S'N'S WHISTLE. BOSUNSWHISTLE_OSC19430204_0303. OREGON HISTORICAL SOCIETY RESEARCH LIBRARY, PORTLAND, OREGON.

careful work to have constructed a second extra Liberty. And it's that *second* extra ship we've got to shoot for this year in renewed vigilance on the safety front.

It can be done because of the 1942 record. For in 1942 the combined experience of the Oregon, Swan Island and Vancouver yards show a *decrease of 10%* in accident frequency per man hour, and a *50% decrease* in time lost because of injuries.

The Vancouver yard had the best safety record for the year, with only one fatal injury in 10,000 man years of work. The three yard average was one fatal injury for each 3,000 man years worked—three times better than the 1941 experience.

There are two danger signs on the horizon that all workers should bear in mind:

Eye injuries increased one-third in 1942 over 1941.

Injuries caused by striking objects increased one-fifth in 1942 over 1941.

> 2 out of every 3 time loss accidents in 1942 resulted from
>
> **EYE INJURIES or HANDLING TOOLS and MATERIALS**
>
> --Lick these two causes of time loss accidents and you'll do a real production job.

PROVED IT IN 1942!

TIME LOSS INJURIES IN 1941 AND 1942

NOTE THAT EYE INJURIES AND "STRIKING OBJECTS" HAVE INCREASED—ALL OTHER CLASSIFICATIONS HAVE IMPROVED

Chapter Nine

X-RAY AND ASBESTOS PERILS EXPOSED

"57 shipyard workers were burned by X-rays and incapacitated . . . some for life . . . in a medical blunder unprecedented in the history of industrial medicine."

—Ed., *Daily News*, Los Angeles, California

"For a whole year after the men were burned, the facts in the cases were kept under cover. For months the men themselves did not know what was wrong with them."

—John Upton Terrell, journalist

On March 16, 1943, the *Daily News* of Los Angeles reported, "Welders Assured." The article opened with the following: "The nation's 100,000 men and women war plant welders were assured tonight they can go on welding without fear of suffering occupational sterility. This was science's answer to rumors, said to have originated in San Francisco [near another Kaiser Co. shipyard], that voltages which produce welding arcs may destroy a welder's fertility." A Dr. Philip Drinker of Harvard University, a consultant to the Maritime Commission and Navy Department, was quoted offering reassurance of the safety of the welding environment. According to the article, Dr. Drinker stated, "while it is a scientific fact that X-rays can produce sterility, the voltage which produces a welding arc falls some 200,000 volts short of creating such a hazard."[1]

The legitimacy of that endangered sterility rumor having been argued, another rumor materialized. Shipyard workers were suffering burns of unknown origin. At the same time Augusta Clawson entered welder training to work at a Portland shipyard, a Southern California shipyard entered the spotlight in a special newspaper story revealing a terrible, unintentional wounding of shipyard workers. This horror occurred within the 175-acre California Shipbuilding Corporation (Calship) yard, "the city built on invisible stilts." Men and machines drove 57,000 piles into Terminal Island to support the building of the yard upon "artificial earth." Henry Kaiser served as a vice president for Calship, which was located between the harbor at Long Beach and the port of Los Angeles.

According to newspaper articles, the unintentional harm occurred inside the very place where workers went for medical support: Calship's first aid station, which was overseen at that time by a Dr. Robert Woodley Stellar, who hired Dr. Isaiah Waterman to cover the day shift at the yard hospital. Stellar also hired a "number of first aid men."[2]

People were talking about this in 1943, but these accidents had happened two years earlier. At the time of the injuries, those in positions of medical authority decided the public and the victim workers were to remain ignorant as to how exactly the fifty-seven men were injured, burned, and maimed at Calship. It would later be proven that the cause was the improper use of an X-ray machine known as an "X-ray fluoroscope." It stands to reason that those in need of X-rays at work were not afraid of a machine called a fluoroscope. At that time—in fact from the 1920s to the 1970s—across the nation shoppers slid their feet inside what they knew as shoe-fitting fluoroscopes under various names like "X-ray Shoe Fitter," "Pedoscope," or "Foot-o-scope."[3]

Apparently, the doctor in charge may have been ill-informed or poorly advised rather than blatantly negligent. Additionally, during later court appearances, Dr. Stellar testified "he never used the X-ray machine, was ill at the time it was used, [and] was not in the yard hospital but was only medical director." Dr. Waterman claimed "some of the burns were inflicted during the night, when he was not in the hospital. Also, he was busy... with emergency surgery and other duties."[4]

Some described the fluoroscope at the shipyard as having been used in an almost playful manner, using long exposures to show each patient—no matter how minimal their injury—what their bones looked like. The demonstrations, unfortunately, greatly extended the risky period of exposure beyond minimal. Those operating the machine were likely oblivious to how deadly a game they were playing. After treatment involving the fluoroscope, many of the trusting shipyard workers were unknowingly destined to lose limbs—fingers, hands, feet, an arm—after suffering open sores, infections, and skin sloughing off the exposed part of their bodies.[5]

Apparently, the frivolous way in which the attendants operated the X-ray machine was not limited to the first aid station at Calship. In May 1943, an advertisement from Pacific Diagnostic Offices in the Los Angeles area announced: "$2 Complete Examination Fluoroscopic X-ray. Examination covers [seventeen] points. See your own organs as shown by our fluoroscopic x-ray examination."

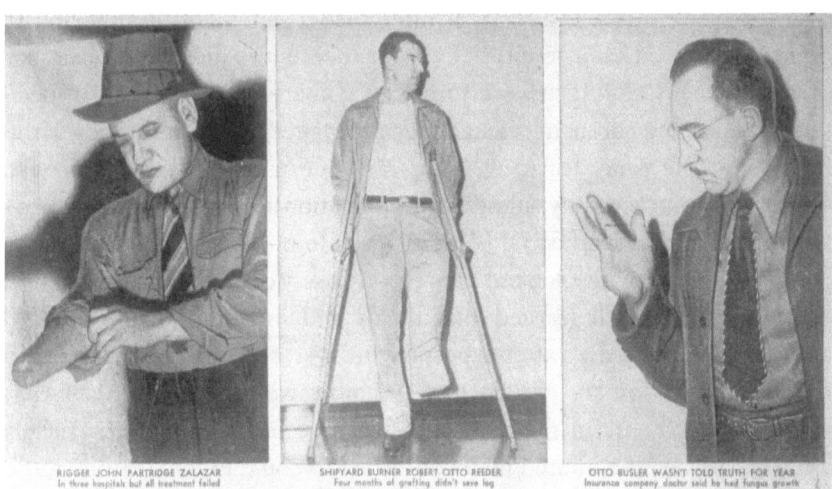

Newspaper images of three men gravely injured by an on-site X-ray machine operated by first aid staff at Kaiser California shipyard, Calship, near Los Angeles.
"HOW X-RAY MAIMED 57 SHIPYARD WORKERS," APRIL 22, 1943, *DAILY NEWS*, HTTPS://WWW.NEWS PAPERS.COM/IMAGE/689235889.

Journalist John Terrell continued to report the ugly truth of what had happened at Calship from September through November of 1941. "[T]he limbs of scores of workers were examined under a fluoroscope by unlicensed and untrained assistants." Terrell revealed that "medical authorities" believed that some of the fifty-seven injured workers "may never be free of the menace." It was stated that all nature of limbs and portions of limbs on the men "may have to be removed because of disintegrating flesh."

Once the affected ship builders learned the deadly secret, they became determined to do something about it. Each of the fifty-seven workers had appeared at the first aid station provided by Liberty Mutual Insurance Co. for assistance regarding a minor injury or wound; some went multiple times.

Apparently, a lot of finger-pointing followed the revelation. Terrell wrote how Calship officials, the insurance company, doctors, and "hospital workers" figuratively threw up their hands claiming no responsibility. A sort of volleying tantamount to a badminton game resulted, as complicated versions of "not me, they're responsible" flew back and forth over the heads of the victims. Calship issued a statement: "As previously pointed out, medical attention of all our men is the direct responsibility of the compensation insurance company." Liberty Mutual (the compensation insurance company) would not accept responsibility to cover the injuries, at the time declaring, "You can't sue us in the superior court. You've got to proceed by filling [sic] application for workmen's compensation before the [I]ndustrial [A]ccident [C]ommission." The workmen's compensation directive lobbed the responsibility of care back at Calship.[6]

However, Terrell learned that burns and infections had begun to appear "within ten days after exposure" in 1941, sending patients back to the first aid station and the doctors and aides working there. At first no one knew the cause of the damage to each patient's body. But, clarifies Terrell, "Still, as the injured men continued to come in for treatment, the medical men began to get suspicious. The suspicion turned into alarm. But it was all kept very quiet. The suspicions were not publicly voiced."[7]

It appears, according to reports that could be found, that no female shipyard workers were involved in this tragic occurrence. One might imagine that such injuries to women workers would have been anathema to the public, perhaps worse to the "players" of the blame game who had previously covered up the harm done to male workers.

In September 1942, the *Daily News* had boldly claimed "Calship Ends X-ray Burn Rumors," saying that "Officials of the California Shipbuilding Corp. yesterday put an end to sinister rumors arising from the fact that 19 men, injured at the plant, have suffered X-ray burns . . . have had fingers amputated . . . And most important of all, the cause of the X-ray burns, which are believed to have resulted from faulty technical operation of clinical X-ray apparatus, has been removed by action of the company." This statement seems to imply that the X-ray machine was removed from the premises. Perhaps the rumor was that the dangerous machine was still in use.

Almost a year later those injured sued for relief. In August 1943, the *Los Angeles Times* announced, "Calship Settles Claims of 39 Workers Burned by X-rays." At the same time, another headline in the *Daily News* stated, "4 More Sue Calship for X-ray Burns." In October, an article in the *Long Beach Sun* declared "X-Ray Burn Victims Ask Huge Sums," followed the next day by the *Daily News* proclaiming, "15 Workers Ask $2,000,000 in Suits over X-ray Burns." The many maimed shipyard workers would persevere and win their suits, receiving financial compensation that would be published in detail including each burn victim's name and the amount awarded them.

These incidents of faulty use of X-ray equipment happened very early in the war years, and months before the attack on the US naval base at Pearl Harbor shocked the nation. Relatively few women had entered shipyard work. Now, the X-ray threat had been removed. Yet plenty of other health threats existed, as previously discussed, such as breathing the toxic fumes that were created while welding. Still, another yet unidentified hazard remained.

Unknown was the risk of working with asbestos. Few if any talked about the dangers of asbestos in World War II industrial jobs. They likely didn't know. Like the experiences of the men gravely injured by

The Shipyard Agent

X-ray exposure, shipyard workers would learn later—only this time after many years passing—what was responsible for their ailments. For some, asbestos fibers were a likely culprit. Specifically, inhaling the fibers could lead to what is now known as asbestosis, a chronic lung disease. Decades later, another chronic lung condition caused by asbestos exposure became well known: mesothelioma. And of course, asbestos exposure could also increase one's likelihood of developing lung cancer.

Unfortunately, and to the eventual detriment of millions of people, since 1939 "asbestos was classified by the US government as a critical material to be stockpiled for future use." And the asbestos "manufacturing companies that provided it hid this fact [its insidious harmfulness] from consumers as well as the military." Vogelzang Law describes the use of asbestos as follows:

> *Asbestos can resist corrosion and withstand high temperatures, so it's an ideal material for building ships, ... By World War II, asbestos was found throughout the ships, in concrete, floor tiles, doors, wall panels, around pipes, in sealants, in boiler cladding furnace firebricks, and welding materials, as well as in insulation.... [It] was also used in some safety equipment and protective gear.*[8]

Unbeknownst to Augusta Clawson and all those working at Swan Island and other shipyards, they were exposed to this hazard, and not until many years later would shipyards be declared "known site[s] of occupational asbestos exposure."[9]

Granted, Augusta and other welders did not *directly* handle asbestos in the course of their daily work, but the material was present virtually everywhere in the yard at dangerous levels. Where there were ships, there was asbestos. Its tiny fibers were easily released into the air to be inhaled inside the hulls where welders and other tradespeople worked. Asbestos exposure was a nationwide problem as shown in a comprehensive study, which lists Kaiser Shipyard as one of many possible asbestos exposure sites:

Alabama Dry Dock	Kaiser Shipyard
Albina Shipyard	Lockheed Shipyard
Barbours Cut Docks	Long Beach Naval Shipyard
Bethlehem Steel Shipyard	Moore Dry Dock
Bremerton Naval Shipyard	Naval Station Everett
Brooklyn Navy Yard	Naval Weapons Station
Caddell Dry Dock	New York Shipbuilding Corporation
California Navy Shipyard	Newport News Naval Shipyard
Charleston Naval Shipyard	Norfolk Naval Shipyard
Consolidated Steel Shipyards	Orange Shipbuilding
Curtis Bay Coast Guard Yard	Pearl Harbor Shipyard
Defoe Shipyard	Pensacola Naval Air Station
Duwamish Shipyard	Portsmouth Naval Shipyard
Galveston Docks	San Diego Naval Shipyard
General Dynamics NASSCO	San Francisco Drydock
GMD Shipyard	Seward Ships Drydock
Groton Naval Base	Sun Shipbuilding
Houston Shipyards	Tacoma Drydock
Hunters Point Naval Shipyard	Todd Shipyards
Ingalls Shipbuilding	Washington Navy Yard
Kane Shipbuilding	Willamette Iron and Steel Works[10]

"The problems associated with asbestos exposure were known by the government as early as 1941." A recommendation was sent to shipyards that "shipyard workers should wear respirators when working with asbestos."[11]

However, providing respirators would incur a large expense and the true dangers of asbestos exposure had not yet been proven, although the potential to harm may have been whispered within the asbestos industry. And so shipyard workers, women welders, and all the rest, with trust and diligence, carried on.

Chapter Ten

MEDICAL CARE FOR ALL

"I see the day when no one need die for lack of medical care, as my own mother died in my arms when I was 16 years old."
—Henry J. Kaiser

"Mayo Clinic for the common man."
—Paul de Kruif, microbiologist and author,
Kaiser Wakes the Doctors

At the age of eighty-five, when asked what he considered the greatest accomplishment of his life, Henry J. Kaiser declared, "The Kaiser Foundation hospitals and health plan."[1] He didn't say it was having helped to win a world war by building ships that most pleased him when thinking about his well-lived life, and it wasn't building those concrete monstrosities called dams, either; it was providing an affordable health care plan for everyday people that brought him the greatest reward. Although considered innovative and compelling at the time it came to the shipyards, Kaiser's health foundation plan did not begin at the shipyards. It was during the industrialist's involvement in building dams as part of the Six Companies, Inc. consortium that the idea had emerged, taken root, and bloomed. In fact, according to an essay published by writer Erich Ebel, "As he had at Grand Coulee Dam, Kaiser brought in Dr. Sidney Garfield to implement a Health Maintenance Organization to keep workers healthy and on the job as much as possible."[2]

Dr. Garfield would wisely "develop and run a successful prepaid family [medical care] plan." Kaiser had wanted a reasonable medical plan to which his workers could subscribe. Dr. Garfield's plan had been so successful at the Grand Coulee Dam project, improving health and increasing productivity, that when Kaiser moved to the Pacific Northwest to construct shipyards, he persuaded Dr. Garfield to come along.

Each shipyard started with, at minimum, first aid stations and perhaps a small medical clinic. Some clinics, although identified as the "Safety Building Clinic," were tantamount to small hospitals, even containing a clinic ward for surgery. In California, only blocks away from the shipyards, a field hospital—described as "a humble, working-class hospital"—was built. There, shipyard workers' families (not yet part of the Permanente Health Plan) could "be cared for in the Field Hospital by their own physicians on a fee-for-service basis."[3]

In the hospital-needy Vancouver area, Kaiser would build a Permanente Hospital. Oregonship and Swan Island shipyard were near hospitals already established in the Greater Portland area. One dire incident occurred on May 3, 1943, a date that would have seen Augusta Clawson still there, still welding together hulls. "Trapped in the forward hold of a tanker at the Swan island shipyard when fire broke out in the vessel, a crew of at least ten workmen were miraculously saved from death late Monday night." Apparently, there had been a broken welding line, which caused gas to overcome all the crew working in the hold and a fire to break out. Eight of the ten listed in the headline were transported from the shipyard on Swan Island to hospitals: three with burns were taken to Good Samaritan Hospital and five sick from fumes were taken to St. Vincent Hospital. Of the five named as having been admitted to St. Vincent, one was named Cora Munson. So, it seems that the "at least ten workmen" included at least one woman welder.

Kaiser's Northern Permanente Foundation helped get the Pacific Northwest hospitals off the ground. In May 1944, page four of the *Bos'n's Whistle* announced, "June 1 is the deadline for all present workers at Vancouver to join the two hospital plans." The article confirmed that 90 percent of the "workers in the yard [were] now members." Employees were given seven days from the date of hire (or re-hire) to decide whether to join the plan. The family plan, the article continued, cost a "fixed fee of thirty cents for the employe[e]'s wife [or husband] and fifteen cents for each child." The article concluded thusly: "The medical and hospital plan at Permanente has been nationally acclaimed as a leading industrial medical plan."[4]

Also, what were identified as "medical centers" were situated in two war housing projects in greater Vancouver: Ogden Meadows and McLoughlin Heights, which was an 1,100-acre development of homes. Shipyard workers living in these projects could easily sign up for the Permanente medical plan inside those medical centers, or at Vancouver first aid stations at the shipyard, or at the Northern Permanente Hospital.[5]

The medical plan was quite comprehensive for the time according to the article, "Now, the Whole Family Gets Hospital Care." The type of coverage contained in the plan included "beds and meals, private rooms and nurses when prescribed by physicians, X-rays, operating rooms and anesthetics, splints and casts, medicines except for vitamins, biologies [sic] or endocrine preparations; laboratory work, basal metabolisms, and electrocardiograms and oxygen as needed."[6]

There were also offered ambulance services—sometimes in the form of a company station wagon—as well as maternity services. The Permanente Hospital can be located on a hand-drawn map, situated on the north side of the Columbia River in Vancouver, Washington, just east of the shipyard men's dormitory, Hudson House. The map also clearly defines the locations of the Kaiser Company, Inc. Vancouver shipyard site, the Oregon Shipbuilding Corporation shipyard site, and the Kaiser Company, Inc. Portland, otherwise known as Swan Island, shipyard site.

According to Paul de Kruif, a microbiologist who wrote about the plan in the *Reader's Digest* in May 1943, his article pronounced "Tomorrow's Health Plan—Today!" In fact, he declared the plan "a triumph of group medicine." To read what he wrote was no surprise to those acquainted with him and his work, for he was a "proponent of socialized medicine," believing that basic medical care was the "fifth human right" beyond the right to food, shelter, clothing, and fuel. "The industrial health care plan ... for the 190,000 workers at Henry J. Kai-

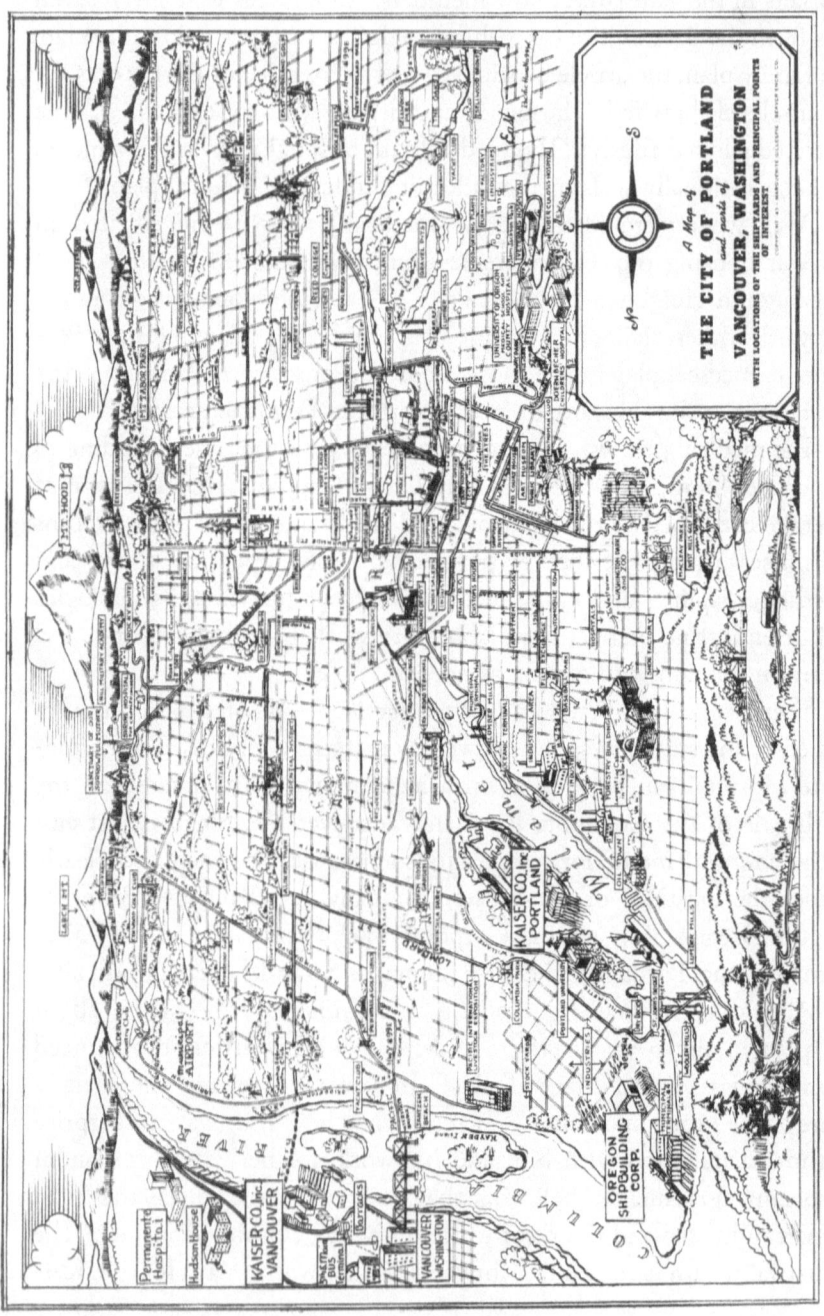

Map of the three northwest Kaiser shipyards, 1943, by Marguerite Gillespie, from *Record Breakers* publication, Oregon Shipbuilding Corporation. COURTESY OF KAISER PERMANENTE HERITAGE RESOURCES.

ser's six West Coast shipyards ... was still considered new in '43, having only begun in March of 1942."[7]

Augusta Clawson witnessed at least one event that required a fellow employee to receive transportation to a hospital directly from the shipyard. While reaching her assigned workspace with another woman welder on the top level of a ship, she realized the gargantuan jib of a "whirley" (construction crane) was hovering with its hoist above an open hatchway. From the hatchway climbed a doctor dressed in white. From the whirley's hoist hung cables which, as a rigger shouted instructions, soon dropped and in minutes lifted a basket that held an injured, unconscious man, from below, plus two other men riding along to watch over the basket and cables as they rose from the dark hatchway. Surely Augusta continued to watch with concern as the basket swung over their heads and began to descend far below to a waiting ambulance, the scene emphasizing the need for medical care in and near a shipyard.[8]

On the West Coast, this newfangled health care plan was first offered in the Kaiser shipyards of Richmond, California. It was there a female physician named Dr. Hannah Peters, born in Germany and trained in New York, "joined the shipyard's medical care team." She hoped to meet the unique problems of health care for women in the workforce. In fact, Dr. Peters further encouraged the medical department to hire a gynecologist to address the needs of the 23,000 women working in the shipyards. For one, women workers were complaining about menstrual problems after starting the physically demanding shipyard jobs. Dr. Peters determined it was a vitamin B deficiency, which she proceeded to treat, helping the women welders and others to stay productive.

Progressive in her approach to the practice of medicine, she began to provide preventative health education in the hope of staving off disease. Realizing that venereal disease especially could be a problem in shipyards with their colossal mixed-gender employee populations, Dr. Peters placed "venereal disease educational materials in all the women's restrooms and shipyard newspapers." She described how this literature was made "easily available in wooden racks which were hung in conspicuous places in every women's restroom."[9]

Henry Kaiser wanted only the best in medical care and care givers for his workforce that spread out for miles and was located across state borders. Dr. Hannah Peters proved herself to be that. She would live to be ninety-seven years old, after publishing research to benefit women's health, specifically regarding reproductive biology and cancer in women. Dr. Peters moved to Copenhagen, Denmark after the war and created the Laboratory of Reproductive Biology.[10]

The Permanente Health Plan was getting noticed and was welcomed by those to whom it was offered. Besides the good health care provided under the auspices of the plan—for only fifty cents a week for almost unlimited medical and hospital care—the hospitals and clinics being built by Kaiser Co., Inc. were free of racial discrimination. They were open to all persons "with no segregation of patients because of creed or color."[11]

"Illness knows no color line here," wrote one journalist. "Red-helmeted men, lady welders, [and] negroes lined up for a checkup by the busy young doctors."[12]

In the Portland–Vancouver area, Vancouver was first to gain a hospital through the Northern Permanente Foundation. An original small shipyard hospital in Vancouver was in serious need of expansion. With a $220,000 grant from the Federal Works Administration, the hospital facilities were able to branch out on the grounds, increasing the capacity of the hospital for Kaiser Company, Inc. employees and their families. New wings added to the structure brought the length of the hospital building to seven hundred feet, housing about three hundred beds. An article about the expansion further explained that the hospital was built for Kaiser Company employees, but "the money allocated is to provide medical facilities for the public in the entire area."[13]

Vancouver Blood Center was also established in Vancouver, where donors lined up to alleviate the "acute" shortage overseas, which led to cargo loads of whole blood being flown to the European fronts. On a Friday designated "Shipyard Day" at the blood center, besides the hundred workers donating blood, Miss Helen Keller, "famed blind woman," appeared. Shaking hands with donors, she praised them for participating in the blood drive. From the blood center to the hospital in Vancouver, with Henry Kaiser's help the city met the healthcare needs of the time.[14]

Kaiser's dedication to providing medical care to keep his dam-project employees healthy led to his first healthcare partnership with Dr. Sidney Garfield, whose out-of-the-ordinary idea of providing "prepayment and preventive care laid the foundation for Kaiser Permanente's future health plan." These two men—a concerned doctor with an excellent, manageable idea and an entrepreneur and builder possessing a mind with no limits—formed a partnership that provided for workers in the shipyards of the West Coast during the frenetic industrial production of World War II. The fruits of the collaboration of that partnership would become something almost immeasurable in the years ahead, spreading across the nation and far into the future.[15]

CHAPTER ELEVEN

MEN VS. WOMEN WELDERS

"The move to bring women into the shipyards met with great opposition because 'they would distract the men.' If you can distract in that outfit, you're good."

—Augusta H. Clawson[1]

Charlotte Carr, assistant to the Deputy Chairman of the War Manpower Commission issued this clarifying statement: "Transition from manpower to womanpower on the war production front is not a female problem but an employment problem—a process of adjusting millions of new workers to new jobs." On May 31, 1943, someone identified only as "one Marinship official" published their opinion about *womanpower* as follows:

> On the whole . . . women have done an excellent job. They are good workmen and can weld and burn as well as any man. Foremen and leadmen have reported that they take direction well, are careful of tools and much easier on them than the men; that they adapt themselves to new conditions readily, have the patience to do repetitive work, require less supervision than men, have established an enviable record on safety and absenteeism and have a low turnover rate.[2]

Notice how the official who published their opinion referred to women in shipyards as *good work*men.

Marinship was the nickname of a shipyard in the bay area of California. As was the custom at the time, the name Marin Shipbuilding Corporation—a division of another productive shipbuilder, W.A. Bechtel Co., whose head was a member of the Six Companies, Inc.—was shortened to Marinship.

The above information was found under the title "Women in Shipyards" in a US Maritime Commission publication, *The Victory Fleet*, described as "a digest of production news with suggestion bulletins." This article covered the subject of women in shipyards with information gathered directly from shipyards across the nation. Science Research Associates' "Women's Work and the War" by Mary E. Pidgeon was cited as a main source of information. Pidgeon, like Augusta Clawson, dedicated her life to advancing the causes of women's freedoms and advancement in society.

The *Victory Fleet* article included some statistics from the Marinship yard as follows: "The average woman at Marinship was found to be between twenty-six and thirty-five years of age, between 5'3" and 5'6" in height, weighed approximately 130 pounds, was married with no children, had had some high school training and previous work experience in the low income occupations." The specific low-income occupations were not named. "The husky women do the heavy work; the small ones are good at fitting in tight spaces." It was believed that women excelled at doing detailed work, or work requiring "finger dexterity," and at being patient enough to take the time to do a task properly.[3]

Augusta put in her two cents, saying, "I have seen many older women of good health and sturdy build on the ship's ways climbing ladders, crossing staging, working from scaffolds, welding ships to send out to their boys."[4]

Interestingly, this *Victory Fleet* article appeared after Augusta had completed her assignment at Swan Island and had written and likely submitted her government report. There are many similarities between this article and her report. One might suggest that this fact testifies to the commonalities of what women were experiencing as they entered the industrial work world of men. Augusta had addressed her shipyard report to "employers, unions, State Directors of Vocational Training, etc.—those who [are] shaping the War Production Training of Women." The report bore no date.

Both her report and the article published by the Maritime Commission addressed the subject of induction. "Much of the bewildering strangeness of a huge shipyard [terms that echo Augusta's description of her experience], which may completely discourage a woman working for the first time in such an atmosphere, is made understandable by the induction schools operated by many yards. Swan Island and Oregon Ship have recently instituted such a course." This "induction course" had been one of Augusta's suggestions in her official report.

Whether bewildered or uncomfortable or both, still women came to the shipyards and offered their hands, heads, and hearts to the war effort. A *Victory Fleet* bulletin titled "Percent of Women in Maritime Shipyards," dated March 1943, lists twenty-eight shipyards across the nation by highest percentage of women workers present. Kaiser Company, Inc.'s Swan Island shipyard and the Oregon Shipbuilding Corporation top the list at 17.8 percent and 15.5 percent, respectively. Only a few lines below that are the Kaiser Company, Inc. Vancouver yard at 14.1 percent and Kaiser's Richmond (California) shipyard at 11.9 percent. According to this list, the Kaiser company led the way in hiring women.[5]

It was true that some male workers at the shipyard could be less than helpful to their female cohorts, according to Augusta. But she is clear about her view (limited to six weeks experience in one area of one shipyard, however) about sexual harassment, although she does not use the term *sexual harassment*. The term did not emerge into the daily vocabulary of the nation until after the passage of the Civil Rights Act of 1964. "During my employment in the Yard," she wrote, "I saw *no* evidence to support the occasional rumor that loose morals in the Yard make it an unsafe place for women."[6]

Some men welcomed women to the shipyard, or at least, cordially accepted them. One employment poster of the period demonstrated a positive male-to-female interaction.

The Shipyard Agent

Poster showing a male and a female together during a lunch break. *"Good work, sister: we never figured you could do a man-size job!" America's women have met the test!* Packer. United States, ca. 1944. New York: Bressler Editorial Cartoons, Inc., May 5. LIBRARY OF CONGRESS. HTTPS://WWW.LOC.GOV/ITEM/97515638/.

Early during her assignment in Portland, Augusta experienced what must have been a welcomed attitude, and which likely produced a smile from her. It came on her first day of work after training. While sitting on a counter stool at a "lunch wagon" in the city, a man seated next to her noticed her welding clothing and asked, "What you going to do?"

"Weld."

"Where?"

"Swan."

"You'll do."[7]

Men vs. Women Welders

Often, women worked in proximity of men while welding. Sometimes they were assigned to the same team. This closeness could not be avoided while working to construct the ship's double bottom segments for assembly. Close inspection of a photograph of welders working inside the bottom hull segments reveals some head scarves peeking out from beneath welding hoods.

Within the pages of *Does Khaki Become You? The Militarization of Women's Lives*, British author Cynthia Enloe explained how those in power "tried to justify the recruitment of women workers without upsetting existing gender ideology and the sexual division of labour."

Connie Field's film *The Life and Times of Rosie the Riveter* includes clips from 1940s American government films aimed at the "mobile woman." Women—all of them white—are shown using electric tools

Revealing image of welders—both men and women—at work seated between longitudinal and transverse stiffeners (beams) within the structure of a double bottom section of a hull being assembled. © THE OREGONIAN. ALL RIGHTS RESERVED. USED WITH PERMISSION. COLLECTION OHS939, OHS.ORG.

to make holes in aircraft wings, as the narrator reassures the audience, "this is just like punching holes in your scouring powder tin." And, for women, it was suggested welding fighter planes (or Liberty ships) was "just like sewing."[8]

After one particularly unpleasant confrontation on the job, which she did not explain, Augusta discovered that her friend and fellow woman welder, Texas, had experienced an equally rough day. Augusta wrote, "It was a comfort to find someone feeling as I did. All the way home in the bus I sang to myself (mentally only):

'Mr. Big Boss, I've been thinking
    What a nice Yard this would be
If the men were all transported
    To coffer-dam or Double-B!'"[9]

    A cofferdam is a narrow, hard-to-access space between the walls of two tanks in the body of the ship. Double-B was a nickname for the area called "double bottom," which was also a notoriously difficult working space. Augusta truly was imagining the worst for the male workers she had encountered that day, while singing the little ditty in her head.
    Before long, a day came when Augusta picked up her assignment and found that she was working under a different boss. She realized quickly that working under his leadership was much more tolerable, even pleasant. Although, her new leadman confessed that he'd once been less than glad on hearing the news that women were coming to work in the shipyard. However, in time, after watching women welders prove themselves on the job, he was very supportive of the work of women.[10]
    Certainly, welder Jean Neil Johnson at Commercial Iron Works shipyard would have agreed. She was a busy, dedicated CIW shipyard employee, who performed well and steadily. By the time the war was over, her determination to do her part to boost the war effort had paid an extra bonus. She'd met her future husband in the shipyard. He was one man who likely did not complain about hardworking women coming onto his

Welder Jean Marsolie Neil (cousin of author's mother) and Rudolph Jonas "Rudy" Johnson, Jean's welding leadman, met at Commercial Iron Works Shipyard on Ross Island in Portland, Oregon. Married in 1944, they continued to work at CIW.
COURTESY OF MARSELLA "MARSE" (JOHNSON) SHOBE.

welding team, especially one rosy-cheeked young woman with a pert cleft in her chin named Jean.

Augusta continually promoted war work for women. Advising women to first visit their doctor to establish if they were "normally healthy," she encouraged healthy women to "establish a record of attendance and production that will help kill all the ridiculous bugaboos that exist about women." She further named some *bugaboos*, stating, "Jealousy, pettiness, resentment are not characteristics restricted to either sex."[11]

"Well selected women have a great deal to offer. They can be efficient, accurate, steady, loyal workers.... Production will win this war," stated Augusta, "and production is what counts now."[12]

Chapter Twelve

A TIGHT SEAM OF SUPPORT

"Women who stepped up were measured as citizens of the nation, not as women... this was a people's war, and everyone was in it."
—Colonel Oveta Culp, Director of WAAC[1]

"I find that many other women dreamed as I did some nights of the first week that we were falling off the edge of the ship," Augusta wrote. "The second week I dreamed four different times that the lights had gone out, that I was seated precariously on a beam or scaffolding high up in mid-air in some tank, and that I mustn't move for fear of falling." After experiencing the fear and "nerve strain" as she called it, like other women welders experienced, Augusta formed an idea, a plan that might help the newest female joiners of steel who would be entering the shipyard. Her concept would provide support and a greater chance to become accustomed to and remain at this new and challenging man's-world work. "If one could draw up a timetable it might read something like this," she wrote:

- "1 week to overcome fear of height and dread of noise
- 2 weeks to develop techniques in climbing and to give time for muscles to develop to meet the stress put upon them
- 3 to 4 weeks to develop sufficient skill, and more important still, confidence in that skill, to do the day's work."[2]

The Shipyard Agent

Hopefully, the camaraderie and friendship that Augusta experienced with the other women welders in the shipyard helped alleviate any remnants of the nightmares she'd suffered of falling from the side of ships. Besides supporting each other through the pressures of the job, the women within Augusta's "lunch bunch" sometimes socialized outside the shipyard, eventually bringing Gus along to family events like birthday celebrations, or to help shop for a daughter's Easter shoes.

"I count them among the most genuine friends I have. They are quiet, almost inarticulate at first, but their loyalty, sincerity, and patriotism are unsurpassed."[3]

Camaraderie among the women welders could not have been stronger, but for Augusta, with that came the risk of secrets—hers—being discovered without her uttering a word.

Another group of women welders who helped keep each other going and working strong in a shipyard were the Hellcats at Oregonship. Along with one helper and their leadman, the seven Hellcats designed the back of their artfully decorated work jackets with the word *Hellcats* boldly printed across the yoke. They felt it presented a most fierce image while doing their part against Axis powers.

Camaraderie and support were not always present in the shipyard, however, as Augusta's tale of her first day reporting to work after training revealed. Stating there had been no formal program of induction (as was the case when she started), she described her first day:

> *The Ways are so large and cover so much ground that one is conscious only of confusion at first. I could not find Checking Station #1 and no one seemed to know its location. After wasting perhaps fifteen minutes, I found it, received a badge, and was turned over to a new welder who knew the Yard from her days as a laborer. We went in quick succession to a shop under one of the Ways for rod boxes, to a lunchroom to leave our lunch boxes, to a tool crib for stinger and brush, to a rod shop for rods and glass, and to the Welders Office to be assigned a day off. My guide, perhaps by way of being perverse, took me through the skids [beams or planks] to get from one Way to another. I could get no sense of direction out of it, with the result that*

A Tight Seam of Support

Women of *Hellcats* welding crew at Oregon Shipbuilding Corporation. *Top row, from left:* Hazel Zimmerman, Georgie Towell, Verna McCaughey, Frances Reid (helper). *Front row:* Mayme Matchett, Mabel Geist, Bess Blankenship, Vivian Sales, Martha Raymond, and Leadman Paul ("Doc") Shade. Photographer: Al Monner. January 18, 1944. © *THE OREGONIAN.* ALL RIGHTS RESERVED. USED WITH PERMISSION. ORGLOT1284.

> *at night I returned my equipment to Welders Lunchroom 14 but got the wrong Way and found it was the Men's Lunchroom. I tracked down the Women's but was five minutes late getting there, so could not get my lunch box. These rooms are supposed to be guarded or locked but the next day, when I returned for my things—gloves, stinger and chipping hammer—[they] had been stolen. . . By then I had delayed too long, and the last bus had left.*[4]

Augusta presents a detailed description of this could-have-gone-better experience, exposing what must have been a growing frustration. Typically, she went on to have a mostly positive experience during her nearly six-week stint at Swan Island.

The Shipyard Agent

So, on the first working day of her first week, after climbing ninety-two steps to reach her leadman, she was finally promised a job. Eventually, a helper appeared who had been instructed to take her to her job site. According to Augusta, the helper, a woman, commented, "You certainly earn your money here just dodging getting killed, there's so much inexperienced help."

Augusta would have something to say about the "help." Her idea of instituting a process of selection would support shipyard rates of production, boost morale of workers already hired, and of perhaps even that of the women who would *not* be working in the ways, no matter how patriotic their desire. Augusta explained her idea:

> *The very nature of the work on the Ways eliminates the advisability of hiring workers who are subject to respiratory disease; who have weak hearts that might be affected by climbing, or by excessive walking; who have extreme aversion to heights; [or] who are subject to epilepsy. Medical authorities should be consulted for a complete list of causes for rejection.... Neither age nor over-weight seems to be a barrier to good performance in many cases.*[5]

Her first day's experience as a woman welder could have left a bad taste in Augusta's mouth; however, befitting her positive personality, she quickly developed a group of friends from within her many coworkers. Her friend Lois, aka Missouri, would remain a friend throughout the years.

Missouri took her lunch break while Augusta was scheduled to take hers. This way, they were able to communicate during the workday, though they worked in different areas of the yard. One day, Missouri described to Augusta how she had walked inside a women's restroom and discovered two male electricians working there. Somehow, she learned that they were not electricians at all, but FBI agents. Soon, rumor had it that a fire extinguisher, dangerously filled with gasoline, had been discovered bearing the fingerprints of a woman. Augusta does not report the results of the agents' posturing, although she wonders why the FBI were conducting such a ruse when they had on file all shipyard employees' fingerprints.[6]

A Tight Seam of Support

Whether via an efficiency expert, a safety expert, a health expert, or a counselor, Kaiser shipyards did initiate plans and programs to benefit their hardworking employees and took steps to meet the special needs of women in an industrial setting; many changes came about because of Augusta's observations and reporting.

Augusta opined that women in general needed to have the right mindset upon entering industrial production work settings with men. Women "should go into it as workers, not as women ... to prove by performance that women can produce and produce well." She reminded her audience they ought not to be worried "about gallantry or exacting the little courtesies we have been accustomed to from men in our private lives."[7]

Commercial shipyards, like those built by the industrialist's Kaiser Company, Inc., were fully engaged in the US Maritime Commission's Emergency Shipbuilding Program doing everything deemed possible to boost production. Anyone who walked into a shipyard knew that there was a great need for ships, and that ships needed to be built as quickly as possible. In this vein, the Kaiser Company supported their workers in many ways. One was by issuing a shipyard publication, the *Bo's'n's Whistle*, publishing an edition tailored for each of Kaiser's three shipyards: Oregonship, Vancouver, and Swan Island. This was one of management's successful attempts to support employees by keeping them informed, encouraged, and celebrated.

Often daily newspapers published cartoons or humorous reports, in order to boost morale, even if only for one moment when a chuckle might bounce the shoulders of a harried war production worker. An example of this type of article was found in the *Spokesman-Review* of Spokane, Washington; it is quoting a small post titled "Preoccupation" from Alameda, California. "Personal note," it begins, "in the employees' plant newspaper at the General Engineering company shipyards: 'Burner Alice Kempton was watching a sailor while on the job, burned a circle around herself and fell through it.'" *Baa-da-bing!*

The Tin Hatters, "Oregon Shipbuilding's swing band entertains the graveyard shift during their lunch break in the early morning." November 15, 1942.
© THE OREGONIAN. ALL RIGHTS RESERVED. USED WITH PERMISSION. PHOTO FILE #2209.

Often, musical entertainment was provided, usually performed in front of large lunch-break gatherings of Kaiser employees, closely packed together, spreading away from the edge of the stage. One band who provided entertainment were called the Tin Hatters, whose own tin hats sparked with reflected light as they performed for fellow shipyard employees and managers.

Employees were especially celebrated when purchasing war savings bonds. "War bonds were sold at [seventy-five] percent of face value (a [twenty-five-dollar] bond sold for [eighteen dollars and seventy-five cents]) and matured over ten years. While the rate of return was below market value, bonds were a stable investment with the bonus of aiding the war effort." The government used money raised by the purchase of war bonds across the nation to help fund the war effort.[8]

A Tight Seam of Support

Augusta explained how employees learned about War Bonds. "Well, it was mostly at Victory Center, I guess. The Center was a raised platform right in the yard and during the lunch hour there would be a rally every [ten] days or so. Beside Victory Center we had a huge bulletin board listing the War Savings record of each group of workers. We passed by it every morning when we came to work."

Author Daniel James Brown in his book *Facing the Mountain: A True Story of Japanese American Heroes in World War II* agreed that all citizens of the United States, no matter their nationality, wanted to help in every way possible during the world conflict. In a brief few lines, Brown says a great deal about the impact of the war and how the citizens of the country came together in even the most challenging of circumstances:

> [T]hey resolved to manifest their best selves, to give, as Lincoln had taught their grandparents and great-grandparents, the last full measure of their devotion to the high ideals underlying their national identity.
>
> So, by the millions they awoke every morning that summer and happily took their coffee without sugar so that the troops could have candy bars on the battlefield. In the evening, they harvested vegetables from the victory gardens in their backyards so that the boys would sometimes have more than K rations to eat. They poured their earnings into War Savings Bonds.[9]

Augusta formed a definite opinion about her fellow welders when it came to purchasing war bonds. "They put some white collar workers to shame.... they were well-informed, eager to help, and buying regularly. Those people are in this sort of work to win the war, and they know that their dollars can help as much as their skilled labor." Apparently, the entire state, not only the Portland area, took the matter seriously. It was declared that "Oregon ranked among top states with [forty-nine] per cent over quota in [a] third war loan."[10]

In her shipyard employment report, Augusta wrote a substantial section titled "Suggestions to the Shipyard Management." She began with praise for a myriad of things from drinking water to award pins as she had observed and experienced them while working as a welder.

> *The Yard is to be highly commended on many things. . . . The condition of the washrooms is excellent. The liberal provision of drinking water on the Ways is equally fine. The work of the Counselors in Women's Services has made a good beginning and can do a great deal. The prospective nursery will offer splendid service. Launchings, the Shipyard paper,* The Bo's'n's Whistle, *the presentation of Maritime Award pins—all do much for morale. Good morale means pride in employment and is translated into production. Surprisingly little things boost morale. I found that a trip through one of the finished ships made one worker feel "like working harder than ever."*[11]

Could that worker's initials have been *A.H.C.*?

"Women have answered the call to service in huge numbers . . . This group of welders and shipfitters, at the Oregon Shipbuilding yards is watching a new Liberty ship take to the water." *Oregon Journal,* June 6, 1943. © *THE OREGONIAN.* ALL RIGHTS RESERVED. USED WITH PERMISSION. OHS.ORG. NEG. NO. ORHI_81549.

Besides being moved by viewing the fruits of their labors, shipyard workers valued the opportunity to witness the ship launchings. Leona Ellis, a marine machinist, remembered the night the last Liberty ship sailed. Thousands of workers from every occupation within the yard gathered that night. "Everybody was down on the dock," Leona reported. "The *Singing Guards* sang 'Aloha-oi.' It was a foggy night. When the ship sailed, you could hardly hear it. It just drifted out and [was] swallowed up by the fog. . . . When that ceremony was over, you could hear the shuffling of the feet in the fog and see all these figures drifting by and nobody said anything. It was just absolutely quiet. . . . all those thousands of people and nobody saying a word. . . . It was just like one big lump in the throat that everybody had. All at once. Everybody."[12]

Augusta Holmes Clawson genuinely cared about the women welders she met at Swan Island shipyard. She cared deeply about the outcome of her investigation and resultant report regarding the conditions present in the shipyards. Women welders and, eventually, any woman who began work in a variety of industrial settings, would benefit from this relatively short but very intense assignment she completed.

Listening to her niece, Ann Henderson Kramer, describe her relationship with Augusta leaves one to draw the conclusion that caring was simply a natural response for Gug. "I loved my aunt," Ann said. "She was awesome . . . an exceptional individual . . . with a heart as big as all outdoors."[13]

Patricia "Pat" Lindley-Clawson, Augusta's grandniece by marriage, agreed that she was always approachable, which seemed like an excellent trait to have when it came to getting other women at the shipyard to share information. "Augusta could talk to anybody," according to Pat, "about anything at any time."[14]

CHAPTER THIRTEEN

RACISM IN THE YARDS

"It was the first time that I ever experienced discrimination."
—Beatrice M., Black shipyard worker[1]

Surely, all citizens who answered the call for help in the war production industry of the Pacific Northwest were anticipating well-paying jobs in the shipyards—as had been advertised—and decent, fair treatment by employers. This was not always the case for people of color. This must have felt like a most distressing rebuff, at the very least. After all, the nation was at war the president said; this was an emergency. All able-bodied persons were needed. They had been asked to come. Some had traveled to the West at government expense to fill production positions. Some had already been trained for the work. President Roosevelt, admirals, and generals had each sent an entreaty for help to the nation, as had Eleanor Roosevelt. So had Augusta H. Clawson in her many essays and during speaking engagements. Yet not every person with hiring responsibilities—usually a white male—was willing to hire all those who came, qualified or not, if an applicant was dark-skinned.

It's easy to speculate that many African Americans were likely trained before traveling away from home for war work, because for one, "seventy-five Black colleges and universities participated in the National Defense Program." These institutions of higher learning, under the Engineering, Science, and Management War Training program, offered new defense-related courses, including welding and other skills useful in shipbuilding.[2]

The Shipyard Agent

Blacks coming from the South to take jobs expected to arrive in a liberal-minded northern city, not one actively practicing bigotry in many of its neighborhoods, including in the center of the city. They did not expect to find more of the same they'd already experienced or heard about in the steamy South. But what southern Black people and other people of color found *was* reminiscent of what they left behind. By 1942, one could walk Portland city streets and find signs indicating *Whites Only*. Or stumble upon a business displaying a sign announcing they were hiring and step forward hopefully, only to read upon closer inspection *only whites need apply*. The settled inhabitants of Portland had not been ready to accept these changes as they arrived—namely, a sudden onrush of twenty-three thousand African American residents. Portland's citizens thought they knew how their town functioned. For hadn't they always "[o]perated within a well-established understanding of acceptable behavior for non-Whites and attempted to create stability by maintaining discriminatory prewar customs and traditions?" This was the case according to Rudy Pearson in "A Menace to the Neighborhood: Housing and African Americans in Portland, 1941–1945."[3]

This unwelcomeness may have been received as a shock by arriving Black citizens. They had come to help and had expected or at least hoped for if not a welcoming embrace, at least acceptance. After all, those seeking jobs might have surmised, wasn't everyone aware of President Franklin D. Roosevelt's Executive Order 8802: Prohibition of Discrimination in the Defense Industry? It's thought-provoking to learn that Executive Order 8802 would later be recognized as "[p]erhaps the most important victory for civil rights since the Fifteenth Amendment."[4]

However, this "victory for civil rights" would not be won overnight.

Interestingly, and perhaps tellingly, only a prediction that 100,000 people—probably predominately Black people—were preparing to march on the nation's capital to "demand an end to discrimination in war industries and the armed forces" finally raised a response from the White House. This threat, as it were, stirred both Roosevelts, meaning the president and the First Lady, to meet with Black leaders. Specifically, A. Phillip Randolph, president of the largest Black workers union in the country who had helped organize the March on Washington, DC Movement (MOWM).

One could say the resulting Order 8802 only existed because of the determination of thousands of citizens directed to march on Washington if it became necessary. The Order had been proclaimed by Roosevelt in June 1941, banning "discriminatory employment practices by federal agencies and all unions and companies engaged in war-related work." A Fair Employment Practices Commission had been established simultaneously with the Order "to enforce the new policy." Yet it took three years and the anticipation of a massive demonstration in the nation's capital to effect change. FDR had been concerned mainly with speeding up production of ships, with little real thought about employee relations—whether racial or gender based—between the workers who were dedicated to meeting his goals.[5]

According to Aaron Randle in his article "'Black Rosies': The Forgotten African American Heroines of the WWII Homefront," Order 8802 prompted participation from Black communities in the war effort. Randle reported that of "one million African Americans who entered paid service for the first time following 8802's signing, 600,000 were women." Imagine that; this was truly an astounding moment in the history of Black women in employment.[6]

In the immediate Kaiser family, there had certainly been no aversion to hiring Blacks. Edgar Kaiser, general manager of the three shipyards in the area, had as a five-year-old boy been close to a Black man who "helped take care of him" in the Kaiser household. This tall man, James A. Shaw, nicknamed "Tote" or "Totem" from the days of carrying Edgar on his shoulders, would remain a friend of the family until his death. Tote met the family in 1908 and worked first for a Mr. Ordway alongside Henry. As Henry's management responsibilities grew, Tote worked for him while he supervised a paving company crew in Spokane, Washington. "When Mr. Kaiser left there, I went with him. I have worked for him in Canada, Washington, California, Cuba, and Oregon." The *Oregonian* article "Negro on Hand for Ceremony" confirms that James Shaw came to Portland and the shipyards in July 1942, taking a job as janitor.[7]

The experience of knowing and working with Tote may explain how the Kaisers became "businessmen who understood the value of workforce diversity and, in their personal lives, moved beyond racial divides decades before the rest of the country."⁸

The question might be asked, on the other hand, why is it that a man with a close personal relationship to the big boss, who was hailed as possessing "problem-solving skills" and who knew how to mix "mud and brains," did not rise above general laborer?

It's documented that the Kaiser yards' race relations problems occurred after the Kaiser shipyards became unionized by allowing the Boilermakers union in. The elder Kaiser felt moved to write an article the *Oakland Tribune* newspaper titled "Class Bitterness Most Serious Problem for Labor, Management" addressing the issue. Published in September 1943, he wrote, "There is no such thing as labor relations. There are only human relations. You are dealing with people, not impersonal problems of finance or electronics. There are [three] sides to every argument—your side, my side, and the right side."⁹

Henry and his manager son, Edgar, were under fire from union representatives who did not like the fact that Blacks, usually referred to at the time as Negroes, were being offered the same work as whites inside the Kaiser shipyards. For instance, the *Herald and News* out of Klamath Falls, Oregon, in an article titled "Kaiser Stands Firm on Use of Negro Workers," reported that "The Henry J. Kaiser company shipyard at Vancouver, Wash., stood firm today behind a decision to use [N]egro workers in skilled jobs despite protests by AFL unions. Tom Ray, boilermakers' union business agent, demanded that the company limit [N]egroes to common labor and segregate their living quarters from the white workers."¹⁰

Though it was said that Kaiser Company stood *for* using Black workers for skilled jobs, the company had been charged otherwise. In November 1942, a group known as the Shipyard Negro Organization for Victory issued a declaration:

> *We the Negro people [notice the statement uses the term* people *not* men, *which implies the inclusion of women] employed by the Kaiser Company maintain that under false pretenses we were brought from east to west to work for defense, and we demand with due process of*

law, the following rights: (1) to work at our trades on equal rights with whites; (2) to go to vocational school or take vocational training on equal rights with whites.[11]

The January 1944 issue of the *Statesman Journal* recalled how just a few months earlier, racial discrimination accusations had been serious enough that the "President's fair employment practices committee hear[d] Negroes' charges of discrimination in Portland area shipyards." Finally, by the end of the year, "Kaiser yards and [the] boilermakers [union were] ordered by [the] president's fair employment practices [committee] to cease racial discrimination."

The Boilermakers union, officially the International Brotherhood of Boiler Makers, Iron Ship Builders and Helpers of America—the same union that Augusta Clawson was required to join—behaved in a shameful, prejudicial manner when the subject of Blacks joining the union was raised. To maneuver around the issue of allowing them to join the previously all-white, all-male union, the Boilermakers created local "auxillary" unions allowing membership to Blacks. These auxiliary unions seemed like a slap in the face to Black shipyard workers, who paid dues equal to whites but received far fewer rights and benefits.[12]

Inside Kaiser's Richmond, California, shipyard, Calship, the same problems existed when they allowed the Boilermakers in. Union leaders insisted on an auxiliary union for Blacks. Like in Portland, this led to lawsuits and eventual intervention by the president's Fair Employment Practice Commission. The commission ruled in favor of Blacks in early 1944 and upheld by the California Supreme Court in January 1945. But of course, "by then the war, and shipyard production was almost over," meaning any feelings of victory won must have been subdued.[13]

In the meantime, skilled women of color were sometimes relegated to duties that could only be categorized as "housecleaning," and in a mighty big house. What these women found was nothing like the work they had hoped for, such as welding, for which some were already trained and quite skilled.[14]

The Shipyard Agent

A white female worker named Leona Ellis remembered an incident of flagrant racism in the shipyard when she witnessed "a black [man] drinking out of a drinking fountain and a white man with a broad southern accent yell[ing] at him to get out of there ... that was for white people only." She seemed pleased to report further that a different white man quickly approached, taking the offending white man who had spewed hatred by the back of his neck, walking and talking with him, explaining that the drinking fountains were for everyone.[15]

Unfortunately, this incident of blatant discrimination was not a rare occurrence in Portland. A young Black woman from Illinois named Beatrice Marshall decided she would take a break from university and contribute to the war effort. After eight weeks of training in Illinois through the National Youth Administration (NYA), she was declared ready to work. However, after traveling at the government's expense to Portland, she was shocked to learn she would not be allowed the work for which she had trained. Beatrice had tried to get work at Oregonship, Kaiser's biggest shipyard in Portland, and was told Blacks would not be hired for skilled positions, but that she could be hired to sweep.

Having begun college studies in Illinois without ever noticing discrimination personally and having experienced the NYA training where Blacks and whites worked harmoniously together, the racism Beatrice encountered in the Portland shipyard left her befuddled and hurt. "I just couldn't understand it when we got to Portland and couldn't get the job."[16]

Leona Ellis, when asked after the war if she thought the attitudes or level of racism changed during the war, stated, "There was definite change, I'd say, more after the war. I think during the war everybody thought it [the large inundation of Black people into the Portland–Vancouver area] was temporary and I think they expected most people to go back to where they came from after the war."[17]

This kind of expectation sounds much like the belief of many male defense workers that females were to return home to resume their role as homemakers after the war, leaving the vocational work world behind.

The arrival of many of the Black citizens who came was a direct result of Kaiser Company's energetic hiring campaign. This did not sit well with many Portlanders. On September 30, 1942, according to the *Oregonian* newspaper, close to five hundred men arrived from New York on a train dubbed the *Kaiser Karavan*; thirty-nine (some accounts say forty) were Black shipyard recruits. According to John Linder's "Liberty Ships and Jim Crow Shipyards," when agents from Kaiser Company had begun hiring in New York City, federal manpower officials reminded them to avoid discriminating.[18]

The Kaiser Vancouver shipyard promised jobs to the Black men aboard the seventeen-car train. All had eagerly boarded in the East to cross the nation happy to be given the opportunity to travel to the West, and to work. According to "Vancouver's Plan . . . For the Utilization of War Housing Projects Located at Vancouver, Wash.," published in March 1945, "The Kaiser Company provided transport then took the fare out of later paychecks." Thus, making it possible for the new hires to start work as soon as possible.[19]

Some on the westbound trains would see "cowboys and Indians" on their way through Montana, a sight they had only before imagined. Others said aloud that if they liked the town, they would bring their families and settle in the Portland–Vancouver area. These men on the train, which had also been labeled the Magic Carpet Special, were tagged "the emigrants of '42." While they traveled along the rails, one shipyard-bound passenger wrote a song, which was soon bursting forth from every hopeful person riding in his train car. It began and ended like this: "Over the top, the top, the top for Henry Kaiser. . . . over the top, the top, the top . . . At dear old Portland."[20]

Black people were not the only non-white people who came to the Kaiser yards in the West Coast states. For example, records state there were fifty Arab employees at Portland's shipyards. A photograph showing some of that number gathered in the city of Portland "at the Central Café" is dated May 23, 1943.[21]

According to the article "Chinese American Service in World War II," there were "many Chinese American women work[ing] in defense industries during World War II. During this period, some estimate that the shipyards of the Bay Area in California [where Kaiser's Richmond shipyards were located] consisted of 15 [percent] Chinese American workers."[22]

Also in the Richmond area, there were a minority of Japanese Americans working in Kaiser's shipyards. But, as the United States officially joined the war after the attack on Pearl Harbor, Japanese Americans working in the war production campaign were not excused from relocating; in the Pacific Northwest as well, President Roosevelt's Executive Order 9066, requiring Japanese residents to relocate inland, affected the shipyards. Most on the West Coast moved to that blight on the history of the United States that were internment camps. It had to have, at least temporarily, reduced the number of workers, as Germans and Italians were named in Executive Order 9066 along with the Japanese. Near Vancouver, Washington, people of these nationalities were forbidden by army orders to live in "southern and western Clark County," an area inundated with shipyard workers and sometimes their families.[23]

The Oregon History Project details how young Native American women also came to participate in defense work:

> *In Oregon, the Chemawa Indian School near Salem sent about forty students to a training facility in Eugene run by the National Youth Administration (NYA)—a program established by the Works Progress Administration during the Depression to help put young people to work. In 1942, the NYA was transferred to the War Manpower Commission and training facilities began to focus on skills such as welding and electrical to prepare students for shipyard work. Most of the trainees in the Eugene facility went on to work for the Kaiser Shipyards in Portland and Vancouver.*[24]

Franklin Roosevelt established the National Youth Administration in 1935, describing its purpose as "To initiate and administer a program of approved projects which shall provide relief, work relief, and employment for persons between the ages of sixteen and twenty-five years who are no longer in regular attendance at a school requiring full time, and who are

"Nine Indian girls" from Chemawa—a Native American school in Salem, Oregon—who were trained at a Eugene, Oregon, National Youth Administration (NYA) School to prepare for work in Portland shipyards, August 1942. PHOTOGRAPH. JOURNAL COLLECTION, CALL NO. 013610. OREGON HISTORICAL SOCIETY RESEARCH LIBRARY, PORTLAND, OREGON.

not regularly engaged in remunerative employment." The president added that the government would help the youth of the nation "because we can ill afford to lose the skill and energy of these young men and women. They must have their chance in school, their turn as apprentices and their opportunity for jobs—a chance to work and earn for themselves."[25]

The NYA program under which the Native Americans were trained was first formed as an offshoot of the Works Progress Administration (WPA), which seems appropriate since the mission of the WPA was to employ adult men and women in public works projects during the Depression. Later the NYA was transferred into the Federal Security Agency (FSA), doubtless because at that time the FSA oversaw education funding. After the start of World War II, the NYA program was transferred to the War Manpower Commission for administration. In 1943, the program closed. At that time, Roosevelt wrote that it was "difficult to evaluate the proportions of the resource which this training of young men and woman has been to America in the war crisis." He continued, saying the program had rendered "a national war service by supplying 30,000 young people, thoroughly trained in some skill [including welding] to essential places in the production program every month."[26]

The Shipyard Agent

Just over forty miles south of Portland, and yet a world away, stood the Chemawa Indian School (an accredited high school) in Salem. The Bureau of Indian Affairs (BIA) was partially responsible for forty students from the school being sent another seventy miles south to the university town of Eugene, Oregon, for NYA training in skills useful for war production jobs. The BIA "supported the integration of Native women into the American workforce ... because it reinforced a policy of cultural assimilation." A. E. Platt wrote in his article "Native American Women from Chemawa Train to Work in Shipyards" that this assimilation raised a question: "Should Native Americans be classified as *colored* or *white?*" Balking at being kept apart from others, Native Americans worked without the burden of "exclusion practices" like those suffered by African Americans. It seems reasonable to suggest that if a war industry worker were Black *and* female, the possibility of suffering discrimination doubled.[27]

Black workers faced a dilemma as the war went on. One might suggest they gained insight. Blacks across the nation, as well as those African Americans working in the war industry, struggled with the reality that "while fighting for democracy abroad" or supporting the fight on the home front, Blacks were "being denied basic rights at home." A man named James G. Thompson wrote a letter to the editor of the *Pittsburgh Courier* in 1942, proclaiming just that idea. The paper took up the cause, calling it the "Double V Campaign ... victory over fascism abroad and victory over racism at home."[28]

Yet positive experiences did exist for Black workers. For instance, Miss Gladys Theus, a Black woman, was hailed as the fastest welder in the yard at Kaiser Co. Calship in Richmond in 1944.[29]

Kathryn Blood with the Department of Labor studied Black women who worked in war industries like Gladys had. In 1945, she wrote that the contribution of African American women was "one which this nation would be unwise to forget or evaluate falsely."

In later years, one wise grandson, Marcus Gardley, whose grandmother had been a "Rosie in Richmond," became a playwright, remembering his grandmother in a stage play called, *This World in a Woman's Hands*. An artist, Rich Black, designed a poster for the play, depicting a black "Rosie" striking a pose mimicking the image of the well-known "We Can Do It" poster of the '40s. His image was different, however, in that the woman, besides being Black, was wearing a welding hood tipped back on her head. It is an appropriate tribute to the strong Black women who performed one of the most difficult jobs in shipbuilding—that of welding.[30]

Chapter Fourteen

A FRACTURED FAILURE AND A COMEBACK

"Poppycock. There was absolutely no failure of welds in this tanker as proved by examination."
—J. F. Lincoln, President, Lincoln Electric Company[1]

"We know definitely it isn't the workmanship, because the break wasn't through the weld."
—John F. Bruns, Principal Hull Inspector, Maritime Commission[2]

"She was loaded too heavy fore and aft without proper ballasting in the middle."
—Earl Ingram, Secretary, Portland Metal Trades Council[3]

The T2-SE-A1 turbo-electric tanker SS *Schenectady*, having been launched on October 24, 1942, and completely fitted out on December 31, completed successful sea trials and returned to her mooring at Swan Island shipyard the following January. Then, with a reverberation heard a mile away, she cracked virtually in half. Buckling in the middle, either end rested on the silt of the river bottom. The ship did not separate completely due to the strength of the construction of the ship's bottom.[4]

The Shipyard Agent

With a noise heard miles around, the SS *Schenectady*, a tanker returned from successful sea trials to dock at Swan Island Shipyard, broke virtually in half, January 16, 1943. HTTPS://COMMONS.WIKIMEDIA.ORG/WIKI/FILE:TANKERSCHE
NECTADY.JPG#/MEDIA/FILE:TANKERSCHENECTADY.JPG

At the very least, this occurrence was a disappointment, for this inaugural tanker, along with its cargo, had surely carried with it the optimism, hope, and promise of all who had touched it. At the occurrence, it must have felt catastrophic to all concerned, while raising unnumbered questions. Likely the most common question was, *Why?* Why had this happened and next, were there other ships sailing the seas in danger of breaking apart? One wonders if the fractured tanker may have been part of the discussion in Augusta Clawson's office. Perhaps the accident persuaded any naysayers who might have existed that Augusta needed to get to the shipyard.

The Kaiser Company, the managers of the shipyard, the providers of ship construction materials and parts, and the men and women welders of Swan Island shipyard had to have felt the implied weight of this event.

Soon, a formidable assemblage of influential men was on its way to Portland to determine the cause of the failure of the hull, which split in half "just aft of the superstructure."[5] Fortunately, only thirty crew members were aboard at the time, who "escaped without injury."[6]

Led by Rear Admiral Howard L. Vickery, the chosen group of men descending on the city to examine the fractured failure included Lieutenant William A. Webber, Vickery's aide; A. A. Norton of Sun Shipbuilding & Drydock; Henry Pierce of New York Shipbuilding Corporation; L. Grover of Air Reduction Co.; James Wilson of the Maritime Commission; A. G. Bissell of the US Navy Department's Bureau of Shipping; E. D. Debes of Bethlehem Steel; J. E. Schmeltzer, Vickery's technical assistant; Louis Luckenbach, president of American Bureau of Shipping; and Lyle Wilson, assistant chief surveyor of the shipping bureau.

For Vickery and "a party of shipping experts," the journey to Portland to examine the broken ship nearly led to a serious, more personal mishap. The *Oregon Daily Journal* reported that Vickery and his shipping experts had flown into a storm when nearing Portland, and "low on gas and its radio out of commission, [the plane] was forced down in an open field by a farmhouse near Condon." In the isolated high plains of Oregon east of the Cascade Mountains in the 1940s, a pilot was eagle-eyed to spot a farmhouse. The names of some of the other small ranching and farming communities in the region where the plane made the emergency landing paint a picture of the territory: Bakeoven, Fossil, Hardman, Antelope, and Lonerock, to name a few. Condon's population is less than seven hundred today.[7]

Having received no communication from Vickery's airplane, authorities feared the plane had crashed. Yet no one was injured in the close-call landing. The helpful farmer drove the admiral and his entourage to the train station in Condon. Edgar Kaiser, along with Carl Flesher of the Pacific Coast division of the Maritime Commission, had attempted to drive to Condon to rescue the party, but a raging winter storm kept them at bay and made the Columbia Gorge Highway on which they needed to travel impassable.[8]

Upon arrival in Portland, although perhaps feeling the effects of the trauma of the near-miss, Vickery was all business. Having been delivered to the Multnomah Hotel—the same hotel where Augusta would stay while working as a welder in the shipyard three months later—he and his entourage left immediately, going directly to Swan Island, refusing to make a statement for reporters who had gathered at the Multnomah Hotel until after he had "visited the yard." Once the admiral was ready to comment, he said, "failures in ship structures are not unknown things; there is always some reason for it, and the job of people in shipbuilding is to find out what's wrong and cure it."[9]

Henry J. Kaiser had been in New York when the tanker came apart on the other side of the country. He, too, left for Portland where he would see the tanker for himself. After that, he planned to join the conferences the admiral intended to hold following the inspection of the fracture and investigation of the incident.

One of those concerned men at the conference was Lewis Luckenbach of the shipping bureau. "This thing has happened before," Luckenbach stated in the *Oregon Daily Journal*. "It just happens that this is an extreme case. Welding is a relatively new art, and welding engineers are working all the time to perfect it. This case may help to bring their studies to a head."[10]

J. F. Lincoln, president of "the world's largest manufacturers of arc welding equipment," mentioned that welding had been used on ships for forty years and was "stronger than the riveted joint." He believed that the *Schenectady* accident could have been caused by "defective steel due to improper scrap." Lincoln's opinions seem to bear merit, but could they have been influenced by the very fact of his livelihood?[11]

"When word got around that whatever the cause of the breakup of the *Schenectady* at the Swan Island dock, it was not due to the quality of workmanship [or] to inexperienced labor . . . a sigh of relief rose from Swan Island's shipbuilders," reported the *Oregon Daily Journal* on the last day of January 1943. "And when it was learned that she could be repaired and put into service without great difficulty," the article continued, "they looked doubly happy. . . . As for the way the Swan Island Boys themselves are feeling—the numbers who showed up for work in spite of the storm is the best gauge of where they stand in the affair. Come snow or high water, they wanted to stay and build ships."[12]

To make that possible, some additional duties befell the shipyard workers that week: shoveling snow. A small article in the *Sunday Orego-*

nian of January 24 read, "Employes [sic] of Portland shipyards have been asked to lend a hand in digging their yards out of the snow."[13]

The state of Oregon was amid their worst winter weather since 1937, with temperatures and conditions fierce enough to freeze portions of the expansive Columbia River at the city of The Dalles, where the river was three hundred feet wide and thirty feet deep or greater.

Snow and ice were not the only source of the chill on Swan Island. And the *Bos'n's Whistle* was not the only employee-targeted news flyer provided to the Swan Island shipyard workers. Apparently, a small piece called the *Finger*, a "scrappy and anonymous little news sheet," was occasionally distributed. Perhaps predictably, an issue suddenly appeared following the *Schenectady*'s collapse. The attitudes shared among workers after the shock of seeing their maiden tanker's broken hull were expressed in the following editorial:

> *Our struggle here is against time. We cannot avoid an accident that has already happened, nor can we afford the time to be gloomy about it or waste moments in regret. This we can do. When we see the* Schenectady *broken in two and helpless, let us each vow to ourselves that she shall be repaired and that the number of her sister ships shall be limited only by our absolute lack of the capacity to do more. Tojo*[14] *and Herr Hitler are grinning because of this. When the* Quebec *[sic], and the Fort Moultrie [sic] and their 50 sister ships sail out, they won't be grinning.*[15]

Notice that the *Oregon Daily Journal* article discussed the feelings of "the Swan Island *Boys*" with no mention of the women who were by now shipbuilders. By January 24, "The FBI said it wasn't sabotage. The [M]aritime [C]ommission said it wasn't faulty welding."[16]

Months later, the topic of the threat of ships coming apart while out to sea was put to rest. In a succinct article summarizing the major events of 1943, a paragraph for each month was dedicated to memorable events. Opening the paragraph for the month of July 1943 is the following: "Charges that Liberty freighters break up at sea proved false at Portland hearing of [H]ouse [M]erchant [M]arine and [F]isheries [S]ubcommittee."[17]

One might imagine a collective sigh of relief spreading across the Swan Island shipyard upon hearing this declaration. For, when the *Schenectady* was launched, a proud Edgar Kaiser had beamed about the shipbuilders, "Their spirit is one that will lead in the building of peace after the war. We will show the men and women of this country what the northwest can do."[18]

And then came the break.

Nearly a year later, there existed a much more celebratory mood among shipyard workers at the Swan Island yard—particularly welders, for they had again shown what they could do. This time they were being celebrated rather than blamed. Swan Island shipbuilders had come through in record time with the highest production of tankers per way in 1943. And now, the coveted Tanker Champs flag would be theirs until and unless another yard surpassed their new record. Both men and women gathered around the flag in a photo where it appears that the workers were quite pleased with themselves, as they ought to have been.

This manufacturing and shipbuilding victory—the highest production of tankers per way (boat slip), 1943—was mentioned again as late as one year later in the *Statesman Journal* newspaper of Salem, Oregon, reminding readers how in "a year of speeding assembly lines and gigantic plans for the future ... The Kaiser Swan Island yard kept pace by earning the nation's [tanker champs] flag." The yard earned the privilege of flying the flag over the shipyard by sending a record-breaking total of four towering ships' hulls down a single way (sometimes known as *slipway*) in the month of September.[19]

Vickery sent a telegram to Swan Island to accompany the awarding of the flag. He instructed the shipyard workers that the flag "is to be flown over your yard for a period of [thirty] days, or as long thereafter as your yard maintains national leadership in tanker construction."[20]

Although found blameless, after swallowing the bitter pill of the *Schenectady* failure—built so earnestly by citizen shipbuilders of Swan Island Shipyard—the winning of the Tanker Champs flag must have tasted that much sweeter.

"Citation for Swan Island: shipyard workers accept the Tanker Champ flag, December 31, 1943." Earning this award was a significant honor among ship builders.
PORTLAND CITY ARCHIVES, AP/7553. VINTAGE PORTLAND. HTTPS://EFILES.PORTLANDOREGON.GOV/RECORD/2859599/.

Chapter Fifteen

BEST WOMAN WELDER IN THE WORLD

"At first I thought I'd probably be nervous with so much at stake . . . but after I got my sparks flying, I just forgot all about the competition and settled down to weld just like I do every night on the ways."
—Mrs. Hermina "Billie" Strmiska[1]

"I'm rather proud of my sex as I've seen it building ships."[2]
—Augusta H. Clawson

In January 1943 someone had a very big idea. Looking to create a means to boost confidence and ignite the competitive spirit in women welders everywhere, the Best Woman Welder in the World competition was declared begun by the Ingalls Shipbuilding Corporation in Mississippi. This competition was open to women welders around the globe, further defined as the United States, Australia, and England. Welding supervisors approached women welders they considered to be their most skilled to offer them an opportunity to compete. Perhaps the contest was seen as a chance to distract the women welders from the ongoing investigation into the failure of a ship built at Swan Island shipyard. Or perhaps it was seen as an opportunity for good-natured sport within the work environment.

Surely, a competition between women welders would have caught the attention of Augusta Clawson. By the time the finals were held in April, Augusta had joined their ranks. It's not a great stretch of the imagination to picture her enthusiastically supporting the contest. Certainly, Augusta would have seen the competition as another opportunity to show the world that women are not only intellectually strong and able to learn—and master—skills required to perform complex tasks but also that they possess the inherent will and stamina to perform work traditionally done by men. Women welders were certainly champions in the shipyards long before any competition was announced.

Whatever the reason driving Mr. Les Voshell, the welding superintendent at Oregonship, he soon called his best women welders to his desk to share the announcement telegram recently received from Ingalls Shipbuilding Corporation. Some women were eager—or at least willing—to compete, including Mrs. Mabel Lionberger, the author's grandaunt, and Mabel's coworker, Lila Dooley.[3]

Excitement for the contest at shipyards like Oregonship spread into outlying towns, with announcements appearing in hometown newspapers. For example, the *Capital Journal* in Salem, Oregon, announced: "Silverton Woman Welder Is Expert." Cecile Peron, a graveyard shift welder at Oregonship, had placed second in her shift.

Large yards such as Henry J. Kaiser's Kaiser Company, Inc. yards participated, while the smaller yards, like Commercial Iron Works (CIW), did not. Welder Jean Neil Johnson, who worked at CIW, was adamant: "We didn't have time for a contest." Supervisors at the larger yards made time for it.

From the Oregon Shipbuilding Corporation yard emerged Mrs. Hermina Strmiska, known as Billie. After moving to Oregon as a teenager, Billie had married and returned to her home state of Texas with her husband, Edward. Then, during the Depression years, they came back to Oregon to work as "migrant pickers" in the orchards and berry fields of the Willamette Valley. During the war, when the cry for help rose from the shipyards, both Edward and Billie took jobs as welders.[4]

"She's never worked before outside of housework in her own home," stated an article in the *Sunday Oregonian* of April 18, 1943, "but when she

"Planning to beat the world . . . Les Voshell, welding superintendent at Oregon [Shipbuilding Corporation] shows two of his topflight welders, Mabel Lionberger [author's grandaunt] and Lila 'Barney' Dooley, the telegram from the Ingalls Shipbuilding corporation that started the world wide contest." *Oregon Journal*, January 10, 1943. Photographer: Al Monner. © THE OREGONIAN. ALL RIGHTS RESERVED. USED WITH PERMISSION. PHOTO FILE #2209. ORGLOT1284.

realized the need for help in Liberty ship building to speed along the end of the war, she decided to give it a try." Interestingly, the article, within which Billie is described as "the blond welderette" and "a little neophyte," was written by a female staff writer for the *Oregonian* newspaper, Bonnie Wiley. The reporter did a fantastic job of describing in fine detail the job of welding that the women were required to perform, no doubt dictated to her by Billie.

Another great motivator to spur Billie on was knowing her two brothers had enlisted in the Army. She was bent on "doing all [she could] at home to help them." Billie had attended a 130-hour welding course at a Portland-area commercial welding school before entering work in the shipyard.[5]

Billie's first day of work after training—much like Augusta's first day—was challenging, to put it mildly. Reporter Bonnie Wiley recorded the impression of that first day as Billie Strmiska told it to her: "There was a clatter, followed by a crash, followed by a boom, followed by a sudden flash of light, followed by a thud. 'I,' said Mrs. Hermina Strmiska to herself, 'have had enough. I,' she added, screaming to make herself heard above the din, 'believe I will be getting out of here.'" But Billie stayed, of course, and thrived at welding. One of her biggest thrills and proudest moments was witnessing the launch of a ship she had worked on, saying, "Why, I helped build that ship. It's part mine."[6]

Now, just as she had heard the cry for help from the shipyards, she heard the cry of a challenge to find the champion woman welder. Billie decided she would compete and see what could happen. What happened was that she was "crowned queen of the women welders in the Oregon yards."

Winners rose through different levels of competition to determine the West Coast woman champion. Billie "won the Oregon Shipbuilding Welderette contest in March 1943, beating out one hundred other women welders in the standard American Bureau of Shipping Test."[7]

Billie placed first over a final field of sixteen "top-flight Kaiser welderettes." Afterward, representing West Coast welders, Billie traveled to Pascagoula, Mississippi, to compete for the prize of war savings bonds and other gifts and privileges. At thirty-five years of age, pleasant Billie Strmiska would perform against the East Coast winner, a Miss Vera Anderson, who was nineteen years old and described as "petite [and] blue-eyed."[8]

"The battle between Billie and Vera took place on a roped-off platform in the Ingalls Shipbuilding Corporation yards, but comparatively few persons witnessed the spectacle as the public was barred and the contest was carried on without interrupting defense work at the yard," outlined the *Oregonian* newspaper back in Billie's adopted hometown of Portland.

Judges of the competition were identified as "representatives of the [N]avy, the [M]aritime [C]omission, and the [B]ureau of [S]hipping."

Mrs. Hermina "Billie" Strmiska from Oregon Shipbuilding Corporation ranks as top woman welder of the three Kaiser Portland–Vancouver shipyards. She traveled to Mississippi to answer a challenge from the best in the Ingalls Shipbuilding Corporation. © *THE OREGONIAN*. ALL RIGHTS RESERVED. USED WITH PERMISSION. COLLECTION OHS939, OHS.ORG.

Billie Strmiska *(right)*, West Coast winner, performs to her best alongside the East Coast winner, Miss Vera Anderson, during their final competition in Pascagoula, Mississippi.
© *THE OREGONIAN*. ALL RIGHTS RESERVED. USED WITH PERMISSION. COLLECTION OHS939, OHS.ORG.

Apparently, Vera Anderson completed the required tasks faster than Billie while welding, for she won all three heats: overhead, vertical, and flat welding. The judges determined that between Billie and Vera, the "quality of the work and rod consumption were about even." Yet young Vera had won the heats (and perhaps a few hearts) and, therefore, the competition.

As the champion woman welder of America, Vera received a two-foot-tall silver loving cup, $350 in war savings bonds, a handbag, and an outfit of summer clothing. Billie "was awarded $175 in war bonds, a handbag, and a slack suit." Both women contestants were invited to visit First Lady Eleanor Roosevelt at the White House. Yet homesick Billie chose to return to Portland, to her husband, and to her friends at Oregonship to get on with the work of war. Vera prepared to travel immediately to Washington, DC, to meet Mrs. Roosevelt.[9]

Billie Strmiska of the Oregon Shipbuilding Corp. wears her name as *Hermina Strmiska*, arm-in-arm with champion Vera Anderson of Ingalls Shipbuilding Corp. Vera was presented a silver loving cup for winning against Billie, and the West.
© *THE OREGONIAN*. ALL RIGHTS RESERVED. USED WITH PERMISSION. COLLECTION OHS939, OHS.ORG.

Eleanor Roosevelt would mention the welding competition in her June 2, 1943, column, "My Day." After listing Vera and Billie's names and their respective shipyards, she wrote: "This is a new occupation for women, and that is why this competition was staged, I imagine. They probably need more women welders and so this should spur the ladies on."[10]

While Billie was away welding her heart out on behalf of everyone back home, her fellow women welders in Portland were anxious for any news of the competition in Mississippi. One woman located a newspaper and gathered others to her. Side by side, the five women sat down wearing rough leather protective clothing and sturdy shoes, welding hoods thrown back from their soot-kissed faces. Reading the latest news about their brave coworker Billie Strmiska, the women welders were excited to learn if she'd won, but mostly to know when she'd be coming home to Oregonship.[11]

"Who Is the Champion Woman Shipyard Welder?" Five women welders from Oregon Shipbuilding Corporation Shipyard search a newspaper. *From left* are Jerry Grant, Margaret Peterson, Reva De Cent, Lila Dooley, and Mabel Lionberger, grandaunt of author. February 3, 1943. Photographer unknown. *THE BO'S'N'S WHISTLE*, VOL. 3, NO. 3. COLLECTION–BW-OSC–THE BO'S'N'S WHISTLE. BOSUNSWHISTLE_OSC19430204_303. OREGON HISTORICAL SOCIETY RESEARCH LIBRARY, PORTLAND, OREGON.

Chapter Sixteen

Augusta Clawson— Beyond War's End

"Her specialty has always been finding new ways to bring people and jobs together harmoniously."
—The *International Altrusan*[1]

"She was awesome . . . an exceptional individual . . . with a heart as big as all outdoors."
—Ann Henderson Kramer, niece of Augusta[2]

There were likely days at the shipyard when Augusta thought, *there is no rest for the weary*. Although she stated many times how she enjoyed the work of welding, perhaps the experience was sometimes bittersweet. And she may have felt some sense of relief following the completion of her assignment there, despite not being anxious to leave. Those who knew her knew she was always ready for something more . . . the next challenge . . . another adventure.

Immediately following the conclusion of her Swan Island Shipyard assignment, Augusta had many other war production sites to observe, from Seattle south to Los Angeles and San Diego and east through Arizona and New Mexico. Augusta was incredibly busy watching over women's work during the war years. Soon came an opportunity in the form of an invitation from the California State Director of Vocational Education "to report [her] experience to his staff." Rather than speaking before a crowd of people, Augusta agreed to work with a member of the "California group," Wava McCullough, whom she identified as "a young woman and an accomplished artist," to create a pamphlet the purpose of which was "to recruit more women to the shipyard. Several thousand [pamphlets] were distributed." Although Augusta gives credit for the development of the pamphlet to McCullough, surely Augusta was involved in the creation of its contextual content. Although she was no longer working in the shipyard, she remained dedicated to those women who were and helped with this project, distributing it for use before the war ended.[3]

"Women in shipyards have been invaluable. We could not have got along without them. Their contribution will be long remembered by a grateful nation," commented Captain Fred M. Earle, US Navy, in 1945.[4] It's commendable that Captain Earle published this statement, shining a light on the women of the nation who had entered shipyards and stuck it out for the duration. Women entering industrial environments like shipyards, aircraft factories, munitions manufacturers, and every sort of business that was needed to support the war effort were proven to have made a crucial difference in winning the war. It seems reasonable to wonder if the war would have been won without the over six million women who reported for war work across the nation. Six million. Captain Earle remarked that women's contributions would long be remembered.

It's easy to imagine Augusta's voice rising, *As well it should be!*

What was likely expected next of women who had entered the male bastion of industrial work during the war period was briefly described by English author Margaretta Jolly in her book, *Dear Laughing Motorbyke: Letters from Women Welders of the Second World War*. She states: "The need for women was balanced by the government's wish to maintain the social order . . . It was assumed that after the war they would return to their primary occupations of wife and mother." This sentiment echoed across the Atlantic to the factories and shipyards of America. As a matter of fact, some women were happy to return to the status quo. Others, enjoying the physical work, the feeling of independence, and the income they'd received while working in the shipyards, were not so eager to return to the life they'd led before.⁵

Augusta remembered her close friend Missouri telling her she had been pleased that she'd worked in the shipyard and done something for her country, that her husband had worked in the shipyard at the same time, and that her mother worked in the yard's childcare center. She was certainly happy to have met Augusta. And she knew she wouldn't weld again.

Other women would continue to weld, such as Jean Neil Johnson, who worked at Commercial Iron Works. She would use her war-honed welding skills repairing equipment and tools and building useful items on their farm in northern Idaho after the war.⁶

Not one to "stay in [her] place," Augusta carried on. In January 1944, she enjoyed seeing her government reports culminate in a small paperback book, *Shipyard Diary of a Woman Welder*, published by Penguin Books, Inc. in New York City. The book was also released in Toronto, Canada, and Middlesex, England, sharing her experience of what it was like for women performing the dirty but essential war production job of welding together the hulls of ships. The bookshop in New Jersey where she'd been affiliated was quick to support her by advertising a February book release. The local newspaper announced that "one of their own" had become an author.

Confessing she'd achieved something she'd not set out to achieve, Augusta insisted she'd "certainly" had "no thought of publishing a book." She'd simply fulfilled her duties. "I was expected to submit a report to my supervisor, Miss Louise Moore, Agent, U.S. Office of Education." She continues:

> *As my reports were received in my home office and circulated to those interested, copies were sent to our publication office. That office sent selected parts to Dodd Meade Publishing Company, Penguin Books, and a magazine [the name of which she could not remember]. When I returned from the West Coast many months later, I found a contract from Penguin to publish my book in paperback to sell for twenty-five cents per copy. I was to receive four cents per copy. . . .*

> *It took considerable time to overcome the strong objection of one whose consent was needed. He felt I had no right to the publicity or monetary rewards since I wrote it as part of my job. When I could prove I wrote it on my own personal time in my hotel room well after midnight, he reluctantly consented.*[7]

After reading Augusta's paperback, one opinionated person, who apparently could not relate to Augusta's cheerful, winning attitude, took up a pen and called the diary a "tip-off to job seekers." This was not meant as a compliment. Using the initials *M. W.*, the reporter for the *Cincinnati Post* had this to say: "This little book contains a number of valuable tips for anyone who contemplates taking a welding job. Aside from that it is tedious reading matter." The pent-up wielder of the pen went on with the critique to proclaim that Augusta had only tried to make the report more interesting by including "exclamations concerning the good-nature, generosity, and general salt-of-the-earthiness of her fellow workers. This looking for the good in everyone, willy nilly, gets extremely monotonous after the first few chapters." M. W.'s final paragraph was succinct: "Getting idle women

Stylish Augusta Clawson, March 1944, two months after publication of her book, *Shipyard Diary of a Woman Welder.*
DIVISION OF WORK AND INDUSTRY, NATIONAL MUSEUM OF AMERICAN HISTORY, SMITHSONIAN INSTITUTION.

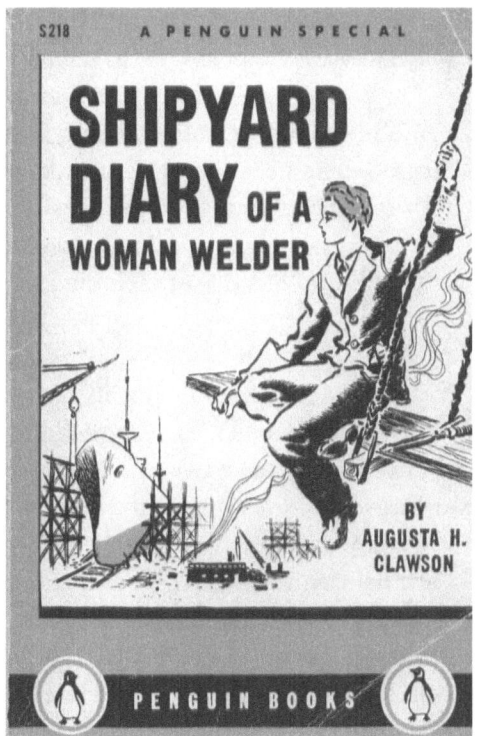

With a vivid scarlet and white cover, Augusta H. Clawson's book, *Shipyard Diary of a Woman Welder, was* published by Penguin Books, Inc. in January 1944. A second publishing followed in April. AUTHOR'S COLLECTION.

interested and employed in war production jobs is of vital concern to the War Manpower commission, but we greatly doubt that the 'Shipyard Diary of a Woman Welder' will recruit even one welder to the ranks. Frankly, if we had ever entertained any thought of becoming a welder, Miss Clawson's experiences would quickly thrust it from our mind."[8]

Occasionally, there came other less-than-positive scrutiny of Augusta and her shipyard work. One woman in the 1980s was heard to remark she had read *The Shipyard Diary* and that it seemed to her Augusta Clawson had simply been on a lark. Who would agree to such an enormous and important task as a "lark"? One might respond that in the minds of those who knew and worked with Augusta, that comment slides down the slipway and sinks.

Whether others liked it or not, Augusta's work as a welder was not her only foray into the world of women employed in challenging industrial labor. In April 1945, the *Courier-News* stated the following: "She has worked in an aircraft factory, as a welder in West Coast shipyards, and now is studying textile industries in the South." Augusta had achieved a great deal in support of war production. And in support of women, saying that she believed women had "gained more self-respect and pride by taking part in the war effort." She was still recommending that women begin a program of "[physical] conditioning ... so they might gain confidence in themselves to endure the 'mud, sweat, and fears' of some of their duties."

During 1945 Augusta followed in the footsteps of family members and friends in Plainfield by becoming a member of the Altrusa International Service Club. Accepting many positions of importance over the years, she contributed to the professional woman's club by serving as the International Relations chairman, a district governor, and the Vocational Services chairman, to name a few positions she held. In late 1947, as "president of the Washington, DC Altrusa Club," she acted as "toastmistress" at a banquet held in the Sapphire Room of the Mayflower Hotel in Washington after earlier attending a "five o'clock" tea given at the White House by Mrs. Harry Truman. The previous day, she and her fellow Altrusans had been guests in J. Edgar Hoover's FBI offices.[9]

That same year another major event would occur, this time involving Augusta's dear friend, Gladys Doane. Gladys and her husband had separated in September 1942. According to an Abstract of Divorce Decree dated May 22, 1947, five years later Gladys divorced her husband, listing the cause of "desertion and abandonment." (During that decade, "divorce was considered to be against the public interest, and civil courts refused to grant a divorce except if one party to the marriage had betrayed the 'innocent spouse.' Thus, a spouse suing for divorce in most states had to state a 'fault' such as abandonment, cruelty, incurable mental illness, or adultery."[10])

Announcing that women could be their own worst enemy, in the March 24, 1950, edition of the *Winston-Salem Journal*, Augusta proclaimed, "Women are not making the contribution they could to the world today." She explained, saying women were victims of "strange dogmas." Augusta identified the dogmas as: "women gossip; women are jealous; women cry; women are emotionally unstable; women won't work for other women." Further saying, "These are false beliefs ... [W]e cut our own executive throats by saying that." Remembering Swan Island, she reminded readers, "We can prove women can do the job. It was proven during the war."[11]

During the war, good friends Gug and Glad had already proven they were of like minds. While Augusta was busy on the West Coast investigating for the benefit of women welders and other female shipyard workers, Gladys had been similarly occupied across the country. In Elkton, Maryland, was "one of the largest munitions factories during the war ... The women who worked at the factory were known as the *Bomb-Bomb Girls*."[12] Having previously worked with the USO (United Service Organizations) clubs, Gladys had accepted a position with the Federal Housing Administration to "act as director of all recreation for 2,500 or more women housed in the Elkton project ... [from] the three munitions plants in the area." Most importantly, she had been given "the responsibility of helping to reduce turnover and absenteeism in the war plants by helping the women war workers to a better adjustment."[13]

After the war years and three years after the divorce, Gladys is recorded as living with Augusta in Arlington, Virginia, in the 1950 federal census. Augusta is recorded as *Agusta*. Her marital status line reads "Never Married (Single)." Her occupation is listed as director of the Hannah Harrison Industrial School. In the column to record age of the occupants, Augusta is forty-six years old and head of a household on Queens Lane. The name entered on the line below hers is Gladys Doane, aged thirty-four. This is a recording error. Gladys Evelyn Doane (née Chase) was born on December 14, 1892, making her fifty-seven years old in the spring of 1950. Identified in the census as a widow engaged in real estate sales, she is further recorded as Augusta's *partner*. (Gladys' ex-husband, F. Clyde Doane had died six months earlier on October 19, 1949, in New York City, where he had remained following their divorce.) A notation on the bottom of the 1950 census form states that the Clawson and Doane lines as recorded were completed using "Information by mother of Miss Clawson. Miss Doane out of U.S." This, of course, would have been Augusta's stepmother, Marion. By all accounts, Augusta and Gladys nurtured a close friendship of at least twenty-two years. This can be determined by counting from the date of the 1933 automobile accident outside Plainfield when Gladys was a passenger in Augusta's car until the death of Gladys in 1955.

Eight years after this census, the *Virginia Chronicle* newspaper published a Show Cause Order for the estate of Gladys C. Doane, listing Augusta as one of the executors of her will. Gladys' death came in September 1955, prompting an obituary that would close with this statement: "At the time of her death she resided with Miss Augusta Clawson, also a former Plainfield resident."

Augusta spent her career dedicated to the vocational education of self-supporting women. In March 1950, the *Evening Star* of Washington, DC, announced the upcoming opening of the Harrison School of Industrial Arts where Augusta had been installed as director. The school had been a dream of and was endowed to the tune of three million dollars by Julius Garfinckel, after whose mother the school was named. In July, the *Newport Daily News*, in the column "Washington Day Book" by Jane Blads, reported: "'[W]orthy women, under the necessity of earning their own livelihood,' was Garfinckel's description of those women who were to be admitted." According to Augusta, wrote Blad, "It's a school to prepare women for jobs, get them jobs, and to provide them with a home during training."

Augusta had further explained that at the time of the opening there were fifteen students, ranging in age from seventeen to fifty-four years old. "Age limits are those set by industry," explained Augusta as she described how the school attempted to fill employment needs as they were presented to the school. For example, "If an industry wants a woman secretary [seventy-five] years old, we'd train one at that age." However, she continued, she found that industry, in fact, wanted younger women for secretarial positions. Augusta added that she believed the "best housekeepers . . . are a vigorous [fifty]."

As director of Hannah Harrison School, Augusta helped set up the curriculum with three courses: "executive housekeeping (for hotel and hospital jobs); commercial food preparation (restaurants, tea rooms, etc.); and secretarial subjects." The staff was hopeful to add courses in the future of "commercial art, transportation management, and needlework." Besides the carefully curated curriculum being offered, every student received a private room in which to reside. Holders of "fellowships" received free room and board in a homey atmosphere "where women who must earn their own living receive vocational training in 'useful and industrial arts.'"[14]

Augusta closed the interview by explaining the desire that had driven Mr. Garfinckel to build the school, saying he "especially wanted to help women suddenly thrown on the labor market through divorce or widowhood, or younger women orphaned and deprived of parental support, who were capable of working but without training, and who desperately needed an income."[15]

In the years after the war, Augusta was sent to various vocational training facilities to study safety, comfort, and even the wages of workers. Two years after the close of the global conflict, on a Vassar Alumnae Register, she listed her occupation as "Director of Training & Employee Services, Government Services, Inc." Describing her responsibilities as "setting up program for [the] company that operates government cafeterias," she took what she learned from that experience and wrote another book, of a different nature. This one was an equipment maintenance and safety manual. Having worked beside kitchen sanitation expert Mary M. O'Donnell, "she developed basic procedures in food production for nationwide application." Along with O'Donnell, she developed charts and extremely detailed instructions for food service workers regarding the use of and care and cleaning of the important equipment with which they worked. This manual was published by Ahrens Publishing Company, Inc. in New York, in 1951.[16]

Within the preface of the manual, Augusta addresses those who may have felt that a manual was not necessary. "The worker will feel the

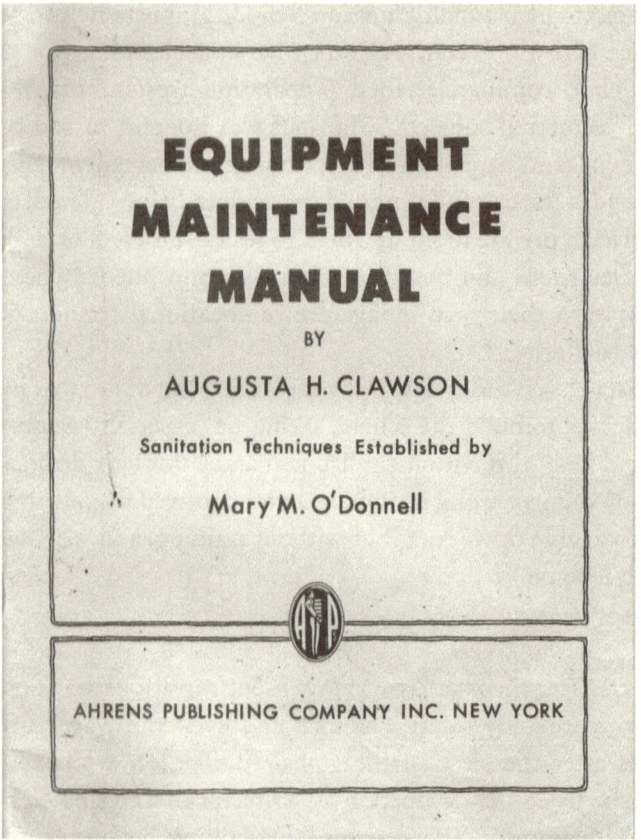

A sage green cover encloses the *Equipment Maintenance Manual* by Augusta H. Clawson, with Mary M. O'Donnell, 1951. Producing this important health and safety manual was one of Augusta's proud accomplishments. AUTHOR'S COLLECTION.

dignity of his job if it is important enough to merit printed instructions," spelled out Augusta, adding that "[p]restige, pride in the job, high morale and consequent job satisfaction are the ingredients that go to make up the efficient, productive employee." She suggested that those responsible for training workers ask these questions: "How high is the repair bill on your equipment? How frequently are replacements needed? How high (or low) are your standards of sanitation? How much time do you consume training a new worker? How effective is that training?" It appears probable that these questions or some similarly constructed might have been used as a guide in her shipyard observations, as well.

In 1961, on the Vassar alumnae register, she identified her title and occupation as "Field Representative, Women's Bureau, U.S. Department of Labor, Washington, D.C." Still sought for speaking engagements, it was before the Virginia Federation of Business and Professional Women's Clubs, in September 1963, that Augusta reiterated, "Woman's place is no longer just in the home. Woman's place is in public life, community life, and in employment." She regarded the President's Commission on the Status of Women—developed to identify barriers to women's employment, and the Manpower Development and Training Act—designed to assure training and retraining programs for unemployed and underemployed workers as two "very significant steps taken by the government."

Serving as part of an Altrusan International panel discussion—beside the likes of Mrs. Chase Going Woodhouse and Lillian Gilbreth—regarding women's fight for equality, Augusta listed three milestones that had occurred in the struggle since the decade of the 1960s began. She listed the December 1961 Executive Order establishing the President's Commission on the Status of Women—"examining remaining barriers to a full partnership of men and women in our society." Next, she mentioned the recently enacted Equal Pay Law. And finally, she explained the benefits of the Manpower Development and Training Act of 1961, which "start with the worker, his [or her] needs, his strengths and his potential ability, which are then matched to a particular job."[17]

By 1965, she was holding yet another position within the Department of Labor. This time identifying herself as a government official, she listed her title as "Chief of the Information and Evaluation Branch and Manpower Specialist in the Manpower office."

The 431 Exchange school in New Orleans invited Augusta to speak at their graduation ceremony in 1967. The 431 Exchange was a school formed by sheer determination on a street called Exchange Place, just off Canal Street. After coming up against fifty-nine refusals to rent from landlords, finally a willing businessman was found. The audience at the graduation ceremony, as well as the school's student body, consisted mainly of Black women. An incredible documentary, *The School That Would Not Die*, may be viewed through a series of YouTube videos. Photos of Augusta's commencement speeches are posted under both the 1967 and 1968 portions.[18]

"The most effective planning for what's ahead will stem from a sharpened awareness of what is," wrote Augusta in 1969 in the *International Altrusan* while serving as chairman of Altrusan Vocational Services. "Today is marked by unrest, conflict, riots; questioning, groping, challenge of old values, disregarding of accepted standards; unemployment and skill shortages; disasters and discovery; affluence and hunger; doubts and fear." Hers was quite a thorough assessment of the condition of American society at the time. Within the article, she goes on to encourage the development of the "employment potential of women." She wanted to help raise the "hopes and aspirations" of what she called "that significant sector of manpower—women."[19]

Augusta believed many women seeking employment were disadvantaged at the get-go (not unlike the women who went to the male-bastion shipyards during World War II to become welders) and continues in the essay to name many types of the "disadvantaged," describing

Altrusa International Service Club official portrait of Augusta Clawson, who held several offices in the long-established "First Service Club for Executive and Professional Women." THE INTERNATIONAL ALTRUSAN. MAY 1969. USED WITH PERMISSION. HTTPS://DMR.BSU.EDU/DIGITAL/COLLECTION/ALTRUSAINTL/ID/43534.

the categories as educationally, culturally, physically, mentally, racially, and socially disadvantaged.[20]

By 1977, Augusta had retired, although she was known to quip, "I'm not retired, I'm recycled!" Writing that she had fulfilled "[fifty] years of employment: all in [the] field of education, industrial training, manpower training, etc.; almost every job [was] one without pattern, experimental in nature, usually involving organization and management."

One can imagine her cheerfully closing the entry with, *That's it in a nutshell!*

It was 1984 when Augusta received bittersweet recognition: Arthritis Patient of the Year. The Washington, DC, Metropolitan Chapter of the Arthritis Foundation recognized her for the qualities that shone through her daily pain, such as perseverance, positivity, and empathy. It seems natural that also in 1984 the Associated Alumnae of Vassar College named her as guest speaker for the sixtieth reunion of her class of '24. She spoke about living with arthritis to those classmates gathered at the reunion, some of whom had gladly pushed her forward in her wheelchair, proudly leading the class of 1924 in the annual reunion parade. From the podium she delivered a speech titled "On Coping." Much of her presentation was published in the *Vassar Quarterly* that year. She presented a message very personalized yet also universal, and one that offered helpful suggestions to others who were suffering:

> *I realized two truths: the pain could increase, and could last a lifetime. I decided I would live now and wouldn't be beaten. So, I developed four rules. 1) Admit the defect is yours. Don't groan and moan at the world when you hurt. It is not their fault. 2) Do something about it. I found the top A-1 rheumatologist in the area. [At this comment, Augusta laughingly apologized to any other rheumatologists in the room.] 3) Never let your good nature slip out of gear. 4) Develop a giant-sized sense of humor. If you can laugh with it, you can live with it. . . . One does tire of constant pain, but I can't afford to develop arthritis of the spirit.*[21]

Much of the same speech was quoted in the *Virginia Gazette* on April 26 that year, written by her friend Dave Robinson. The title, "McLean's Augusta Holmes Clawson: 80 and Rollin'," was befitting of her and her lifelong encouraging, can-do attitude. Robinson had visited Augusta at home. He shared much of their conversation, opening his article with this: "You should see me go through one of those airport metal detectors. Boy! Do I light up the place!" Dave continued:

And then she throws her head back and laughs, this bionic woman with hip joints of stainless steel, funny bone of activated quicksilver, and soul of hammered gold. The hammer that has forged that soul is called Osteoarthritis, a bone-crunching bludgeon of a disease that leaves all too many of its victims in bed, in pain, in despair. But when it began to better Augusta Holmes Clawson, it produced instead, a work of art. An original. Maybe even a masterpiece.[22]

The *Gazette* article revealed more of what Robinson witnessed that evening. A happy memory burst forth when Augusta noticed a photograph resting on her bookshelf, "'*There's* Missouri! There's my old shipyard pal. . . . Missouri and I still keep in touch,' she smiles." She next remembered friends made during her time at Vassar College, sharing with Robinson that she had never missed a reunion of her graduating class. "I love seeing my old classmates, and I'm fascinated by what they are all doing."

Suddenly she added, as though she'd been building a list of characteristics for Dave, "Oh, I collect kids." After telling how children liked to be around her and often helped her at church, as an example, she declared, "I'm gonna get a Pied Piper license!" Augusta's niece, Ann, would agree to these statements, confirming that all the children in the extended Clawson family were drawn to the "kid collector." No wonder, as Augusta would unfailingly bring a book when she came to visit, reading aloud to the youngsters when they piled across the covers of her bed each morning.

Finally, Augusta slowly searched in her bedroom, returning to show Robinson what she'd received as a gift when she had turned eighty years old. She was tickled by looking at the vibrant purple sweatsuit, white pip-

Portrait of Augusta Holmes Clawson at the age of eighty-four in 1987.
COURTESY OF MARGARET "MEG" SONDEY.

ing adding pizazz, with the words *Augusta—80 and rollin'* embroidered above her heart. Apparently, when she received it, she had immediately dressed in the suit to attend a slide show to which the friend had invited her. The "slide show" was instead a surprise birthday party. "Oh, I tell you," she said to Robinson, "you've *got* to live to be 80. Did I have a party!"[23]

Besides a good party, Augusta greatly enjoyed her work, often offering her opinion about the great achievements, noble goals, and ideas of suitable compensation for women. "On you depends not only your own success but expanded opportunities for all women." With the flavor of a mantra, this was one of the statements Augusta had suggested the Office of Education staff tell women trainees who were hired by the shipyards. She lived this belief. Her own life reflected the strength of her convictions regarding the betterment of the lives of working women, especially those who by choice or of necessity were self-supporting.[24]

Augusta's extended career remained focused on building the confidence and job security of women. Vassar College and their archived biographical files are a treasure trove of bits of memorabilia that had been collected and saved. It is an opportunity to "hear" her voice. Following is an accumulation of entries from the reunion forms detailing her work and interests, in Augusta's own words:

1929, Teacher at Elizabeth Girls Continuation School—Teaching "related academic subjects."

1938, Placement Guidance and Apprentice Supervisor or Coordinator, Edison Vocational School, Elizabeth, New Jersey—Enrollment of pupils, assignment to courses, organization of new courses, supervision of student government and Alumnae organization, coordinator contacting industry and school to build [a] market for students trained, to place in jobs for which trained, and to follow up. This includes organization of Advisory Board for every trade department comprising outstanding members active in these trades.

1947, Director of Training and Employee Services, Government Services, Inc.—Setting up program for company that operates government cafeterias, directing employee services.

1957, Management Analyst, U.S. Navy Department, Executive Office of the Secretary— Head of Navy Directives System.

1961, Field Representative, Women's Bureau, U.S. Department of Labor, Washington, D.C.

1965, Government Official, Manpower Development Specialist— Chief, Information and Evaluation Branch, Manpower Office, U.S. Department of Labor, where she noted, her nickname was 'Gus or 'Gusta.

1977, Retired. [Fifty] years of employment, all in the fields of education, industrial training, manpower training, etc. Almost every job [was] one without pattern, experimental in nature, usually involving organization and management.

Her most significant previous occupations were recorded by Augusta in 1984 on the Alumnae House form:

1941–1945 U.S. Office of Education, Training Specialist

1949–1951 Hannah Harrison School (resident, vocational), Director

1952–1957 U.S. Department of the Navy, Head, Navy Directive System

Volunteer work:

- Altrusa International Service Club, projects of community service as well as serving as Governor of the Southeast region in 1949.
- Washington (DC) Personnel Association, a private industry group where she served as vice president from 1950 through 1951.
- Washington (DC) Area Group of Hard-of-Hearing, member from 1973 through 1975.
- Northern Virginia Hotline, a volunteer, anonymous answering service operating twenty-four hours a day, seven days a week, year-round. Served as listener, board member, and trainer from 1980 through 1984.
- Arthritis Foundation Hotline, a listener from 1983 through 1984.
- Federal Club Toastmistress, President, Washington, DC.

Honors and awards:

- Government Superior Performance Award for leadership in developing Older Worker Program to expand training and employment opportunities.
- Government Meritorious Award for "outstanding pioneering contributions to the Experimental Manpower and Development Programs."
- Woman of the Year Award from the Altrusa Club of Alexandria, Virginia and from the McLean Virginia Business and Professional Women's Club.

- Publication of *Shipyard Diary of a Woman Welder* by Penguin Books, Inc., recording her incognito work in a Kaiser shipyard during the war.
- Publication of her *Equipment Maintenance Manual* by Ahrens Publication Company, listing techniques for operation, cleaning, and maintenance of hotel and restaurant foods equipment.
- Publication of many articles in professional journals and other periodicals.
- Listed in *Who's Who of American Women*.
- One of seventeen government employees selected for a six-month release from her job (with full salary) to train for higher administrative posts in government, which led to her post in the Navy Department.[25]

After a lifetime of service to others, Augusta died on May 13, 1997, at her home in McLean, Virginia, from complications of arthritis.

Augusta Holmes Clawson, surviving twin of a darling set of girls, led an extraordinary life, achieving much to improve the world for other women. But for all of that, it's apparent that Augusta—Gusta, or Gus, or Gug, as she was called by family members and dear friends—cherished most her close relationships throughout her life. It is also clear that she was treasured in return. One example of this comes in the form of a letter written to Augusta in her eighty-first year. The letter came from her friend, David Robinson, whom she called Dave and identified as "an editor at *National Geographic* magazine and a writer for the *Virginia Gazette* as a hobby." This is a portion of his letter, written on simple lined note paper and dated April 20, 1984.

> *Dear Gug,*
> *I remember when I came to the home of a welder who once danced with Sandburg. In appreciation, I now break out my finest stationery to thank you for one of the greatest evenings I've had in a long time.*

You should be declared a strategic natural resource—a renewable resource, for your strength and good humor and love of life seem to renew themselves every day. . . .

Thanks also for the delightful Sandburg vignette. I couldn't use it, as it didn't fit gracefully into the story line, but it was fascinating all the same.

Someday when I'm 99 and sitting here with a bionic big toe and an artificial spleen and a head transplant, I'll tell some wide-eyed reporter from the Intergalactic Gazette that I once spent a beautiful evening with Gug.

He signed his name *David* beneath the body of the affectionate letter and bid farewell by fondly drawing a small heart.[26]

It seems a fitting *adieu* to one who so willingly gave the best of her heart—and her mind—to supporting other working women, to helping win a worldwide war, and to continuing to believe into her ninety-third year in a world of work where every woman of the future might realize . . . well, whatever she wishes.

Welding helmet donated by Augusta Clawson to the Smithsonian's National Museum of American History to be displayed in "The Price of Freedom: Americans at War" exhibition.
DIVISION OF WORK AND INDUSTRY, NATIONAL MUSEUM OF AMERICAN HISTORY, SMITHSONIAN INSTITUTION.

NOTES

CHAPTER 1: A NATION'S CALL FOR HELP

1. In the introduction to Amy Kesselman's book, *Fleeting Opportunities: Women Shipyard Workers in Portland and Vancouver During World War II and Reconversion* (Albany: State University of New York Press, 1990), I read this plea made by Admiral Nimitz. It seemed a fitting inclusion in this opening chapter.

2. From *Her War, Her Story: WWII*, edited by Jim Karpeichik, Ocean State Video, Rhode Island. (Tim Gray Media/WWII Foundation @2022). Scenes of Eisenhower during opening of documentary.

3. See Fred Hampson, "Working in Shipyards Makes Women All Sisters Under Skin," *Statesman Journal*, August 17, 1943, https//www.newspapers.com/image/80117619/.

4. Read "War Jobs for Women," Office of War Information, Magazine Section, 1942, 3, 20. Received at OWI on November 17, 1942, a detailed informative booklet aimed at the women of the nation. https://www.loc.gov/item/42038951/.

5. See "Vancouver's Plan . . . For the Utilization of War Housing Projects Located at Vancouver, Wash.," March 20, 1945, Vancouver Housing Authority. This is a comprehensive overview of the development of the city of Vancouver and Greater Vancouver before, during, and after the war years. This plan completely describes how the community desired to restore itself once the war was over.

6. See "V-Mail Is Speed Mail" with contributor Kim Guise at the National WWII Museum online. https://www.nationalww2museum.org/war/articles/mail-call-v-mail. Accessed January 18, 2025.

7. See La Verne Bradley, "Women at Work," *National Geographic Magazine*, August 1944, 193–220. Author's collection.

8. Found at cbi-theater.com/yank_marilyn/Marilyn.html, "Marilyn Monroe and YANK—The Army Weekly."

9. Norman Rockwell's vision of *Rosie the Riveter* graced the cover of the May 29, 1943, issue of the *Saturday Evening Post*. An outstanding version of the concept of "Rosie," most people thought the familiar fist-raised torso of a woman commissioned for a Westinghouse factory in-house recruitment drive was the only true depiction.

10. Bradley, "Women at Work," 193–220.

11. A family letter describing her wartime work in Pasadena, California, at California Institute of Technology (CIT) building rocket-powered weapons: "I am head of the

machining dept. in the experimental development of all the new rockets; we carry out the orders for each new type of propellant for the rockets." From the author's grandaunt, Edith Lionberger Alkire, January 3, 1945.

12. See Donna L. Sinclair, "Part III, Riptide on the Columbia: A Military Community Between the Wars, Vancouver, Washington and the Vancouver National Historic Reserve, 1920–1942," Center for Columbia River History. Funded by National Park Service, Fort Vancouver National Historic Site, Vancouver, Washington, January 2005.

13. See complete article, "First Woman Welder Finally Identified," *Bos'n's Whistle*, May 26, 1944, 4, digitalcollections.ohs.org/the-bosns-whistle-swan-island-edition-volume-04-number-16.

14. From a family letter from the author's grandaunt, Edith Lionberger Alkire, January 3, 1945.

15. Oregon Historical Society Research Library, oral history interview of Lois L. Housman. Collection 883, Northwest Women's History Project, 1981. Reference code: SR11502.

16. From "Women in Defense—Each Day Finds an Ever-Increasing Number of Women Doing Man-Sized Jobs in Defense Industry," in the *La Grande Observer* (La Grande, OR), June 1942, www.newspapers.com.

17. See Robert R. La Du, *Her Finest Hour: Shipbuilding in the Portland Area During World War II (1941–1945)*. Published in 2016, this modest book packs a lot of information inside. This is a very complete, if brief, history of the city of Portland when building ships during World War II.

18. Bradley, "Women at Work," 193–220.

19. A *way* is "the sloping dry dock in which a ship is built and from where it is launched." En.wiktionary/wiki/shipway.

20. This photo appears along with the article "The Audacious Americans" by Allan Nevins, who writes about decades of "bold experimentation," using the example, "Henry Kaiser and others revolutionized shipbuilding." *LIFE Magazine*, January 2, 1950, 79, 85. Author's collection.

CHAPTER 2: AUGUSTA CLAWSON—UNTIL WAR'S END

1. From a telephone interview by the author with Ann Henderson Kramer, niece of Augusta Clawson, on October 6, 2024. Ann's mother was Barbara Clawson, the youngest of Augusta's half-siblings.

2. Over the years, the seminary was also known as the Plainfield College for Young Ladies, Plainfield Seminary for Young Ladies and Children, and Miss Kenyon's Seminary.

3. This three-paragraph article written by Vassar College Professor Burgess Johnson in 1922, included under the title, "Modern Girl Wins Defenders in High Places and She Is Declared to be 'All Right,'" defended the "modern college girl" in several ways. The article is found in the *Evening World* of New York, 28.

4. Taken from 1929 Alumnae Address Register form contained in Alumnae Association of Vassar College Biographical File 1924 Clawson.

5. From a lengthy article discussing the life and work of Augusta Clawson. Written by Flora Ann Winfree under the heading "Riveting, Dealing with Chefs Part of Speaker's

Past: Miss Clawson Wrote Book on War Work," it was published in the *Winston-Salem Journal* on March 24, 1950, 27. www.newspapers.com.

6. Information found in a Memorandum from the Vocational Bureau written by Zita L. Thornbury, director, on February 23, 1943. Alumnae Association of Vassar College Biographical File 1924 Clawson.

7. From "Contemporary Notes—The Classes," *Vassar Quarterly*, vol. XVI, num. 3, July 1, 1931, 250, https://newspaperarchives.vassar.edu.

8. A description from an obituary for Gladys Doane in the September 19, 1955, issue of the *Courier-News* of Bridgewater, New Jersey. According to the *Courier-News*, Gladys also had "studied voice at the New England Conservatory of Music in Boston and coached with Hubert Linscott and Ellmer Zoller in New York City." See "Mrs. Gladys Doane Named to FHA Recreation Post" in the December 28, 1943, issue of the *Courier-News*, 3.

9. "Mrs. Gladys Doane Named to FHA," 3.

10. Taken from the 1929 Alumnae Address Register form contained in Alumnae Association of Vassar College Biographical File 1294 Clawson.

11. See Augusta H. Clawson's essay, "An Evening with Carl Sandburg," in the *Vassar Club of Washington Newsletter*, McLean, Virginia, December 1, 1982. Copy of the original is in Alumnae Association of Vassar College Biographical File 1294 Clawson.

12. Telephone interview by the author with Ann Henderson Kramer, October 6, 2024.

13. Taken from 1929 Alumnae Address Register form contained in Alumnae Association of Vassar College Biographical File 1924 Clawson. Note by Zita L. Thornbury, director, Vocational Bureau, Vassar College.

14. More from Augusta Clawson can be found on page 14 of the March 24, 1950, edition of the *Winston-Salem Journal* under the heading, "Women Held Worst Enemy to Own Sex."

15. See "Welder on the Ways: The Story of 'Jersey Gus' from the Office of Education," publication unknown, no date, 13. Courtesy of Margaret "Meg" Sondey collection.

16. See Augusta Clawson's article in March 1943 *Vassar Alumnae Magazine*, vol. XXVIII, no. 4, "The Time is Now!", 6, https://newspaperarchives.vassar.edu. This article was informative and also likely inspirational for those young college women contemplating going into war production work.

17. Clawson, "The Time Is Now!"

18. See "Report on Welding Training and Shipyard Employment" by Augusta H. Clawson, Special Agent, Training Women for War Production, US Office of Education, Washington, DC, 1943. Courtesy Margaret "Meg" Sondey collection.

19. Clawson, *Shipyard Diary*, vii.

Chapter 3: Henry's Pacific Shipyards

1. Clawson, *Shipyard Diary of a Woman Welder*.

2. From "Women in Shipyards," the *Victory Fleet*, U.S. Maritime Commission, Division of Public Relations, vol. 1, no. 48, 6. Oregon Historical Society Research Library, ohs.org.

3. See "Shipbuilding in Washington," at Wikipedia.com. Retrieved from https://en.wikipedia.org/w/index.php?title=Categary:Shipbuilding_in_Washington_(state)&oldid=1122312855.q.

4. Read the complete article, "Year 1943 Is Eventful in Oregon; Much of News Related to War, Postwar: Opens With Storms; War Effort Claims Major Attention," in the January 2, 1944, issue, p. 11, of the *Statesman Journal* of Salem, Oregon. Available on newspapers.com.

5. Description taken from caption of photo "The Liberty" on p. 6 of the December 29, 1944, issue of the *Bos'n's Whistle*, https://digitalcollections.ohs.org/the-bosns-whistle.

6. Read "Oregon Yard Launches 100th 'Liberty,'" in the *Oregonian* November 23, 1942 issue to learn more about Oregon Shipyard Corporation's accomplishments.

7. See "Year 1943 Is Eventful in Oregon, 11, and the article "Wreath Awarded Oregon Shipyard" in the *Oregonian* of October 30, 1943, 20, from newspapers.com.

8. See "The British Merchant Shipping Mission in the United States and British Merchant Shipbuilding in the Second World War," an essay by Lewis Johnman and Hugh Murphy, in the *Northern Mariner*, 2002, 10, 15.

9. Both the shipyard burner who witnessed the suspect and a cab driver who delivered the man along with another man from Richmond to Oakland early one morning not long after the fire would testify against the man. "Alleged Nazi Is Tried for Firing Oakum Warehouse," *Santa Cruz Sentinel*, December 18, 1942, https://www.newspapers.com/image/570334763/.

10. From a lengthy and comprehensive article regarding the building career of Henry J. Kaiser, industrialist. "Builder No. 1" by Frank J. Taylor in the *Saturday Evening Post* on June 7, 1941. Inland Northwest Special Collections, Northwest Room Biographical Files, Spokane Public Library.

11. See Henry J. Kaiser letter dated October 27, 1944, to employees praising them for record-setting work building tankers for use by the US Navy. From the World War II collection at the Oregon Historical Society Research Library, Portland, Oregon. Note he begins the letter, "Men and Women of Swan Island." He acknowledges that both sexes were busy in the Yard.

12. A. R. Nieman letter, also dated October 27, 1944. Although he opens with the greeting, "Fellow Workers," his first sentence declares "you men and women here at Swan Island . . ." From the World War II collection at the Oregon Historical Society Research Library, Portland, Oregon.

13. La Du, *Her Finest Hour*.

14. Sinclair, "Part III, Riptide on the Columbia."

15. Read the essay, "President Franklin Roosevelt, on a Secret Tour of National Defense Plants and Military Facilities, arrives at Fort Lewis on September 22, 1942" by Duane Colt Denfeld, PhD., on HistoryLink.org, Essay 11190, posted February 20, 2016. "This essay made possible by: Cultural Resources Program, Joint Base Lewis-McChord." https://historylink.org/File/11190.

16. See Erich R. Ebel, *Exploring Maritime Washington: A History and Guide* (Charleston, SC: The History Press, 2023), https://www.arcadiapublishing.com/pages/the-history-press.

17. "Year 1943 is Eventful in Oregon," 11.

18. *American Vocational Association Inc. Journal and News Bulletin*, Washington, DC, n.d., cover page, 1943.

NOTES

CHAPTER 4: WHO WAS HENRY JOHN KAISER?

1. From "After the War . . . What?," an article publishing an address by Henry J. Kaiser to business and civic leaders in San Francisco on September 29, 1942. The *Bo's'n's Whistle*, vol. 2, no. 20, October 22, 1942, 2–3.

2. From a lengthy article in *LIFE Magazine* of June 29, 1942, titled, "No. 1 Shipbuilder: Henry J. Kaiser applies dam-construction methods to launch a third of the U.S. shipbuilding program and set the pace for the rest of it" by Gerard Piel.

3. See John Caldbick's article, "Panic of 1893 and Its Aftermath," the cause and effect of the Panic of 1893, the event that tarnished America's "Gilded Age." Caldbick describes in detail the many issues affected across the nation during this time. Go to HistoryLink.org to read the article, identified as Essay 20874, dated October 1, 2019.

4. From the article, "Henry J. Kaiser Still Happy to Be Working," in the May 9, 1967, issue of the *Spokane Daily Chronicle*. At Inland Northwest Special Collections, Northwest Room Biographical Files, Spokane Public Library.

5. From about.kaiserpermanente.org/who-we-are/our-history/henry-j-kaiser-americas-health-care-visionary.

6. Notes from "Biography of the Month—Henry J. Kaiser," *White's Biographical Bulletin*, vol. IX, no. 1, January 1946. Inland Northwest Special Collections, Northwest Room Biographical Files, Spokane Public Library.

7. Piel, "No. 1 Shipbuilder."

8. "City's Population for 1920 104,204," *Spokane Press*, May 7, 1920. Retrieved from https://en.wikipedia.org/wiki/History_of_Spokane,_Washington#cite_note-98 on August 10, 2024.

9. From an unidentified newspaper dated March 12, 1933, comes an article titled "$7 A Week Man Here Rises High." Inland Northwest Special Collections, Northwest Room Biographical Files, Spokane Public Library.

10. From Northwest Digital Collections, Ned M. Barnes Northwest Room archives, Spokane Public Library, spokanelibrary.org/northwest-room/digital-collections/.

11. From Ancestry.com site after performing search for the name Bess Fosburgh. View copy of 1920 Federal Census record of New Paltz, New York.

12. It's interesting and says something about the closeness of the family—and perhaps Henry's eagerness for his sons to learn the business—that they traveled with him for his work. This is from Piel, "No. 1 Shipbuilder."

13. Notes from "Biography of the Month—Henry J. Kaiser."

14. "The Men of Six Companies," from PBS.org, *American Experience*, https://www.pbs.org/wgbh/americanexperience/features/hoover-companies/.

15. "Henry Kaiser's Career Began in Local Store," the *Spokesman-Review*, August 25, 1967. Inland Northwest Special Collections, Northwest Room Biographical Files, Spokane Public Library.

16. See "The Permanente Richmond Field Hospital" at *Kaiser Permanente* online. February 22, 2021. https://about.kaiserpermanente.org/who-we-are/our-history/the-permanente-Richmond-field-hospital-proud-reminder-of-health.

17. Alan Allport, *Britain at Bay: The Epic Story of the Second World War, 1938–1941* (Alfred A. Knopf, 2021), 370–371.

THE SHIPYARD AGENT

18. Description taken from caption of photo "The Victory" on page 6 of the December 29, 1944, issue of the *Bos'n's Whistle*, https://digitalcollections.ohs.org/the-bosns-whistle.

19. Found at about.kaiserpermanente.org/who-we-are/our-history/an-industrial-revolution-all-their-own-world-war-ii-women-stand-, this statement raises questions such as: Was the union anti-Kaiser and his hiring practices? Did Kaiser also promote hiring Black women? As the quote reads, "he integrated the shipyards—hiring black men directly and hiring women from the United States Employment Service." Note that in general the statement references "Black people," but the specifics mention "hiring black men . . . and hiring women" without mentioning the race of the women.

20. Read "After the War . . . What?" from an address by Henry J. Kaiser in the *Bos'n's Whistle*, October 22, 1942, issue, vol. 2, no. 20, 3, https://digitalcollections.ohs.org/the-bosns-whistle.

21. See "Mr. Stalin's Visitors" by Henry McLemore, September 30, 1942, in the *San Francisco Examiner*, 15. www.newspapers.com.

22. See the April 8, 1943, issue, vol. 3, no. 7, for the article and photograph titled "Gold Eagle for Oregon." The *Bos'n's Whistle*, https://digitalcollections.ohs.org/the-bosns-whistle.

23. It's likely the *Sidney Daily News* had a reporter present in Pullman, Washington, while Henry Kaiser was present and during the creation of the tribute to Henry Kaiser. The article, "Kaiser Is Said to Outdo Ancient," was short, sweet, and complete. One can discover a great deal about Kaiser's accomplishments just by reading this article. It reflects the great contributions made by one man. From https://www.newspapers.com/image/880062402.

CHAPTER 5: HOUSING SHIPYARD WORKERS

1. From the July 22, 1943, issue of *The Bos'n's Whistle*, vol. 3, no. 14, Oregon Shipyard Corporation edition, "Homes for 19,646 Shipbuilders," https://digitalcollections.ohs.org/the-bosns-whistle-volume-03-number-14.

2. From "After the War . . . What?" an article publishing an address by Henry J. Kaiser to business and civic leaders in San Francisco on September 29, 1942. *The Bos'n's Whistle*, vol. 2, no. 20, October 22, 1942, 2–3. Kaiser could easily have been thinking about Vanport, the large housing project the Kaiser Co. built for shipyard workers.

3. See "Vancouver's Plan . . . For the Utilization of War Housing Projects Located at Vancouver, Wash.," a comprehensive report published by the Vancouver Housing Authority, March 20, 1945.

4. Kit Oldham, "Kaiser Shipyard in Vancouver Launches Its First Escort Aircraft Carrier on April 5, 1943," essay no. 5266 posted on HistoryLink.org on February 21, 2003, historylink.org/File/5266.

5. See Clawson, "Report on Welding Training and Shipyard Employment."

6. This comment by Carl Abbott regarding racial prejudice being present in the Vanport City housing project is supported by a following paragraph. This is a portion: "Vanport was racially segregated. For the record, HAP [Housing Authority of Portland] stated that the clearly demarcated color lines there and at smaller war-housing projects were the result of free choice among available apartments, but tenants were steered to different sections on the basis of race. Vanport's Black residents found integrated schools but segregated medical facilities." Carl Abbott, "Vanport," Oregon Encyclopedia, https://www.OHS.org.

7. Sinclair, "Part III, Riptide on the Columbia."
8. See the article, "Houses on West Coast Follow Ship Workers," published October 23, 1945, on page 9 of the *Daily Olympian* of Olympia, Washington. Found on newspapers.com.
9. "Dormitory Fire Kills Eight Men, Injures Seven," was the title of the article on page 1 in the *Herald and News* (Klamath Falls, OR) issued on January 10, 1944. This can be found at https://www.newspapers.com/image/104619295/.
10. This information was found at https://gallery.multcolib.org/collection/temporary-wartime-housing. Under the heading, "Temporary wartime housing," an image of a wartime pamphlet, "War Housing Projects," provided a map along with the list of housing projects and their respective number of dwelling units. Multnomah County Library, Portland, Oregon.
11. Sinclair, "Part III, Riptide on the Columbia."
12. This article was taken from one of the *Bos'n's Whistle* shipyard publications, vol. 3, no. 17, 11, dated September 2, 1943, digitalcollections.ohs.org/the-bosns-whistle-volume-03-number-17. The article includes photographs taken inside the dormitories.
13. The Grand Coulee Dam was built by Consolidated Builders, Inc., which included the Six Companies, Inc. consortium of contractors of which Henry J. Kaiser was general chairman.
14. Read the complete article, "Housing Unit Opens Sunday: 2088 Single Persons to Get Quarters," of the January 9, 1944, issue of the *Sunday Oregonian*, page 15. Found on newspapers.com.
15. See "Swan Barracks to Close After 3 Years Service," in the May 4, 1945, issue of the *Bos'n's Whistle*.
16. From "Welder on the Ways."
17. This information was discovered on the Oregon Historical Society Research Library website, ohs.org. Several other photos are available for viewing there, including the Church of God building: https://digital collections.ohs.org/church-at-meadowlark-trailer-camp-for-shipyard-workers-st-johns.
18. From the website PDX History, where one can find pleasant color images of the original Multnomah Hotel. http://www.pdxhistory.com/html/multnomahhotel.html. Accessed on October 28, 2024.

Chapter 6: Celebrated Childcare Center

1. "Working Mothers Face Problem: Child Care Causes Concern," published by *Oregon Daily Journal* on February 21, 1943, page 20. www.newspapers.com.
2. See the *Columbian* of Vancouver, Washington, article, "Eleanor 'Rings Bell;' Batting Eye Perfect," in the April 5, 1943, issue, page 1, www.newspapers.com.
3. See "War Jobs for Women," *Office of War Information*, Magazine Section. Received on November 17, 1942, 19, https://www.loc.gov/resource/gdcmassbookdig.warjobsforwomen00unit_0/.
4. "Women in Shipyards," *The Victory Fleet*, vol. I, no. 48, 1–4. Division of Public Relations, U.S. Maritime Commission. Oregon Historical Society Research Library.
5. Wolff and Phillips, Architects, "Designed for 24-Hour Child Care: Kaiser's Child Service Centers Serving Portland Shipyards Are a Community School Facility of a

New and Important Type," *Architectural Record*, March 1944, Oregon Historical Society Research Library, ohs.org.

6. See "Wartime Shipyard Child Care Centers Set Standards for Future," at https://about.kaiserpermanente.org/who-we-are/our-history/wartime-shipyard-child-care-centers-set-standards-for-future. Accessed on November 30, 2024.

7. "Wartime Shipyard Child Care Centers Set Standards."

8. See "Service Byword of Child Care Center" in the November 17, 1944, issue of *Bos'n's Whistle*, 5, https://digitalcollections.ohs.org/the-bosns-whistle-swan-island-edition-volume-04-number-41.

9. "Center Aids Graveyard Parents: Kids Slumber There," *Bos'n's Whistle*, Oregon Shipyard edition, March 31, 1944, vol. 4, no. 8, 5. https://www.OHS.org.

10. From the Oregon Historical Society Oregon History Project, "Child Service Centers, Swan Island Shipyards," oregonhistoryproject.org/articles/child-service-centers-swan-island-shipyards/. Retrieved October 5, 2024.

11. See Carl Abbott, "Vanport," Oregon Encyclopedia, http://www.OHS.org.

12. The short article "Child Center Cuts Service to One Shift" on page 5 of the *Bos'n's Whistle* of April 6, 1945, ought to have been reassuring. The shipyard would continue to accommodate those in need.

CHAPTER 7: TRAINING WOMEN TO WELD

1. Clawson, "Report on Welding Training and Shipyard Employment," 1.
2. Clawson, "Report on Welding Training and Shipyard Employment," 1.
3. Clawson, "Report on Welding Training and Shipyard Employment," 2.
4. Taken from a full-page advertisement found in the Maidenform Collection, Archives Center, National Museum of American History, Smithsonian Institution at sova.si.edu/record/nmah.ac.0585.
5. Clawson, "Report on Welding Training and Shipyard Employment," 2.
6. Clawson, "Report on Welding Training and Shipyard Employment," 6.
7. Clawson, "Report on Welding Training and Shipyard Employment," 2.
8. Clawson, "Report on Welding Training and Shipyard Employment," 3.
9. Clawson, "Report on Welding Training and Shipyard Employment," 3.
10. "Welder on the Ways," 13.
11. Clawson, "Report on Welding Training and Shipyard Employment," 7–9.
12. See Anne Wallace's essay, "Why Women Leave the Plant," 1–2, 6. November 3, 1943. Courtesy of Margaret "Meg" Sondey collection. The essay is essentially Wallace's memory of Augusta's speech about her work in the shipyard.

CHAPTER 8: HAZARDS IN THE HULLS

1. Clawson, *Shipyard Diary*, 111.
2. See Augusta H. Clawson's article, "Safety Clothing for Women in War Production Industries" in the *Journal of Home Economics*, December 1942, vol. 34, no. 10, 727–729.
3. Clawson, "Report on Welding Training and Shipyard Employment," 3.
4. "Report of the Investigation of Fume Hazards at the Oregon Shipbuilding Company (Kaiser Company) at St. Johns, Portland, Oregon by Special Committee." From

the reading room of the OHSU library: "Forrest E. Rieke collection on the Oregon Shipbuilding Corporation (Kaiser Company), 1937–1945," 4. Collection 2007-007. Oregon Health & Science University, Historical Collections and Archives in Portland, Oregon. The OHSU hospital is located on what the locals have always called "Pill Hill," because the children's and veteran's hospitals and OHSU are all located there overlooking the city of Portland.

5. "Report of the Investigation of Fume Hazards," 2.
6. "Report of the Investigation of Fume Hazards," 3.
7. "Report of the Investigation of Fume Hazards," 7.
8. "Report of the Investigation of Fume Hazards," 21–22.
9. "Report of the Investigation of Fume Hazards," 23.
10. See "Eye Specialist Needed to Aid at Shipyards," in the August 11, 1942, issue of the *Corvallis Gazette-Times*, www.newspapers.com.
11. Clawson, "Report on Welding Training and Shipyard Employment," 3.
12. Jean Marsolie (Neil) Johnson (cousin of author's mother), interviewed by author on February 15, 2016, in Sandpoint, Idaho.
13. Memorandum from Dr. Rieke from the reading room of the OHSU library: "Forrest E. Rieke collection on the Oregon Shipbuilding Corporation (Kaiser Company), 1937–1945." Collection 2007-007. Oregon Health & Science University, Historical Collections and Archives in Portland, Oregon.
14. Wallace, "Why Women Leave the Plant," 5.
15. Clawson, "Report on Welding Training and Shipyard Employment," 4.
16. "Welder on the Ways," 13.
17. "Year 1943 Is Eventful in Oregon," 11.

Chapter 9: X-Ray and Asbestos Perils Exposed

1. "Welders Assured," originally published on March 16, 1943, by the *Daily News* of Los Angeles, page 9. newspapers.com.
2. John Upton Terrell, "Mankind Owes Large Debt to X-rays Properly Applied," Los Angeles *Daily News*, April 24, 1943, 3.
3. Wikipedia efficiently explains the acceptance of the X-ray fluoroscope during the time of World War II, when the burn accidents happened at Calship. See https://en.wikipedia.org/wiki/Shoe-fitting_fluoroscope#.
4. Terrell, "Mankind Owes Large Debt," 3.
5. Journalist John Upton Terrell wrote two detailed stories to expose the truth about injuries sustained by shipyard workers at the California Shipbuilding Corporation (Cal-Ship) yard near Los Angeles in 1941. First, "How X-ray Maimed 57 Shipyard Workers," *Los Angeles Daily News*, April 22, 1943, 3–4; and on the next day, "Doctors Came Late to Shipyard Maimed," also the *Daily News*, April 23, 1943, 3, 22.
6. Terrell, "Doctors Came Late," 22.
7. Terrell, "How X-ray Maimed," 4.
8. See "Asbestos Exposure in Shipyards," presented on May 27, 2022, by Vogelzang Law Webmaster at https://vogelzanglaw.com/blog/asbestos-information/asbestos-exposure-in-shipyards/.

THE SHIPYARD AGENT

9. See Asbestos.com, "Shipyard Workers and Asbestos" at https://www.asbestos.com/occupations/shipyard-workers/.

10. Asbestos.com, a website "Brought to you by The Mesothelioma Center," besides providing copious information regarding asbestos exposure, includes a list of "possible asbestos exposure sites" and more. https://www.asbestos.com/shipyards.

11. See "Swan Island Shipyard Overview" at Mesothelioma.com for additional details. https://www.mesothelioma.com/asbestos-exposure/jobsites/shipyards/swan-island-shipyard/. Accessed November 14, 2024.

CHAPTER 10: MEDICAL CARE FOR ALL

1. "Henry J. Kaiser Still Happy to Be Working," *Spokane Daily Chronicle*, May 9, 1967. Inland Northwest Special Collections, Northwest Room Biographical Files, Spokane Public Library.

2. Erich Ebel, "Henry J. Kaiser (1882–1967)," February 27, 2024, HistoryLink.org Essay 22897, https://www.historylink.org/File/22897.

3. See "The Permanente Richmond Field Hospital" at Kaiser Permanente, February 22, 2021, https://about.kaiserpermanente.org/who-we-are/our-history/the-permanente-Richmond-field-hospital-proud-reminder-of-health.

4. See "Sign-up Ends June 1 for Hospital Plans" in the May 19, 1944, issue of the *Bos'n's Whistle*, 4, volume unknown, https://digitalcollections.ohs.org/the-bosns-whistle.

5. From "Now, the Whole Family Gets Hospital Care" in the April 8, 1943, issue of the *Bos'n's Whistle* vol. 3, no. 7, https://digitalcollections.ohs.org/the-bosns-whistle.

6. "Now, the Whole Family Gets Hospital Care."

7. See "Good Medicine Brought Within Reach of All," at *Kaiser Permanente*, written by Paul de Kruif, microbiologist, for the May 1943 edition of *Reader's Digest*. https://about.kaiserpermanente.org/who-we-are/our-history/good-medicine-brought-within-reach-of-all. August 10, 2017.

8. Clawson, *Shipyard Diary*.

9. See "Hannah Peters, MD, Provides Essential Care to 'Rosies'" on *Kaiser Permanente*, April 25, 2023, https://about.kaiserpermanente.org/who-we-are/our-history/hannah-peters-plays-vital-role-as-doctor-to-the-rosies.

10. "Hannah Peters, MD."

11. See "Kaiser Permanente's History of Nondiscrimination" on Kaiser Permanente website, dated August 25, 2021, https://about.kaiserpermanente/who-we-are/our-history/early-leaders-in-equity-and-inclusion.

12. From "Patients Don't Object If They Can't Pick Doctor at Henry J. Kaiser Clinic," dated October 7, 1943, in the *Progress-Bulletin* (Pomona, CA), www.newspapers.com.

13. See "New Hospital Facilities for Vancouver," in the *Bos'n's Whistle*, vol. 3, no. 7, 13, April 8, 1943, issue, https://digitalcollections.ohs.org/the-bosns-whistle.

14. See "Helen Keller Praises Vancouver Donors" in the January 5, 1945, issue of the *Bos'n's Whistle*, vol. 5, no. 1, 5, https://digitalcollections.ohs.org/the-bosns-whistle.

15. See "Henry J. Kaiser: America's Health Care Visionary" at *Kaiser Permanente* online, dated May 3, 2024, https://about.kaiserpermanente.org/who-we-are/our-history/henry-j-kaiser-americas-health-care-visionary.

Notes

Chapter 11: Men vs. Women Welders
1. Comment in a letter from Augusta Clawson to Margaret "Meg" Sondey, dated March 18, 1988. Courtesy of Margaret "Meg" Sondey collection.
2. From "Women in Shipyards," the *Victory Fleet*, vol. 1, no. 48, 1, U.S. Maritime Commission, Division of Public Relations.
3. "Women in Shipyards," 1.
4. Read "What of the Older Woman?" by Augusta H. Clawson in the February 1944 issue of the *International Altrusan*, where Clawson discusses work after war for women. Ball State University's digital collections.
5. "Women in Shipyards," 1.
6. Clawson, "Report on Welding Training and Shipyard Employment," 10.
7. Wallace, "Why Women Leave the Plant," 3.
8. See Cynthia Enloe, *Does Khaki Become You? The Militarization of Women's Lives* (London: Pandora, 1988).
9. Clawson, *Shipyard Diary*, 144.
10. Clawson, *Shipyard Diary*, 145.
11. Clawson, "What of the Older Woman?"
12. Clawson, "Report on Welding Training and Shipyard Employment," 10.

Chapter 12: A Tight Seam of Support
1. See "A Conversation with Margaret Spalluzzi, WWII Shipyard Worker" on YouTube, Boston NHP (National Parks of Boston), January 28, 2019. Viewed January 18, 2025.
2. Clawson, "Report on Welding Training and Shipyard Employment."
3. "Welder on the Ways."
4. Clawson, "Report on Welding Training and Shipyard Employment," 7.
5. Clawson, "Report on Welding Training and Shipyard Employment," 4.
6. Clawson, *Shipyard Diary*.
7. Augusta Clawson as speaker for Women's Canadian Club in Toronto January 1944. This observation of Augusta's would oft be repeated.
8. Sarah Sundin, "World War II War Bonds," November 28, 2022, https://www.sarahsundin.com/world-war-ii-war-bonds/.
9. Highly recommended: Daniel James Brown's *Facing the Mountain: A True Story of Japanese American Heroes in World War II* (New York: Viking, 2021), 112.
10. "Year 1943 Is Eventful in Oregon," 11.
11. Clawson, "Report on Welding Training and Shipyard Employment."
12. Oregon Historical Society Research Library, oral history interview of Leona E. Ellis. Collection 883, Northwest Women's History Project, 1981. Reference code: SR9077.
13. From Ann Henderson Kramer's interview by author on October 6, 2024. Ann's mother was Barbara Clawson, the youngest of Augusta's much-loved half-siblings.
14. From author interview on November 2, 2024, of Patricia "Pat" Lindley-Clawson, grandniece-by-marriage of Augusta. Pat and Augusta worked together in the Navy Department, Executive Office of the Secretary. Augusta's title was "Head, Navy Directives System." It was during this time that Augusta introduced young Pat to her future husband, Gusta's grandnephew, Frank T. Clawson II. His father, F. Wells Clawson Jr., was Augusta's beloved nephew, son of her half-brother, F. Wells Clawson.

CHAPTER 13: RACISM IN THE YARDS

1. Oregon Historical Society Research Library, oral history interview of Beatrice G. Marshall. Collection 883, Northwest Women's History Project, 1981. Reference code: SR9081.
2. See the National World War II Museum, "The Double V Victory: African Americans on the Home Front During World War II," https://www.nationalww2museum.org/war/articles/double-v-victory.
3. Rudy Pearson, "'A Menace to the Neighborhood': Housing and African Americans in Portland, 1941–1945," *Oregon Historical Quarterly*, vol. 102, no. 2, Summer 2001, 159. At Oregon Historical Society website.
4. John Linder, "Liberty Ships and Jim Crow Shipyards: Racial Discrimination in Kaiser's Portland Shipyards, 1940–1945," published in the *Oregon Historical Society Quarterly*, vol. 120, no. 4, 2019.
5. In the National Archives, "Executive Order 8802: Prohibition of Discrimination in the Defense Industry (1941)," https://www.archives.gov/milestone-documents/executive-ordewr-8802#.
6. Aaron Randle, "'Black Rosies': The Forgotten African American Heroines of the WWII Homefront," History.com, updated September 12, 2023, https://www.history.com/news/black-rosie-the-riveters-wwii-homefront-great-migration.
7. "Negro on Hand for Ceremony" in the July 7, 1943, issue of the *Oregonian*, p. 27, newspapers.com.
8. See "Henry Kaiser's Racial Acceptance Began with One of First Employees," *Kaiser Permanente*, June 15, 2010, https://about.kaiserpermanente.org/who-we-are/our-history/henry-kaisers-respect-for-people-of-all-races-dates-from-african.
9. See "When Labor and Management Work Side by Side," *Kaiser Permanente*, August 28, 2019, https://about.kaiserpermanente.org/who-we-are/our-history/when-labor-and-management-work-side-by-side.
10. "Kaiser Stands Firm on Use of Negro Workers," *Herald and News*, October 21, 1942, 1, newspapers.com/image/93023962/.
11. Sinclair, "Part III, Riptide on the Columbia."
12. Linder, "Liberty Ships and Jim Crow Shipyards."
13. See "The World War II Kaiser Richmond Shipyard Labor Force," *Kaiser Permanente*, January 9, 2015, https://about.kaiserpermanente.org/who-we-are/our-history/the-world-war-ii-kaiser-richmond-shipyard-labor-force.
14. "Year 1943 is Eventful in Oregon," 11.
15. Oregon Historical Society Research Library, oral history interview of Leona E. Ellis. Collection 883, Northwest Women's History Project, 1981. Reference code: SR9077.
16. Oregon Historical Society Research Library, oral history interview of Beatrice G. Marshall. Collection 883, Northwest Women's History Project, 1981. Reference code: SR9081.
17. Oregon Historical Society Research Library, oral history interview of Leona E. Ellis. Collection 883, Northwest Women's History Project, 1981. Reference code: SR9077.
18. Linder, "Liberty Ships and Jim Crow Shipyards."

Notes

19. See "Vancouver's Plan ... For the Utilization of War Housing Projects Located at Vancouver, Wash.," a comprehensive report published by the Vancouver Housing Authority, March 20, 1945.

20. "Magic Carpet Special Bearing Kaiser Crews Approaches Vancouver" by Lawrence Barber, editor at the *Oregonian*. Barber wrote this article after boarding the Kaiser train in Missoula, Montana, to ride to Vancouver with the shipyard crews who were coming from the East.

21. See the photo "Part of the [Fifty] Arab Employees at Oregon Shipbuilding Corp. & Kaiser Co. Swan Island, at the Central Café," taken May 23, 1943, at https://librarycatalog.ohs.org/O90000/OPAC/Search/AdvancedSearch.aspx. Accessed January 23, 2025.

22. Read "Chinese American Service in World War II," online at en.wikipedia.org/wiki/Chinese-American_service_in_World_War_II. Page last edited March 15, 2024.

23. Sinclair, "Part III, Riptide on the Columbia."

24. From "Native American Women from Chemawa Train to Work in Shipyards," https://www.oregonhistoryproject.org/articles/nine-native-american-women-from-chemawa-train-to-work-in-shipyards/. Retrieved October 5, 2024.

25. From the "Social Welfare History Project, National Youth Organization" on the Virginia Commonwealth University Libraries website, https://socialwelfare.library.vcu.edu. Accessed October 20, 2024.

26. "Social Welfare History Project, National Youth Organization."

27. "Native American Women from Chemawa Train to Work in Shipyards."

28. From the *National Park Service: Inequality and Racism* see "The Double V Campaign," https://www.nps.gov/poch/learn/historyculture/the-double-v-campaign.htm.

29. From about.kaiserpermante.org/who-we-are/our-history/an-industrial-all-their-own-world-war-II-women. Retrieved on October 5, 2024.

30. See "Image of Rosie Broadens to Embrace African American Women," Kaiser Permanente, https://about.kaiserpermanente.org/who-we-are/our-history/image-of-rosie-broadens-to-embrace-african-american-women.

Chapter 14: A Fractured Failure and a Comeback

1. J. F. Lincoln was president of Lincoln Electric Co., "said to be the world's largest manufacturers of arc welding equipment." According to the *Oregon Daily Journal* of January 28, 1943, he was certain that the break(s) in the hull of the SS *Schenectady* were not caused by defective welding techniques.

2. The principal hull inspector for the Maritime Commission, John F. Bruns, stated that the break "wasn't through the weld" in the article "Vickery Will Seek Cause of Ship Split," in the *Oregon Daily Journal* on January 20, 1943. This must have been an encouraging bit of news for the shipbuilders at Swan Island, most surely for the welders, and perhaps especially for the women welders who worked so hard to prove themselves as able.

3. Earl Ingram was the secretary of the Portland Metal Trades Council. In the January 27, 1943, issue of the *Oregon Daily Journal*, the article "Ship Break Report to Be 'Scientific'" stated that Ingram had "voiced his personal opinion that wrong loading caused the crack-up."

4. From a brief article, "SS *Schenectady*," at https://www.mastermariners.org.au/storeis-from-the-past/3031-ss-schenectady, with the article's source cited as wikiwand.com. Accessed December 21, 2024.

5. "SS *Schenectady*."

6. The *Oregon Daily Journal* of January 24, 1943, in an article without a heading, mentioned the thirty-man crew aboard the *Schenectady*.

7. An observation worth sharing from Daniel O. Lionberger, writer, researcher, and brother of the author.

8. The article "Group Here After Peril" in the *Oregon Daily Journal* of January 22, 1943, explains how close Rear Admiral Vickery and the others came to disaster while on their way to Portland to investigate the tanker breakup, 1.

9. "Group Here After Peril," 1.

10. "Tanker Breakup Has Good Side: Cause Still Undetermined," *Oregon Daily Journal*, January 24, 1943, issue, p. 5.

11. "Lincoln Says 'Poppycock:' Welding Charge Discounted," *Oregon Daily Journal*, January 28, 1943, p. 6, https://www.newspapers.com/image/10908019031/.

12. "Group Here After Peril."

13. "Shipyard Employes [*sic*] Asked to Dig Snow," appeared in the January 24, 1943, issue of the *Sunday Oregonian*, front page, in a small announcement.

14. "Tojo," as referenced in the article from *The Finger* on Swan Island shipyard, is referring to General Hideki Tojo, who was appointed prime minister of Japan in October 1941. He was a vicious leader who would eventually pay for his crimes against humanity—including against his own countrymen—and be hanged.

15. One of many articles discussing the fracturing of the tanker *Schenectady*'s hull at the Swan Island shipyard, "Tanker Builders Rarin' to Go, Appreciate Value of Time," in the January 31, 1943, issue of the *Oregon Daily Journal*, p. 19, did not mention women workers specifically, but they would have been actively involved in the building of the SS *Schenectady*.

16. The *Oregon Daily Journal* of January 24, 1943, in an article without a heading, mentioned the FBI involvement in the investigation of the *Schenectady* catastrophe.

17. "Year 1943 Is Eventful in Oregon," 11.

18. Lawrence Barber, marine editor, "Tanker Production Schedule Upped by Swan Island Yard," *Sunday Oregonian*, January 10, 1943, p. 16.

19. "Year 1943 Is Eventful in Oregon," 11.

20. The flag photo and a further explanation can be found at Vintage Portland website under the title, "Swan Island Shipyard, 1943," https://vintageportland.wordpress.com/2021/03/16/swan-island-shipyard-1943/.

Chapter 15: Best Woman Welder in the World

1. "Billie Makes the Sparks Fly," the *Sunday Oregonian*, April 18, 1943, 85, https://www.newspapers.com/image/1083185790/.

2. Clawson, *Shipyard Diary*, 144.

3. Find the image at Oregon Historical Society Library, "Women Welders at Oregon Shipbuilding Corporation," taken January 5, 1942. Photographer Al Monner. digitalcollections.ohs.org/woman-welders-at-oregon-shipbuilding-corporation.

4. "Hermina Strmiska, welder: 'I guess they needed us, so they put up with us.'" By Mary Bryan Curd on the Oregon History Project website is a capsule description of Mrs. Hermina Strmiska (Billie), https://www.oregonhistoryproject.org/articles/herminia-billie-strmiska-oral-history/

5. "Billie Makes the Sparks Fly," 85.

6. "Billie Makes the Sparks Fly," 85.

7. Curd, "Hermina Strmiska."

8. "Mississippi Lassie Welds to World's Championship," the *Oregonian*, May 29, 1943, 1, https://www.newspapers.com/image/1084027929/.

9. "Mississippi Lassie Welds," 1.

10. Eleanor Roosevelt's "My Day, June 2, 1943," is accessed at *The Eleanor Roosevelt Papers Digital Edition* (2017), https://www2.gwu.edu/~erpapers/myday/displaydocedits.cfm?_y=1943&_f=md056511.

11. Find the photograph of five women welders seated on a bench above the title "Who Is the Champion Woman Shipyard Welder?" in the February 3, 1943, issue of the *Bos'n's Whistle*, vol. 3, no. 3, at Oregon Historical Society Research Library, digitalcollections.ohs.org/the-bosns-whistle.

Chapter 16: Augusta Clawson—Beyond War's End

1. A consolidation of what could have served as a brief biography appears in the May 1969 issue of the *International Altrusan*, page 21. As expected, the article highlights how "as 'special agent' with the U.S. Office of Education, to test the efficacy of wartime shipyard training, she became a shipyard welder."

2. From a telephone interview by the author with Ann Henderson Kramer, niece of Augusta Clawson, on October 6, 2024. Ann's mother was Barbara Clawson, the youngest of Augusta's half-siblings.

3. Excerpts from a letter written to Meg Sondey by Augusta H. Clawson on February 4, 1988, while Augusta still owned the rights to her book, *Shipyard Diary of a Woman Welder*. Augusta describes how the official report became a published book offered for public consumption. Permission to use her letters and reports in her thesis was sent from Augusta to Meg Sondey. Courtesy of Margaret "Meg" Sondey.

4. From Capt. Fred M. Earle's "Employment of Women in the Navy Yards," found under the title, *United States Naval Institute Proceedings*, vol. 71/9/511, September 1945, https://www.usni.org/magazines/proceedings/1945/September/employment-women-navy-yards.

5. *Dear Laughing Motorbyke: Letters from Women Welders of the Second World War*, edited by Margaretta Jolly (London: Scarlet Press, 1997), 16–17.

6. Interview with Jean Neil Johnson by author on February 15, 2016, in Sandpoint, Idaho.

7. Letter written to Meg Sondey by Augusta H. Clawson, February 4, 1988.

8. "Diary of Woman Welder Is Tip-Off to Job Seekers," by M. W. was published on July 19, 1944, six months after the book release, in the *Cincinnati Post*; one can find the complete article on p. 6.

9. The article "Altrusans Return from Washington" in the *Charlotte News* of North Carolina, dated November 11, 1947, gives a concise report of twelve Altrusans, including Augusta Clawson, who had attended a weekend-long meeting of the organization.

10. Under the title, "Divorce in the United States," Wikipedia presents a good discussion of the subject. Find it online at https://en.wikipedia.org/wiki/Divorce_in_the _United_States.

11. More from Augusta Clawson can be found on page 14 of the March 24, 1950, edition of the *Winston-Salem Journal* under the heading "Women Held Worst Enemy to Own Sex."

12. On the Veterans Outreach Ministries website, read Lishamarie Hunter's article about the women who worked in munitions factories in Elkton, Maryland, during the war. Accessed February 7, 2025, veteransoutreachministries.org.

13. "Mrs. Gladys Doane Named to FHA Recreation Post," *Courier-News* (Bridgewater, NJ), December 28, 1943, p. 3, www.newspapers.com.

14. From the reverse side of a photograph of unidentified older women relaxing in a private room together at the Hannah Harrison School of Industrial Arts. Date unknown.

15. A brief but information-packed article about the Hannah Harrison School of Industrial Arts written by Jane Blads and published in her "Washington Day Book" column. In the July 6, 1950, issue of *Newport Daily News*, Rhode Island, p. 8.

16. Augusta H. Clawson, *Equipment Maintenance Manual: Sanitation Techniques Established by Mary M. O'Donnell* (Ahrens Publication Company: New York: 1951), preface.

17. "Women's Status—Panel Conclusions," *International Altrusan*, September 1963 issue, p. 11, Ball State University archives.

18. To view the photos of Augusta at the 431 Exchange school's graduation ceremony, go to 431exchange.org/photo-album-adult-education-center.

19. Augusta H. Clawson, "Take a Fresh Approach to Service in Vocational Services," *International Altrusan*, May 1969, vol. 46, no. 9, pp. 19–20. Used with permission. Ball State University and Altrusan International.

20. Clawson, "Take a Fresh Approach to Service," 19–20.

21. Augusta Clawson, "On Coping," *Vassar Quarterly*, June 1984, Alumnae Association of Vassar College Biographical File 1924 Clawson.

22. Dave Robinson, "McLean's Augusta Holmes Clawson: 80 and Rollin'," the *Virginia Gazette*, April 26, 1984, p. 11. Courtesy Margaret "Meg" Sondey collection.

23. Robinson, "McLean's Augusta Holmes Clawson," 11.

24. Clawson, "Report on Welding Training and Shipyard Employment," 8.

25. Details taken from various Vassar College Alumnae forms completed by Augusta H. Clawson through the years. Alumnae Association of Vassar College Biographical File 1924 Clawson.

26. Copy of letter to Augusta from David Robinson. Alumnae Association of Vassar College Biographical File 1924 Clawson.

BIBLIOGRAPHY

Sources used only in passing are not included in this bibliography.

1900 United States Federal Census. Clawson, Frank J. ancestry.com/search/?name =Frank+J_Clawson&event=_new+jersey-usa.
1910–1950 U.S. Federal Censuses. Clawson, Augusta H. ancestry.com/search/?name =Augusta+H_Clawson&event=_new+jersey-usa.
Abbott, Carl. "Vanport." Oregon Encyclopedia, Oregon Historical Society. https://www .OHS.org. Last updated September 26, 2023.
"After the War . . .What?" *Bo's'n's Whistle.* October 22, 1942, 2–3. https://digitalcollec tions.ohs.org/the-bosns-whistle.
Alkire, Edith Lionberger. Letter to Jerrold Dean Lionberger, Edith's nephew and author's father. Sent from Altadena, California, on January 5, 1945. Author's collection.
"Alleged Nazi Is Tried for Firing Oakum Warehouse." *Santa Cruz Sentinel* (Santa Cruz, CA), December 18, 1942. https://www.newspapers.com/image/570334763.
Allport, Alan. *Britain at Bay: The Epic Story of the Second World War, 1938–1941.* Alfred A. Knopf, New York: 2021, 370–371.
"Altrusans Return from Washington." *Charlotte News* (Charlotte, NC), November 11, 1947, 25. https://www.newspapers.com/image/617906958.
"Alumnae to Meet." *Evening Star* (Washington, DC), March 13, 1944, 16. https://www .loc.gov/resource/sn83045462/19440313/ed1/?dl=page&q=%22Augusta+Claw son%22&sp=16.
American Vocational Association Inc. Journal and News Bulletin, n.d., cover page. 1943.
"Asbestos Exposure in Shipyards." https://www.asbestos.com/shipyards/. Accessed November 14, 2024.
"Augusta Clawson Goes to Capital." *Courier-News* (Bridgewater, NJ), September 22, 1941. https://www.newspapers.com/image/219756338.
"Augusta Clawson to Tell of Women in War Industry." *Courier News* (Bridgewater, NJ), March 18, 1944. https://www.newspaper.com/image/220046452.
Barber, Lawrence. "'Magic Carpet' Special Bearing Kaiser Crews Approaches Vancouver." *Oregonian* (Portland, OR), September 30, 1942, 1. https://www.newspapers.com /image/1084122546/.

———. "Tanker Production Schedule Upped by Swan Island Yard." *Sunday Oregonian* (Portland, OR), January 10, 1943, 16. https://www.newspapers.com/image/1081869541/.

Beadle, Roy. "Group Here After Peril: Admiral, Others Arrive to Check Tanker Breakup." *Oregon Daily Journal* (Portland, OR), January 22, 1943, 1. https://www.newspapers.com/image/1090808207/.

"Best Woman Welder Contest Is Planned." *Daily Times* (New Philadelphia, OH), May 15, 1943, 7. https://www.newspapers.com/image/84233487.

"Billie Makes the Sparks Fly." *Sunday Oregonian* (Portland, OR), April 18, 1943, 85. https://www.newspapers.com/image/1083185790/.

"Biography of the Month—Henry J. Kaiser." *White's Biographical Bulletin*, January 1946. Inland Northwest Special Collections, Northwest Room Biographical Files, Spokane Public Library, Spokane, WA.

Blads, Jane. "Washington Day Book." *Newport Daily News* (Newport, RI), July 6, 1950, 8. https://www.newspapers.com/image/57023512.

Bourne, Nick. "Patients Don't Object If They Can't Pick Doctor at Henry J. Kaiser Clinic." *Progress-Bulletin* (Pomona, CA), October 7, 1943, 14. https://www.newspapers.com/image/623298869/.

Bradley, La Verne. "Women at Work." *National Geographic Magazine*. August 1944, 193–220. Author's collection.

Brown, Daniel James. *Facing the Mountain: A True Story of Japanese American Heroes in World War II*. New York: Viking, 2021, 112.

"Cadet Nurse Corps." https://www.gilderlehrman.org/history-resources/spotlight-primary-source-/cadet-nurse-corps-1943#.

Caldbick, John. "Panic of 1893 and Its Aftermath." HistoryLink.org Essay 20874, October 1, 2019. https://historylink.org/file/20874.

"Calship Ends X-ray Burn Rumors." *Daily News* (Los Angeles, CA), September 14, 1942, 5. https://www.newspapers.com/image/689255466/.

"Calship Settles Claims of 39 Workers Burned by X-rays." *Los Angeles Times* (Los Angeles, CA), August 28, 1943, 2.

"Center Aids Graveyard Parents: Kids Slumber There." *Bos'n's Whistle*. Oregon Shipyard ed., March 31, 1944, 5. https://digitalcollections.ohs.org/the-bosns-whistle.

"Child Center Cuts Service to One Shift." *Bos'n's Whistle*, Swan Island ed., April 6, 1945, 5. https://digitalcollections.ohs.org/the-bosns-whistle.

"Child Service Centers, Swan Island Shipyards," Oregon Historical Society Research Library. https://www.oregonhistoryproject.org/articles/child-service-centers-swan-island-shipyards/. Accessed October 5, 2024.

Clawson, Augusta. "On Coping." *Vassar Quarterly*, June 1984. Alumnae Association of Vassar College Biographical File 1924 Clawson.

Clawson, Augusta H. "An Evening with Carl Sandburg." *Vassar Club of Washington Newsletter* (McLean, VA), December 1, 1982.

———. "Report on Welding Training and Shipyard Employment," n.d., 1–12. Typewritten by Clawson. Courtesy of Margaret "Meg" Sondey collection.

Bibliography

———. "Safety Clothing for Women in War Production Industries." *Journal of Home Economics.* American Home Economics Association, December 1942.

———. *Shipyard Diary of a Woman Welder.* New York: Penguin Books, 1944.

———. "Take a Fresh Approach to Service in Vocational Services." *International Altrusan*, vol. 46, no. 9, 19–20. Altrusa International, Inc., May 1969. Ball State University. https://dmr.bsu.edu/digital/collection/AltrusaIntl.

———. "The Time Is Now!" *Vassar Alumnae Magazine, Vassar Quarterly*, vol. XXVIII, no. 4, 6–8, March 1943. https://newspaperarchives.vassar.edu.

———. "What of the Older Woman?" *International Altrusan*, vol. XXI, no. 15, February 1944. Ball State University. https://dmr.bsu.edu/digital/collection/AltrusaIntl.

"Clawson Speaks on Job Opportunities in War Industries." *Vassar Miscellany News*, February 1943. https://newspaperarchives.vassar.edu/?a=d&d= miscellany19430224-01.

"Complete Examination Fluoroscopic X-ray" advertisement. *Los Angeles Times*, May 16, 1943, 8. https://www.newspapers.com/image/380830036/.

"Contemporary Notes—The Classes." *Vassar Quarterly*, 193, 250. https://newspaperarchives.vassar.edu.

"A Conversation with Margaret Spalluzzi, WWII Shipyard Worker." Quote by Colonel Oveta Culp Hobby. YouTube. Boston NHP (National Parks of Boston). January 28, 2019. Viewed January 18, 2025.

Curd, Mary Bryan. "Hermina Strmiska, welder: 'I guess they needed us, so they put up with us.'" https://www.oregonhistoryproject.org/articles/herminia-billie-strmiska-oral-history/.

Dear Laughing Motorbyke: Letters from Women Welders of the Second World War, Ed. Margaretta Jolly, pp. 16–17. London: Scarlet Press, 1997.

Denaro, Adrienne. "Jantzen." *Oregon Encyclopedia*. https://www.oregonencyclopedia.org/articles/jantzen/.OHS.org. Accessed January 24, 2024.

Denfeld, Duane Colt, PhD. "President Franklin Roosevelt, on a Secret Tour of National Defense Plants and Military Facilities, Arrives at Fort Lewis on September 22, 1942." HistoryLink.org. Posted February 20, 2016. https://historylink.org/File/11190.

"Diary of Woman Welder Is Tip-Off to Job Seekers." *Cincinnati Post*. July 19, 1944, 6. https://www.newspapers.com/image/762225792.

"Dormitory Fire Kills Eight Men, Injures Seven." *Herald and News* (Klamath Falls, OR) January 10, 1944, 1. https://www.newspapers.com/image/104619295/.

"The Double V Campaign." *National Park Service: Inequality and Racism.* Updated June 24, 2024. https://www.nps.gov/poch/learn/historyculture/the-double-v-campaign.htm.

"The Double V Victory: African Americans on the Home Front During World War II." National World War II Museum. https://www.nationalww2museum.org/war/articles/double-v-victory.

Earle, Captain Fred M. "Employment of Women in the Navy Yards." *United States Naval Institute Proceedings*, vol. 71/9/511. September 1945. https://www.usni.org/magazines/proceedings/1945/September/employment-women-navy-yards.

Ebel, Erich. "Henry J. Kaiser (1882–1967)." HistoryLink.org Essay 22897, February 27, 2024. https://historylink.org/file/22897.

Ebel, Erich R. *Exploring Maritime Washington: A History and Guide*, 210. Charleston, SC: History Press, 2023. Spokane Public Library, Spokane, WA.

Enloe, Cynthia. *Does Khaki Become You? The Militarization of Women's Lives*. London: Pandora, 1988.

"Estate of Gladys C. Doane." *The Virginia Chronicle* (Falls Church, VA), September 12, 1958. https://virginiachronicle.com/.

"Executive Order 8802: Prohibition of Discrimination in the Defense Industry (1941)." National Archives website. https://www.archives.gov/milestone-documents/executive-order-8802#.

"Eye Specialist Needed to Aid at Shipyards." *Corvallis Gazette-Times* (Corvallis, OR), August 11, 1942. https://www.newspapers.com/image/383242577.

"[Fifteen] Workers Ask $2,000,000 in Suits Over X-ray Burns." *Daily News* (Los Angeles, CA), October 23, 1942, 3. https://www.newspapers.com/image/689207420/.

"First Woman Welder Finally Identified." *Bos'n's Whistle*, May 26, 1944, 4. digitalcollections.ohs.org/the-bosns-whistle-swan-island-edition-volume-04-number-16.

"Food, Comfort, and Care: Women Workers at Kaiser's WWII Child Service Centers." https://www.ohs.org/blog/women-wwii-childcare-workers.cfm. March 22, 2022.

"Forrest E. Rieke collection on the Oregon Shipbuilding Corporation (Kaiser Company), 1937–1945." Collection No. 2007-007. Oregon Health & Science University, Historical Collections and Archives, Portland, OR.

"[Four] More Sue Calship for X-ray burns." *Daily News* (Los Angeles, CA), September 14, 1943, 17. https://www.newspapers.com/image/689223466/.

"Fraternity to Hear of Women's Job in War Factories." *Courier-News* (Bridgewater, NJ), April 19, 1945. https://www.newspapers.com/images/221409472.

"Gladys Doane, Soprano, Dies." *Courier-News* (Bridgewater, NJ), September 19, 1955. https://www.newspapers.com/image/221455101.

"Gold Eagle for Oregon." The *Bos'n's Whistle*, April 8, 1943, vol. 3, no. 7. https://digitalcollections.ohs.org/the-bosns-whistle.

"Gold Wreath to Shipyard; Oregon Company Wins First Such Award After Other Honors." *New York Times*, October 30, 1943, 13. https://www.nytimes.com/1943/10/30/archives/gold-wreath-to-shipyard-oregon-company-wins-first-such-award-after.html.

"Good Medicine Brought Within Reach of All." Kaiser Permanente online. August 10, 2017. https://about.kaiserpermanente.org/who-we-are-/our-history/good-medicine-brought-within-reach-of-all.

Good Work, Sister! Women Shipyard Workers of World War II: An Oral History. Produced by Northwest Women's History Project. Portland, OR: NW Documentary, 2006, DVD.

"Governor's Wife to Break Bottle on Ship." *Corvallis Gazette-Times* (Corvallis, OR), September 17, 1941. https://www.newspapers.com/image/383144043.

"'Gus' Comes Back—Welder-Author Visitor." *Bo's'n's Whistle*, Swan Island ed. May 12, 1944, 2. https://digitalcollections.ohs.org/the-bosns-whistle.

Hampson, Fred. "Working in Shipyards Makes Women All Sisters Under Skin." *Statesman Journal* (Salem, OR), August 17, 1943. https://www.newspapers.com/image/80117619.

Bibliography

"Hannah Harrison School to Open This Month." *Evening Star* (Washington, DC), March 10, 1950. https://www.newspapers.com/image/868255949.

"Helen Keller Praises Vancouver Donors." *The Bos'n's Whistle*, January 5, 1945, vol. 5, no. 1, 5. https://digitalcollections.ohs.org/the-bosns-whistle.

Henderson Kramer, Ann, interviewed by telephone by author on October 6, 2024.

"Henry Kaiser Married—Spokane Man Weds Secretly in Boston." *Spokesman-Review*. (Spokane, WA), April 14, 1907. https://www.newspapers.com/image/566282595.

"Henry Kaiser's Career Began in Local Store." *Spokesman-Review* (Spokane, WA), August 25, 1967, 6. Inland Northwest Special Collections, Northwest Room Biographical Files, Spokane Public Library, Spokane, WA.

"Henry Kaiser's Racial Acceptance Began with One of First Employees." *Kaiser Permanente*. June 15, 2010. https://about.kaiserpermanente.org/who-we-are/our-history/henry-kaisers-respect-for-people-of-all-races-dates-from-african.

"Henry J. Kaiser: America's Health Care Visionary." May 3, 2024. https://about.kaiserpermanente.org/who-we-are/our-history/henry-j-kaiser-americas-health-care-visionary.

"Henry J. Kaiser Still Happy to Be Working." *Spokane Daily Chronicle* (Spokane, WA), May 9, 1967. Inland Northwest Special Collections, Northwest Room Biographical Files, Spokane Public Library, Spokane, WA.

Her War, Her Story: WWII. Edited by Jim Karpeichik, Ocean State Video, Rhode Island. Tim Gray Media/WWII Foundation @2022. Television documentary.

"Houses on West Coast Follow Ship Workers." *Daily Olympian* (Olympia, WA). October 23, 1945, 9. https://www.newspapers.com/image/801806974.

"Housework Will Call Women Back." *Evening World-Herald* (Omaha, NE), November 28, 1944. https://www.newspapers.com/image/882401459.

"Housing Unit Opens Sunday: 2088 Single Persons to Get Quarters." *Sunday Oregonian* (Portland), January 9, 1944, 15. https://www.newspapers.com/image/1081838402/.

Hunter, Lishamarie. Article. Veterans Outreach Ministries. Accessed February 7, 2025. https://www.veteransoutreachministries.org/patriotism/the-women-of-elkton-during-wwii/.

Iadarola, Lea. "Shipyard Worker 'Betsy the Burner' Dies at 83." *Tampa Bay Times*. July 10, 2002. https://www.tampabay.com/archive/2002/07/10/shipyard-worker-betsy-the-burner-dies-at-83.

"Identify 5 of 7 Fire Victims." *Capital Journal* (Salem, OR), November 16, 1942. https://www.newspapers.com/image/94709504.

"Image of Rosie Broadens to Embrace African American Women." Kaiser Permanente. August 2, 2013. https://about.kaiserpermanente.org/who-we-are/our-history/image-of-rosie-broadens-to-embrace-african-american-women.

"Industry Calling Women." *Los Angeles Times*. April 28, 1942. https://www.newspapers.com/image/380758279.

Johnman, Lewis and Hugh Murphy. "The British Merchant Shipping Mission in the United States and British Merchant Shipbuilding in the Second World War." *The Northern Mariner/Le marin du nord*, XXII, no. 3, July 2002, 10, 15. https://tnm.journals.yorku.ca/index.php/default/article/view/576/552.

Johnson, Burgess. "Modern Girl. Wins Defenders in High Places and She Is Declared to Be 'All Right': Educators and Editors Are Warm Champions, and College Students, Boys and Girls, Are Sure There's Nothing the Matter with Her But—'She lives at Tremendous Rate of Speed.'" *Evening World* (New York, NY), February 3, 1922, 28. https://www.newspapers.com/image/85469979/.

Johnson, Jean Marsolie (Neil). Interviewed by the author on February 15, 2016. Sandpoint, ID.

Johnson, Jean Marsolie (Neil). Interviewed by her daughter, Marsella "Marse" Irene (Johnson) Shobe in 2016. Sandpoint, ID.

"Kaiser Is Said to Outdo Ancient." *Sidney Daily News* (Sidney, OH), August 7, 1943. www.newspapers.com/image/880062402.

Kaiser, Henry J. "After the War . . . What?" *Bo's'n's Whistle.* October 22, 1942. https://digitalcollections.ohs.org/the-bosns-whistle.

"Kaiser Permanente's History of Nondiscrimination." Kaiser Permanente. August 25, 2021. https://about.kaiserpermanente.org/who-we-are/our-history/early-leaders-in-equioty-and-inclusion.

"Kaiser Stands Firm on Use of Negro Workers." *Herald and News* (Klamath Falls, OR), October 21, 1942, 1. https://www.newspapers.com/image/93023962/.

Kesselman, Amy. *Fleeting Opportunities: Women Shipyard Workers in Portland and Vancouver During World War II and Reconversion.* Albany: State University of New York Press, 1990.

La Du, Robert R. *Her Finest Hour: Shipbuilding in the Portland Area During World War II.* New York: Page Publishing, Inc., 2016.

"Lady Welders to Vie for Championship." *Oregon Statesman.* (Salem, OR), May 12, 1943. https://www.newspapers.com/image/80008135.

"Lincoln Says 'Poppycock,' Welding Charge Discounted." *Oregon Daily Journal* (Portland), January 28, 1943, 6. https://www.newspapers.com/image/1090809031/.

Linder, John. "Liberty Ships and Jim Crow Shipyards: Racial Discrimination in Kaiser's Portland Shipyards, 1940-1945." *Oregon Historical Quarterly*, vol. 120, no. 4 (Portland), 2019, 522–27. https://www.ohs.org/oregon-historical-quarterly/back-issues/upload/09_Linder_Liberty-Ships-and-Jim-Crow-Shipyards_OHQ-Winter-2019_web.pdf.

Lindley-Clawson, Patricia "Pat," interviewed by telephone by author on November 2, 2024.

"Maritime Awards Due This Month." *Capital Journal* (Salem, OR), November 12, 1943. https://www.newspapers.com/image/96226790.

McLemore, Henry. "Mr. Stalin's Visitors." *San Francisco Examiner.* September 30, 1942, 15. https://www.newspapers.com/image/458481221/.

"The Men of Six Companies." PBS.org. American Experience. https://www.pbs.org/wgbh/americanexperience/features/hoover-companies/.

"Miss Clawson to Give Talks." *Fort Collins Express-Courier* (Fort Collins, CO), July 14, 1944. https://www.newspapers.com/image/589070133.

"Mississippi Lassie Welds to World's Championship." *Oregonian* (Portland), May 29, 1943. https://www.newspapers.com/image/1083185790/.

Bibliography

"Monday Afternoon Club to Resume Meetings and Social Activities Next Week: Augusta Clawson to Speak with Mrs. R. W. Cornelison at Guest Meeting and Tea." *Courier-News* (Bridgewater, NJ), October 17, 1942. https://www.newspapers.com/image/219854664.

"Mrs. Clawson Dies Suddenly." *Courier-News* (Bridgewater, NJ), June 27, 1903. https://www.newspapers.com/image/221005619.

"Mrs. Gladys Doane Named to FHA Recreation Post." *Courier-News* (Bridgewater, NJ), December 28, 1943, 3. https://www.newspapers.com/image/219695433/.

"Mrs. Roosevelt Christens First Vancouver Carrier." *Bo's'n's Whistle*, Vancouver ed., April 8, 1943. https://digitalcollections.ohs.org/the-bosns-whistle.

"Mrs. Suffern Sells Interest in Book Shop." *Courier-News* (Bridgewater, NJ), June 11, 1926. https://www.newspapers.com/image/218884746.

"Negro on Hand for Ceremony." *Oregonian*. (Portland), July 7, 1943, 27. https://www.newspapers.com/image/1082023565/.

Nevins, Allan. "The Audacious Americans: Bold Experimentalism Gave Us Five Decades of Dazzling Achievement. That Was Our Adolescence; Now We Have Come to Responsible Maturity." *LIFE Magazine*, January 2, 1950, 79, 85. Author's collection.

"New Hospital Facilities for Vancouver." *Bos'n's Whistle*, Vol. 3, No. 7, 13. April 8, 1943. https://digitalcollections.ohs.org/the-bosns-whistle.

"Nine Victory Ships Scheduled for May." *Bos'n's Whistle*, April 28, 1944. https://digitalcollections.ohs.org/the-bosns-whistle.

"Now It's Dorms for Women." *Bos'n's Whistle*, September 2, 1943, 11. https://digitalcollections.ohs.org/the-bosns-whistle.

Oldham, Kit. "Kaiser Shipyard in Vancouver Launches Its First Escort Aircraft Carrier on April 5, 1943." HistoryLink.org, February 21, 2003. https://historylink.org/File/5266.

Oregon History Project. (2015). *Bos'n's Whistle*. Oregon Shipbuilding Corporation ed. https://www.oregonhistoryproject.org/articles/the-bosns-whistle.

Pearson, Rudy. "'A Menace to the Neighborhood': Housing and African Americans in Portland, 1941–1945." *Oregon Historical Quarterly*, vol. 102, no. 2, Summer 2001, 159, 168, 174–75, 177. https://www.ohs.org/oregon-historical-quarterly/upload/Pearson_A-Menace-to-the-Neighborhood_OHQ-102_2_Summer-2001.pdf.

"The Permanente Richmond Field Hospital." Kaiser Permanente. February 22, 2021. https://about.kaiserpermanente.org/who-we-are/our-history/the-permanente-Richmond-field-hospital-proud-reminder-of-health.

Piel, Gerard. "No. 1 Shipbuilder: Henry J. Kaiser Applies Dam-construction Methods to Launch a Third of the U.S. Shipbuilding Program and Set the Pace for the Rest of it." *LIFE Magazine*. June 29, 1942. Inland Northwest Special Collections, Northwest Room Biographical Files, Spokane Public Library, Spokane, WA.

"Plainfield Musical Club Begins Season on Oct. 18." *Courier-News* (Bridgewater, NJ), October 8, 1932. https://www.newspapers.com/image/220916988.

"Plainfield Seminary, 123 W. Seventh St., Will Reopen." *Courier-News* (Bridgewater, NJ), November 7, 1907, 2. https://www.newspapers.com/image/220771013/.

Platt, A. E. "Native American Women from Chemawa Train to Work in Shipyards." www.oregonhistoryproject.org/articles/nine-native-american-women-from-chemawa-train-to-work-in-shipyards/. Retrieved September 15, 2024.

"Preoccupation." *Spokesman-Review* (Spokane, WA), August 8, 1943, 1. https://www.newspapers.com/image/568516217.

"Price of Freedom: Americans at War, The Changing Gender Roles on the Home Front." https://americanhistory.si.edu/explore/exhibitions/price-of-freedom.

Randle, Aaron. "'Black Rosies': The Forgotten African American Heroines of the WWII Homefront." Updated September 12, 2023. Accessed December 31, 2024. https://www.history.com/news/black-rosie-the-riveters-wwii-homefront-great-migration.

"Report of the Investigation of Fume Hazards at the Oregon Shipbuilding Company (Kaiser Company) at St. Johns, Portland, Oregon." Collection 2007-007. 1942. Oregon Health & Science University, Historical Collections and Archives. Portland, OR.

Robinson, Dave. "McLean's Augusta Holmes Clawson: 80 and Rollin,'" *Gazette* (McLean, VA), April 26, 1984, 11. Courtesy Margaret "Meg" Sondey collection.

Robinson, David. Personal letter to Augusta Clawson, written April 20, 1984. Alumnae Association of Vassar College Biographical File 1924 Clawson.

Roosevelt, Eleanor. "My Day, June 2, 1943." *The Eleanor Roosevelt Papers Digital Edition* (2017). https://www2.gwu.edu/~erpapers/myday/displaydocedits.cfm?_y=1943&_f=md056511. Accessed December 28, 2024.

"Rosie the Riveter." History.com editors. April 23, 2010, updated February 20, 2024. https://www.history.com/topics/world-war-ii/rosie-the-riveter.

"Rosie the Riveter." Marcy Kennedy Knight. *Saturday Evening Post.* July 1, 2013. https://www.saturdayeveningpost.com/2013/07/rosie-the-riveter/.

The School That Would Not Die. Documentary: The 431 Exchange, New Orleans, LA. 1967–1968. https://www.youtube.com/watch?v=xDdQAkB-InU.

"Service Byword of Child Care Center." *Bos'n's Whistle*, November 17, 1944, 5. https://digitalcollections.ohs.org/the-bosns-whistle-swan-island-edition-volume-04-number-41.

"[Seven Dollars] A Week Man Here Rises High." Unidentified newspaper. March 12, 1933. Inland Northwest Special Collections, Northwest Room Biographical Files, Spokane Public Library, Spokane, WA.

"Ship Break Report to Be 'Scientific.'" *Oregon Daily Journal* (Portland), January 27, 1943, 19. https://www.newspapers.com/image/1090808981/.

"Shipyard at Normal After Big Event—Mrs. Roosevelt Receives Special Serenade at Post-launching Affair." *Columbian* (Vancouver, WA), April 6, 1943. https://www.newspapers.com/image/809629815.

"Shipyard Employes [sic] Asked to Dig Snow." *Sunday Oregonian* (Portland, OR), January 24, 1943, 1. https://www.newspapers.com/image/1083761055/.

"Sign-Up Ends June 1 for Hospital Plans." *Bos'n's Whistle*. May 19, 1944, 4. https://digitalcollections.ohs.org/the-bosns-whistle.

"Silverton Woman Welder is Expert." *Capital Journal* (Salem, OR), March 22, 1943. https://www.newspapers.com/image/94755213.

Bibliography

Sinclair, Donna L. "Part III, Riptide on the Columbia: A Military Community Between the Wars, Vancouver, Washington and the Vancouver National Historic Reserve, 1920–1942." Center for Columbia River History. National Park Service, Fort Vancouver National Historic Site, Vancouver, Washington, January 2005. https://www.nps.gov/fova/learn/historyculture/upload/VNHRHistoryPartThree1920_1942-Accessible-PDF.pdf. Accessed January 16, 2025.

Snyder, Lois Wilkie. "Eleanor 'Rings Bell;' Batting Eye Perfect." *Columbian* (Vancouver, WA), April 5, 1943, 1. https://www.newspapers.com/image/809629742.

Sundin, Sarah. "World War II War Bonds." November 28, 2022. https://www.sarahsundin.com.

"Swan Barracks to Close After 3 Years Service." *Bos'n's Whistle*. May 4, 1945, 5. https://digitalcollections.ohs.org/the-bosns-whistle-swan-island-edition.

"Swan Island Shipyard Overview." Mesothelioma.com. https://www.mesothelioma.com/asbestos-exposure/jobsites/shipyards/swan-island-shipyard/. Accessed November 14, 2024.

"Tanker Breakup Has Good Side: Cause Still Undetermined." *Oregon Daily Journal* (Portland, OR), January 24, 1943, 5. https://www.newspapers.com/image/1090808402/.

"Tanker Builders Rarin' to Go, Appreciate Value of Time." *Oregon Daily Journal* (Portland, OR), January 31, 1943, 19. https://www.newspapers.com/image/1090809320/.

Taylor, Frank J. "Builder No. 1." *Saturday Evening Post*. June 7, 1941, 9–11, 120, 122, 124. Inland Northwest Special Collections, Northwest Room Biographical Files, Spokane Public Library, Spokane, WA.

Taylor, Frank J. "Meet America's No. One . . . Axis Smasher." Publication not listed. August 31, 1942, 4. Inland Northwest Special Collections, Northwest Room Biographical Files, Spokane Public Library, Spokane, WA.

"Temporary Wartime Housing." War Housing Project. Pamphlet with map and housing project data. https://gallery.multcolib.org/collection/temporary-wartime-housing. Multnomah County Library, Portland, OR.

"[Ten Thousand] Shipyard Workers Wanted at Swan Island, Vancouver, Oregon Ship." *Oregon Daily Journal* (Portland) September 20, 1942, 9. https://www.newspapers.com/image/1091291565/.

Terrell, John Upton. "How X-ray Maimed 57 Shipyard Workers." *Daily News* (Los Angeles), April 22, 1943, 3–4. https://www.newspapers.com/image/689235889.

——— "Doctors Came Late to Shipyard Maimed." *Daily News* (Los Angeles), April 23, 1943, 3, 22.

"[Thirty-eight] X-ray Damage Cases Settled." *Daily News* (Los Angeles), September 8, 1943, 3. https://www.newspapers.com/image/689223267/.

Thomas, Kathleen. *Don't Call Me Rosie: The Women Who Welded the LSTs and the Men Who Sailed on Them*. Tigard, OR: Thomas/Wright, Inc., 2004.

"Two Accident Actions Filed." *Courier-News* (Bridgewater, NJ, Bureau), March 7, 1934. https://www.newspapers.com/image/221030857.

"Two-Fisted Mother." *Medford Mail Tribune* (Medford, OR), April 16, 1942. https://www.newspapers.com/image/97191536.

"V-Mail Is Speed Mail." Kim Guise, contributor. National WWII Museum online. https://www.nationalww2museum.org/war/articles/mail-call-v-mail. Accessed January 18, 2025.

"Vancouver's Plan . . . for the Utilization of War Housing Projects Located at Vancouver, Wash." Vancouver Housing Authority, March 1945. https://dahp.wa.gov/sites/default/files/VancouverPlanWarHousing.pdf. Accessed January 16, 2025.

"Vickery Will Seek Cause of Ship Split." *Oregon Daily Journal* (Portland), January 20, 1943, 1. https://www.newspapers.com/image/1090808061/.

Vodra, Bettie. "Member of the Month, Augusta Holmes Clawson." *In The Spotlight*. (Lewinsville Church, McLean, VA). Courtesy of Margaret "Meg" Sondey collection.

Vogelzang Law Webmaster. "Asbestos Exposure in Shipyards." Vogelzang Law. May 27, 2022. https://vogelzanglaw.com.

Wallace, Anne. "Why Women Leave the Plant." Essay, 1–2, 6. November 3, 1943. Courtesy of Margaret "Meg" Sondey collection.

"War Jobs for Women." Office of War Information, Magazine Section (Washington, DC), 1942, 3, 19–20. https://www.loc.gov/resource/gdcmassbookdig.warjobsforwomen00unit_0/.

"Wartime Shipyard Child Care Centers Set Standards for Future." About Kaiser Permanente website. https://about.kaiserpermanente.org/who-we-are/our-history/wartime-shipyard-child-care-centers-set-standards-for-future. Accessed November 30, 2024.

"Welder on the Ways: The Story of 'Jersey Gus' from the Office of Education," author and publication unknown, 13. Courtesy of Margaret "Meg" Sondey collection.

"Welderettes Await Tests, Title Chance." *Oregon Journal* (Portland), March 22, 1943.

"Welders Assured." *Daily News* (Los Angeles), March 16, 1943, 9. https://www.newspapers.com/image/689332113/.

"Who Is the Champion Woman Shipyard Welder?" The *Bos'n's Whistle*, vol. 3, no. 3, February 3, 1943. https://digitalcollections.ohs.org/the-bosns-whistle.

Willingham, William F. "Swan Island." Updated May 2, 2022. *Oregon Encyclopedia*. https://www.oregonencyclopedia.org.

Winfree, Flora Ann. "Riveting, Dealing with Chef's [sic] Part of Speaker's Past." *Winston-Salem Journal* (NC), March 24, 1950, 27. https://www.newspapers.com/image/934574037/.

Wolff and Phillips, Architects. "Designed for 24-Hour Child Care: Kaiser's Child Service Centers Serving Portland Shipyards Are a Community School Facility of a New and Important Type." *Architectural Record*. March 1944. Oregon Historical Society Research Library. https://www.ohs.org/research-and-library/.

"Women Held Worst Enemy to Own Sex." *Winston-Salem Journal* (NC), March 24, 1950, 14. https://www.newspapers.com/image/934573953.

"Women in Defense—Each Day Finds an Ever-Increasing Number of Women Doing Man-Sized Jobs in Defense Industry." *La Grande Observer* (OR), June 1942. https://www.newspapers.com/image/135550499.

Bibliography

"Women in Shipyards." *Victory Fleet.* Division of Public Relations, U.S. Maritime Commission, 1–4, bulletin no. 34. Oregon Historical Society Research Library. https://www.ohs.org/research-and-library/.

"Women Like Factory Work—Part in War Effort Adds to Respect." *Evening World-Herald* (Omaha, NE), November 29, 1944. https://www.newspapers.com/image/882402230.

"Women Must Prove Selves as Workers." *Windsor Star* (Windsor, Ontario, Canada), January 20, 1944. https://www.newspapers.com/image/501170938.

"Working Mothers Face Problem: Child Care Causes Concern." *Oregon Daily Journal* (Portland), February 21, 1943, 20. https://www.newspapers.com/image/1090546421/.

"The World War II Kaiser Richmond Shipyard Labor Force." *Kaiser Permanente.* January 9, 2015. https://about.kaiserpermanente.org/who-we-are/our-history/the-world-war-ii-kaiser-richmond-shipyard-labor-force.

"Wreath Awarded Oregon Shipyard." *Oregonian* (Portland), October 30, 1943, 20. https://www.newspapers.com/image/1082354354/.

"X-Ray Burn Victims Ask Huge Sums." *Long Beach Sun* (Los Angeles), October 22, 1943. https://www.newspapers.com/article/the-long-beach-sun/94735373/.

"Year 1943 Is Eventful in Oregon; Much of News Related to War, Postwar: Opens With Storms; War Effort Claims Major Attention." *Statesman Journal* (Salem, OR), January 2, 1944, 11. https://www.newspapers.com/image/80180623.

ACKNOWLEDGMENTS

Oregon Historical Society (OHS), where would we be without you and your magical research library? Thank you for keeping the faith that safekeeping the documents and images of our forebears is important and worth the effort. I particularly appreciate the efforts of these persons: Nikki Koehlert and Renato Rodriguez, reference librarians, and Robert Warren, digital collections photographer. Thank you for your patience, and for excellent service. And thanks for assisting my brother, Dan, who came in my stead when it was impossible for me to travel the 355 miles between my house and yours. Thanks to my son, Brian, for chauffeuring me into the city during a visit and spending time at OHS with me. Thanks, too, for driving me to Swan Island. It was a treat to be there and imagine it solely occupied by thousands of like-minded citizens working together across a shipyard producing vessels of superiority.

As someone who was raised reading the *Oregon Journal* and *Oregonian* newspapers, it was fun to select vintage images from the OHS website. It was a pleasure to garner those digital files from Dave Killen, photographer and videographer for the *Oregonian*, an understanding man. Thank you, Dave, for the very best assistance to me and to my editor, Brittany Stoner, when we needed a cover image. Also, thanks to David Kukla and Alexis Holloway for making certain I got my invoices and the publication got paid.

Thank you especially to Dean M. Rogers, library coordinator at Vassar College Archives and Special Collections. After I contacted your office to ask if anything was available regarding 1924 graduate Augusta

Clawson, it wasn't long before you sent fifty-four individual images from her archived file. Opening those emails was like walking into a sparkling gold mine.

To Kay Peterson, Archives Center, National Museum of American History Rights and Reproductions, Smithsonian Institution, thank you for delivering an important group of images.

For coming through in the eleventh hour, many thanks to Alanna Smollen, archives collections specialist at Ball State University, who solved the unknown word mystery.

Thanks are due to Steve Duckworth, University Archivist and associate professor at Oregon Health and Sciences University Historical Collections and Archives in Portland. That title is a mouthful. I appreciate your flexibility in letting me come in without much notice, and your guidance along with John Durant while I was there. To my brother, Dan, again, thanks for being there and helping me research. But especially thanks for escorting me on my first ride on the OHSU tram up "Pill Hill"—even if the young man running the fares machine thought we were a couple of doddering old people. *Hey, man, we got this!*

For other images and nuggets of information I need to thank the following people, whose contact may have been a single email, but was precious just the same: Megan Huff, curator, Fort Vancouver National Historic Site; Ayshea Khan, City of Portland Archives and Records Management Division; Lindsey Vesperry, Ball State University Archives and Special Collections; Melissa Diaz, administrative assistant, Altrusa International, Inc.; Leopoldo "Leo" Villardi, managing editor, *Architectural Record*, and Matthew Hickman who directed me to him; Sarah Stroman, oral history librarian, Oregon Historical Society; Eben Dennis, manager, Special Collections Department, Enoch Pratt Free Library/State Library Resource Center; staff of Kaiser Permanente Heritage Resources; and staff at Spokane Public Library, Inland Northwest Special Collections.

Then, who knew Ancestry.com would reveal three new sprouts on a branch of a family tree and, in the process, bring me three new friends? While researching Augusta's life, I had a bright idea. *Wait a minute,* I thought. *I'll build Augusta's family tree!* I knew it would serve as a tool

Acknowledgments

to keep her family members organized in my mind. Posting a note on my resulting Clawson Family Tree page, I explained it was strictly for research; she was no relation of mine. Somehow now it feels like she is.

After discovering a few links had appeared on my Clawson page and, although beneath the publishing-a-book hoopla I'm a shy person, I decided to reach out. First, I found Margaret "Meg" Sondey. Having worked on a thesis in the past that included researching Augusta's shipyard welding experience, Meg had the privilege of staying in Augusta's home in Virginia. I'm green with envy. Lucky Meg. But mostly, lucky me for meeting Meg, who besides being a lovely woman I hope to meet in person someday, proceeded to pass forward a plethora of research. This book is so much better because Meg's mother obviously taught her how to share!

The three sprouts I mentioned—Augusta's family members—to whom I owe enormous thanks are Roger Price, Ann Henderson Kramer, and Patricia "Pat" Lindley-Clawson. After a few Ancestry.com-mail conversations, Roger was able to connect me with Ann, who connected me with Pat. Ann and Pat, thanks for the memories. Your clearly remembered stories made her come alive.

I must mention Lyons Press acquisitions editor, Brittany Stoner, to whom I owe a shipload of thanks. Thanks to assistant acquisitions editor, Justine Connelly, as well. I'm glad Debra Murphy, assistant editor at TwoDot Books, sent my book proposal on to you. I'm grateful you believe in Augusta's story, too. Thank you, as well, for your patience and compassion as I navigated around some unexpected rogue waves and rocky reefs this past year. Thank you, too, to senior production editor Alden Perkins, copyeditor Emily Natsios, and proofreader Annette Van Deusen, who helped assure smooth sailing for the manuscript during production. Your immense work is appreciated. I must also thank the design team for the fantastic job they did in creating the cover image for the book.

To my team—go team!—of beta readers, Ruth Bragg, Daniel Lionberger, Liz Gilbert, Brian Parsons, Mitch Williams, Laura Williams, and Paul Manly, how can I ever thank you enough? Dan, I'm lucky you are my brother for many reasons. I'm fortunate you love research, too. Special thanks for keeping emails and texts with documents and photographs coming to me down to the wire. Everyone who agreed to read, your willingness to comment and offer critique made all the difference for me while shaping the best version of Augusta's biography. You made my year!

I mustn't forget to thank my cousin, "Marse" Johnson Shobe, who helped inspire me to keep going and write this book, which includes tales of her mother, Jean Neil Johnson as a woman welder during World War II. The photos and stories you provided, Marse, were like the icing on the cake. I'm also grateful that "Aunt" Jean was willing to record her memories during that long-ago interview in Sandpoint.

Finally, I need to apologize if I've neglected to name anyone who deserves a measure of gratitude. I hope forgiveness and understanding will be forthcoming.

To my daughter, Laura, son-in-law, Mitch, son, Brian, and daughter-in-law, Ashley—for unwavering support and never-ending encouragement, I love you more. To my husband, Tom, who once steered haze grey ships through darkest storms and dove to the deepest of deep sea depths, your courage today continues to inspire me.

INDEX

AAUW. *See* American Association of University Women
Abbott, Carl, 67, 194n6
Abstract of Divorce Decree, 174
accidents, 102; automobile, 28–29, 176; burn, 197n3; Oregon's State Industrial Accident Commission, 93, 96, 100; SS *Schenectady*, 154, 156, 157; sterility, 107–8; toolbox, 101
acetylene torch, 12, *13*
Aero Mechanic (newspaper), 47
African Americans, 151, 194n19; childcare for, 79; housing projects for, 67; "A Menace to the Neighborhood" on, 142; racial discrimination, 120, 141, 142, 143, 145, 147, 150; racial prejudice, 67, 79, 145, 194n6; racism, 144–45, 146–47, 150; Shipyard Negro Organization for Victory and, 144–45
air hose, 10, 92, 98
Alazon Bay, U.S.S. (all-welded carrier), 47, *48*, *49*, 75
Alkire, Edith Lionberger, 14, 189n11, 190n14
all-feminine launching, 39, 40
Altrusa International Service Club, 169, 174, 179, 180–81, 204n9
ambulance services, 117, 119
American Association of University Women (AAUW), 90

American Vocational Association Inc. Journal and News Bulletin, 51–52
Anderson, Vera, 164, *165*, *166*, 167
Ann (cousin), 21–22
Ann, Blossom, 17
Arab employees, 147
Arc Flash, 100
Architectural Record, 76, 77
Army Micro Photographic Mail Service (V-mail), 8
arthritis, 181, 182, 185, 186
Arthritis Foundation, 181, 185
Arthritis Patient of the Year, 181
asbestos fibers, 111–13, 198n10
assembly line production, 37, 38
Associate Alumnae, Vassar College, 29
associations, professional organizations and, 30
"The Audacious Americans" (Nevins), 190n20
automobile accident, 28–29, 176
auxiliary unions, 145
Awards, from Maritime Commission, U.S., 40, 44–46, *45*, 62, 138
awards, honors and, 185–86
A way, 17, 39, 190n19
Axis powers, 11, 132
"Axis Smasher," 63
Ayre, Amos, 40

Barber, Lawrence, 201n20
barracks, 66, 70
Bataan, 35, 62

Bauer, Al, 63
Best Woman Welder in the World, competition, 161–62, *163*, 164, *165*, *166*, *167*
Betsy the Burner, 12
BIA. *See* Bureau of Indian Affairs
Big Elmer (nickname), 70–71
Black, Rich, 151
Black people. *See* African Americans
"Black Rosies" (Randle), 143
Blads, Jane, 176
Blankenship, Bess, *133*
Blood, Kathryn, 150
Blood Center, Vancouver, 120–21
blood drive, 120–21
blowers, 98
boilermakers union, 144–45
Bomb-Bomb Girls (factory women workers), 175
Bo's'n's Whistle (shipyard publication), 14, 62, 65, 116–17, 135, 138; on childcare at Swan Island Shipyard, 78–80, 196n12; Roosevelt, E., in, 47
Bradley, La Verne, 8, 11, 15
Bridgewater, New Jersey, 28, 32, 191n8
Brown, Daniel James, 137
Bruns, John F., 153, 201n2
Bureau of Indian Affairs (BIA), 150
burns, 100–101, 107, 108–9, 110–11, 116, 197n3

Caldbick, John, 55, 193n3
California Institute of Technology (CIT), 189n11
California Shipbuilding Corporation (Calship), 108, *109*, 110, 197n5
California State Director, of Vocational Education, 169–70
camaraderie, of women welders, 3–4, 132–33
cancer: lung, 112; skin, 101; women workers and, 120
Capital Journal (newspaper), 162
Carr, Charlotte, 123

Carroll, Mary C., 14
Catalpa, U.S.S. (naval vessel), 39
certificate, of availability, 81
Chase, Gladys. *See* Doane, Gladys
Chemawa Indian School, 148, *149*, 150
childcare, 75–76, *77*, 78–80, 171, 196n12
Chinese Americans, 147–48
Church of God, 72
Cincinnati Post (newspaper), 172–73
CIT. *See* California Institute of Technology
Civil Rights Act, of 1964, 125
CIW. *See* Commercial Iron Works
"Class Bitterness Most Serious Problem for Labor, Management" (Kaiser, H.), 144
Clawson, Augusta Holmes "Gus or Gug," *23*, *52*, *172*, *173*, *180*, *183*; as Jersey Gus, *36*; signature identification card, *82*; Vassar College senior portrait, *26*; in welding gear, *83*. *See also specific topics*
Clawson, Augustus Holmes (brother), 21, 25
Clawson, Barbara "Bobbie" (half-sister), *23*, 190n1, 199n13
Clawson, Ellen Augusta Holmes (mother), 21
Clawson, Frances Myra (sister), 21–22
Clawson, Franklin W. "Wells" (half-brother), *23*, 199n14
Clawson, Frank Titsworth (father), 21, 22, 32, 199n14
Clawson, Jeanette "J." (half-sister), *23*
Clawson, Margaret "Margie" (half-sister), *23*
Clawson, Marion (stepmother), 22
Codding, Clarence, 70
cofferdam, 128
Columbian (newspaper), 75–76
Columbia River, 7, 38, 49, 60, 67–68, 117, 157
commencement speech, for 431 Exchange school, 179, 180

INDEX

Commercial Iron Works (CIW), 38–39, 100, 128, 171; Johnson, J., at, 128, *129*, 162; LCS, *16*
commercial shipyards, 135–36
Commission on the Status of Women, 179
competition, for women welders, 161–62, *163*, 164, *165*, *166*, *167*
complaints, against Oregon Shipbuilding Corporation, 93, 96, 98–99, 101
conditions, on shipyards, 93, *94*, *95*, 96–101, 138
Conover, David, 10
continuation school, 27, 184
counsellors, Kaiser Company, 79, 82
Courier-News (newspaper), 28, 32, 174
Culp, Oveta, 131
Curd, Mary Bryan, 79

Daily News (newspaper), 107, 111
Daily Olympian (newspaper), 68
Dear Laughing Motorbyke (Jolly), 170
debris, 69, 92, 101–2
De Cent, Reva, *167*
"Degree of Visible Fume Condition," 96–97
Denfeld, Duane Colt, 47
Department of Labor, U.S., 93, 150, 179, 184
disadvantages, of women workers, 180–81
discrimination: racial, 120, 141, 142–43, 145–46, 147, 150; women workers and, 4, 35
disintegrating flesh, *109*, 110
divorce, 26, 174, 175, 177, 204n10
Doane, F. Clyde, 28, 31, 174, 175
Doane, Gladys "Glad" (née Chase), 28–29, 31, 174, 175–76, 191n8
Does Khaki Become You? (Enloe), 127
dogmas, about women workers, 175
Don't Call Me Rosie (Thomas), 14
Dooley, Lila "Barney," 162, *163*, *167*
dormitories, 38, 65, 68–70, 117
double bottom, 102–3, 127, 128

Dougherty, Norma Jeane (Marilyn Monroe), 10
Drinker, Phillip, 107–8
dwelling units, 69, 195n10

Earle, Fred M., 170
Ebel, Erich, 115
education: Girls' Vocational School, 1, 27, 29; New York University, 1, 29; Plainfield Seminary, 23–25, 30, 190n2; Vassar College, 1, 23, 25–28
Eisenhower, Dwight D., 5, 6, 7
electrocution, 86
Elizabeth, New Jersey, 27, 30, 32, 184
Elkton, Maryland, 175
Ellis, Leona, 139, 146
Emergency Shipbuilding Program, 38, 39, 42, 61, 135
employee relations, 143
Enloe, Cynthia, 127
Equal Pay Law, 179
equipment, for women welders, 82–85
Equipment Maintenance Manual (Clawson, Augusta), 177, *178*
escort aircraft carrier, 47, 194n4
Eugene, Oregon, 148, *149*, 150
Evening Star (newspaper), 176
exclusion practices, 150
Executive Order 8802, 142, 143
Executive Order 9066, 148
exposures: to asbestos fibers, 111–13; toxic fumes, 96, 97, 99; X-ray, 109, 110, 111–12
eye injuries, on shipyards, 100
eye injury, 100

Facing the Mountain (Brown), 137
Fair Employment Practices Commission, 143, 145
FBI, 134, 157, 174, 202n16
Federal Housing Administration, 175
Federal Security Agency (FSA), 32, 33, 149
Federal Works Administration, 120

223

Field, Connie, 127–28
financial compensation, for burns, 111
fine dust, 98, 101
The Finger (shipyard publication), 157, 202n14
fires, 44, 68–69, 100, 116, 192n9
fireside address, of Roosevelt, Franklin Delano, 2, 5, 66
first aid stations, 42, 96, 108, 109, 110, 116, 117
flash burns, 100
Fleeting Opportunities (Kesselman), 189n1
Flesher, Carl, 155
flooding, of Vanport City, 67–68
flu, 103
fluoroscope machine, 108–11, 197n3
foot injuries, on shipyards, 14
Fosburgh, Bessie H. *See* Kaiser, Bessie H.
Fosburgh, Edgar F., 56, 58
431 Exchange school, 179–80
fracture, of SS *Schenectady*, 154–55, 156
FSA. *See* Federal Security Agency
fume conditions, 93, 96–97, 99–100
Furnold, Clara, 14

Gardley, Marcus, 151
Garfield, Sidney, 115–16, 121
Garfinckel, Julius, 176, 177
Gazette (newspaper), 182
Geist, Mabel, *133*
Gilbreth, Lillian, 179
Gilmore, J. F., 71–72
Girls' Vocational School, 1, 27, 29
Gold Eagle Merit Award Flag, 62, *63*
Good Samaritan Hospital, 116
Good Work, Sister! (oral history of women workers), 18
Government Girls, 12
government reports, 72, 102, 124–25, 171
Grand Coulee Dam, 59, 60, 62, 70, 115–16, 195n13
Grant, Jerry, *167*

graveyard shifts, 17, 79–80, 97, *136*, 162
Great Depression, 18–19, 148, 149, 162
gynecologist, 119

Hampson, Fred, 5
Hannah Harrison Industrial School, 175, 176–77, 185, 204n14, 204n15
HAP. *See* Housing Authority of Portland
Hawkins, Layton S., 34
Head Start program, 78
health care plan, 115, 116–21
health hazards, 99; burns, 100–101, 107, 108–9, 110–11, 116; lung and organ injury, 101; ultraviolet radiation injury, 100
Hellcats, at Oregonship, 132, *133*
Herald and News (newspaper), 15, 144
Her Finest Hour (La Du), 15, 17, 190n17
hiring practices, of Kaiser, H., 61, 194n19
Hitler, Adolf, 10–11, 63, 157
Holmes, Augustus Dole (grandfather), 21
home, of Clawson family, *22*
honors, awards and, 185–86
Hoover, J. Edgar, 174
horrible driver, 29
hospitals: ambulance services, 117, 119; Good Samaritan Hospital, 116; OHSU, 196n4; Permanente Hospitals, 56, 116–17, 120–21; shipyard, 80, 108–9, 120; St. Vincent Hospital, 116; workers, 110
Housing Authority of Portland (HAP), 69, 194n6
housing projects, 65–69, 79–80, 194n2, 194n6, 195n10
Housman, Joe, 18, 50
Housman, Lois "Missouri," 14, 18–19, 50, 51; FBI and, 134; friendship with Clawson, Augusta, 2, 171, 182
hulls, *18*, 39, *43*, 46, 90; double bottom section of, 102–3, 127, 128; fumes in, 3; height of, 101–2; of SS *Schenectady*, *154*, 155, 157, 158
Hymes, James L., 78

Index

induction process, for shipyards, 125, 132, 133–34
industrial environments, 91–92, 107–8, 135, 139, 170
industrial jobs, 34, 35, 83, 111, 124, 170
Ingalls Shipbuilding Corporation, 161, 162, *163*, 164, *165*, *166*
Ingram, Earl, 153, 201n3
injuries, on shipyards, 14, 28, 92, 100; flouroscope machine causing, 108, *109*, 110; workmen's compensation for, 96, 110, 111
instructions, for welding trainees, 88–89
International Altrusan (newspaper), 169, 180, 203n1
In the Spotlight (Vodra), 22–23

Jantzen Knitting Mills, 11
Japanese Americans, 148
Jersey Gus "Gus" (Clawson, Augusta), 36, 53
Jim Crow Shipyards, 147
Johnson, Burgess, 25–26, 190n3
Johnson, Jean Neil, 100–101, 128, *129*, 162, 171
Johnson, Lyndon, 78
Join Us in a Victory Job (poster), 8
Jolly, Margaretta, 170
Joseph N. Teal (Liberty ship), 47
Journal of Home Economics (Clawson, Augusta), 33, 91–92
judges, of women welding competition, 164, 166

Kaiser, Bessie H. (née Fosburgh), 56–59, *133*
Kaiser, Edgar F., 13–14, 58, *63*, 66–67, 80, 143; childcare centers designed by, 76, *77*; Flesher and, 155
Kaiser, Henry J., 7, 13–14, 37–38, 115, 192n11, 193n12; Calship and, 108; "Class Bitterness Most Serious Problem for Labor, Management," 144; early life of, 55–56; Gold Eagle Merit Award Flag received by, 62, *63*; hiring practices of, 61, 194n19; on housing, 65; Kaiser, B., and, 56–59; Kaiser, E., and, 66–67; letter from, 44–45; *Sidney Daily News* on, 62–63, 194n23; Six Companies, Inc. and, 59–60, 65, 195n13; Tote and, 143–44; war production influenced by, 61–63
Kaiser Company, 44, 59, 80, 135, 162; assembly line production at, 37, 38; counsellors at, 79, 82; employee relations, 143; escourt aircraft carrier launched by, 47, 194n4; flu at, 103; map of shipyards in, *118*; Permanente Health Plan, 116, 120; Permanente Hospitals, 56, 116–17, 120–21; racism and, 144–45, 146–47; Richmond shipyard, 37–38, 60, 68–69; safety record at, 103; signature identification card for, *82*; Vancouver shipyard, 7, 40, 47, *48*, 75, 147; women welders employed at, 15. *See also Bo's'n's Whistle*
Kaiser Foundation, 115
Kaiser home, in Spokane, 57, *58*
"Kaiser Is Said to Outdo Ancient," 62–63, 194n23
Kaiser Karavan, 147, 201n20
Kaiser's Child Service Centers, 76, 77, 78–80
Keefe, Mary Doyle, 10–11
Keller, Helen, 120–21
Kenyon, Eliza Elvira, 24, 25
Kesselman, Amy, 189
Key, Ella Nora, 70
Knickerbocker Village, New York City, 31
Kramer, Ann Henderson (niece), 139, 169, 182, 190n1, 191n12, 199n13
Kruif, Paul de, 115, 117–18

Laboratory of Reproductive Biology, 120
labor market, 177
La Du, Robert R., 15, 17, 46, 190n17

La Grande Observer (newspaper), 14–15
Landing Craft Infantry (LCI), 39
Landing Craft Support (LCS), 39
Landreth, Catherine, 78
launches, from shipyards, 46, *138*; A way, 17, 39, 190n19; all-feminine, 39, 40; Ellis on, 139; *Joseph N. Teal*, 47; SS *Schenectady*, 153; SS *Star of Oregon*, 39–40, *41*; Strmiska, H., on, 164; USS *Alazon Bay*, 47, *48*, 75
LCI. *See* Landing Craft Infantry
LCS. *See* Landing Craft Support
Lend-Lease Act, of 1941, 60
Liberty Mutual Insurance Co., 110
Liberty ships, 17, 40, 62, 157; Ellis on, 139; Jim Crow and, 147; *Joseph N. Teal*, 47; SS *Star of Oregon*, 39, *41*; Strmiska, H., on building, 163; women welders watching launch of, *138*
"Liberty Ships and Jim Crow Shipyards" (Linder), 147
The Life and Times of Rosie the Riveter (movie), 127–28
Life magazine, 17, 59, 193n2
Lincoln, Abraham, 31, 137
Lincoln, J. F., 153, 156, 201n1
Lincoln Electric Company, 153, 201n1
Lindbergh, Charles, 42
Linder, John, 147
Lindley-Clawson, Patricia "Pat" (grandniece), 139, 199n14
Lingenfelder, Fred (Mrs.), 39
Lionberger, Daniel O., 202n7
Lionberger, Mabel, *87*, 162, *163*, *167*
Long Beach Sun (newspaper), 111
Los Angeles Times (newspaper), 111
Luckenbach, Lewis, 156
lunch wagon, 126
lung cancer, 112
lung injury, 101
Lyle, Cornelia E., 27

Magic Carpet Special, 147, 201n20
Maidenform Company, 83

maim, 108, *109*, 111
manpower, 5, 6, 123, 147, 180, 181
Manpower Development and Training Act, of 1961, 179
map of shipyards, Kaiser Company, *118*
March on Washington, DC Movement (MOWM), 142–43
Marin Shipbuilding Corporation (Marinship), 123–24
Maritime Commission, U.S., 17, 201n2; Awards from, 40, 44–46, *45*, 62, 138; Bruns and, 153, 201; childcare funded by, 75; Emergency Shipbuilding Program, 38, 39, 42, 61, 135; Gold Eagle Merit Award Flag, 62, *63*; *The Victory Fleet* publication for, 76, 124, 125
Marshall, Beatrice, 141, 146
Martin, Jane, 5–6
masters in personnel administration, from New York University, 1, 29
Matchett, Mayme, *133*
McCaughey, Verna, *133*
McCullough, Wava, 170
McGowan Bros., 57
"McLean's Augusta Holmes Clawson: 80 and Rollin'" (Robinson), 182
McLemore, Henry, 62
Meadowlark Trailer Camp, 71, *72*
Medford Mail Tribune (newspaper), 13, 14
medical centers, 38, 116, 117
medical questionnaire, on shipyard conditions, *94*, *95*
Mein Kampf (Hitler), 10–11
"A Menace to the Neighborhood" (Pearson), 142
mesothelioma, 112, 198n10
metal burns, 100
Metal Trades Council, of Portland, 93, 153, 201n3
Missouri. *See* Housman, Lois
modern college girl, 25–26, 190n3
"Modern Girl" (Johnson, B.), 190n3
Monday Afternoon Club, 24, 30
Moore, Louise, 32

INDEX

morale, on shipyards, 62, 89, 101, 134, 135, 138
MOWM. *See* March on Washington, DC Movement
Multnomah Hotel, 50, 72, *73*, 155–56
Munson, Cora, 116
M. W. (reporter), 172–73, 203n8
"My Day" (Roosevelt, Eleanor), 167

National Geographic Magazine, 8
National Youth Administration (NYA), 146, 148–50
Native Americans, 148, *149*, 150, 201n24
"Native American Women from Chemawa Train to Work in Shipyards" (Platt), 150
Nazis, 44, 192n9
Negroes. *See* African Americans
Neil, Clara, 16
Neil, Jean, 16
nerve strain, 131
Nevins, Allan, 190n20
New Jersey: Bridgewater, 28, 32, 191n8; Elizabeth, 27, 30, 32, 184; Girls' Vocational School, 1, 27, 29; Plainfield, 1, *24*; Plainfield Book Shop, Inc., 27–28; Plainfield Seminary in, 23–25, 30, 190n2
Newport Daily News (newspaper), 176
New York City, 30–31, 147, 171
New York University, 1, 29
Nieman, A. R., 46, 192n12
Nimitz, Chester W., 5, 7, 189n1
noises, 3, 87–88, 103, 131
Northern Permanente Foundation, 116–17, 120
NYA. *See* National Youth Administration

Oakland Tribune (newspaper), 144
oakum, 44
O'Dea, Mark, *63*
O'Donnell, Mary M., 177, *178*
Office of Education, U.S., 3, 33, 34, 36, 72, 183, 185
Office of War Information (OWI), 6–7, 10

OHSU. *See* Oregon Health & Science University
Oldham, Kit, 66
Olsen, Betty, 14
Ordway, Mr., 143
Oregon: Eugene, 148, *149*, 150; Ross Island, 16, 39, 100, *129*; University of Oregon Medical School, 93. *See also* Portland
Oregon Daily Journal (newspaper), 75, 157–58, 201n1, 201n2; Ingram in, 201n3; Luckenback in, 156; SS *Schenectady* mentioned in, 202n6, 202n15, 202n16; on Vickery, 155, 202n8
Oregon Employment Services, 81
Oregon Health & Science University (OHSU), 196n4
Oregon Historical Society, 38, 79
Oregon History Project, 148
Oregonian (newspaper), 143, 147, 163, 164, 201n20
Oregon Shipbuilding Corporation (Oregonship), 7, *12*, *18*, *138*; all-feminine launching, 39, 40; competition for women welders at, 161–62, *163*, 164, *165*, *166*, *167*; complaints against, 93, 96, 98–99, 101; dormitories at, 70; Hellcats at, 132, *133*; Peron at, 162; racism at, 146; *Report of the Investigation of Fume Hazards* at, 93, *94*, *95*, 96–101; SS *Star of Oregon*, 39, *41*. *See also* women welders
Oregon's State Industrial Accident Commission, 93, 96, 100
Oregon Trail (tanker), 49
organ injury, 101
orientation meetings, 50, 51
OWI. *See* Office of War Information

Pacific Diagnostic Offices, 109
Pacific Northwest, 65, 71, 148; Columbia River in, 7, 38, 49, 60, 67–68, 117, 157; Grand Coulee Dam, 59, 60,

227

62, 70, 115–16, 195n13; shipyard workers in, 2, 7, 59, 60; war production in, 141; women welders in, 3, 11
Panic, of 1893, 55–56, 193n3
"Panic of 1893 and Its Aftermath" (Caldbick), 193n3
Pasadena, California, 12, 189n11
Pathfinder (booklet), 55
patriotism, 4, 75, 132, 134
Pearl Harbor, Hawaii, 1–2, 62; attack on, 15–16, 60, 148; X-rays and, 111, 113
Pearson, Rudy, 142
Penguin Books Inc (publishing company), 2, 171, 186
"Percentage of Women in Maritime Shipyards," 37–38, 125
Permanente Health Plan, 116, 120
Permanente Hospitals, 56, 116–17, 120–21
Peron, Cecile, 162
Peters, Hannah, 119–20
Peterson, Margaret, *167*
Pidgeon, Mary E., 124
pinup girls, 8
Pittsburgh Courier (newspaper), 150
Plainfield, New Jersey, 1, *24*, 175, 176; Clawson family home in, *22*; rally in, 34
Plainfield Book Shop, Inc., 27–28
Plainfield High School Alumnus (pseudonym), 32
Plainfield Seminary, 23–25, 30, 190n2
Platt, A. E., 150
Portland, Oregon, 155; CIW, *16*, 38–39, 100, 128, *129*, 162, 171; HAP, 69, 194n6; *Her Finest Hour* on, 15, 17, 190n17; Jantzen Knitting Mills, 11; Metal Trades Council of, 93, 153, 201n3; Port of, 42; Post Office, 81; Willamette River, 7, 17, 36, 39, 49. *See also* Swan Island Shipyard
Port of Portland, 42
posters, for war effort, 8–10, *9*, *12*, 151

poster slogans, 8–10
Post Office, of Portland, 81
Poughkeepsie, New York, 25, *26*
prepared family meals, 78, 79, 80
prevention care, 100, 119–20, 121
professional organizations, associations and, 30
protective devices, 92, 98–99, 100–101
published articles, 33

racial discrimination, 120, 141, 142–43, 145–46, 147, 150
racial prejudice, 67, 79, 145, 194n6
racism, 144–45, 146–47, 150
radial wheel plan design, 77, 79
rally, for Women in Action, 34
Randle, Aaron, 143
Randolph, A. Phillip, 142
Raymond, Martha, *133*
Reader's Digest, 117–18
Reagan, Ronald, 10
Reid, Frances, *133*
Report of the Investigation of Fume Hazards at the Oregon Shipbuilding Company at St. Johns, Portland, Oregon, 93, *94*, *95*, 96–101
"Report on Welding Training and Shipyard Employment" (Clawson, Augusta), 36, 84–85, 137–38, 139, 171
Research Library, Oregon Historical Society, 38
respiratory problems, 3, 99, 113, 134
retirement, 181
reunion forms, 23, 26–27, 184–86
Rieke, Forrest E., 99–100, 101
"Riveting, Dealing with Chef's Part of Speaker's Past" (Winfree), 190n5
Robinson, Dave, 182–83, 186–87
rocket-fuel propelled weapons, 12, 189n11
Rocket Girls, 12
Rockwell, Norman, 10–11, 189n9
rods, for welding, 85, 86, 88, 132, 166
Roedel, Heinrich, 44

INDEX

Roosevelt, Eleanor, 47, *48*, *49*, 75–76, 141, 166–67
Roosevelt, Franklin Delano, 7, 39, 141; Executive Order 8802 and, 142, 143; Executive Order 9066 and, 148; fireside address by, 2, 5, 66; NYA established by, 148–49; shipyards visited by, 47; WPA classes, 11, 16
Rosie the Riveter, 10–11, 151, 189n9
Ross Island, Oregon, 16, 39, 100, *129*
routine, at Swan Island Shipyard, 2

Safety Building Clinic, 116
safety clothing, 33, 91–92
safety lectures, 86
"Safety Pays" (employee newsletter), *104*, *105*
Sales, Vivian, *133*
Sandburg, Carl, 30–31, 186, 187
San Francisco Examiner (newspaper), 62
Santa Cruz Sentinel (newspaper), 44
Saturday Evening Post (newspaper), 44
Schenectady, SS, *154*, 155–58; Best Woman Welder in the World competition as distraction from, 161; launch of, 153; *Oregon Daily Journal* on, 202n6, 202n15, 202n16
The School That Would Not Die (documentary), 180
sea trials, 153, *154*
Secondary Teacher's Club, 30
Secret Service, 47
sexual harassment, 125
Shade, Leadman Paul, *133*
Shaw, James A., "Tote," 143–44
sheet metal, 15
shipfitters, 89, 97, 102, 103, *138*
Shipyard Diary of a Woman Welder (Clawson, Augusta), 2, 102–3, 171–73, *173*, 186, 203n3
shipyard employment report. *See* "Report on Welding Training and Shipyard Employment"

Shipyard Negro Organization for Victory, 144–45
shipyard publications: *Bo's'n's Whistle*, 14, 47, 62, 65, 78–80, 116–17, 135, 138, 196n12; *The Finger*, 157, 202n14
shipyards: a way, 17, 39, 190n19; Arab employees in, 147; asbestos exposure on, 113; childcare on, 75–76, *77*, 78–80, 171; Chinese Americans in, 147–48; commercial, 135–36; conditions on, 93, *94*, *95*, 96–101, 138; dormitories at, 38, 65, 68–70, 117; health care plan on, 115, 116–19, 120; hospital for, 80, 108–9, 120; induction process for, 125, 132, 133–34; Japanese Americans in, 148; Jim Crow, 147; La Du describing, 17; Martin on, 5–6; medical centers on, 38, 116, 117; morale on, 62, 89, 101, 134, 135, 138; musical entertainment on, 136; Native Americans and, 148, *149*, 150, 201n24; noises on, 3, 87–88, 103, 131; orientation meetings at, 50, 51; Pacific Northwest, 2, 7, 59, 60; production and repair of war-bound vessels at, 38–40; protective devices at, 92, 98–99, 100; racial discrimination and, 120, 141, 142–43, 145–46, 147, 150; racial prejudice and, 67, 79, 145, 194n6; racism and, 144–45, 146–47, 150; venereal disease in, 119–20; workers housing projects for, 65–66. *See also* injuries; Kaiser Company; launches, from shipyards; Swan Island Shipyard; women welders
Shorty McGinnis (nickname), 70–71, 102
Sidney Daily News (newspaper), 62–63, 194n23
signature identification card, *82*
Six Companies, Inc., 59–60, 65, 115, 195n13
skin cancer, 101
slag burns, 100

229

Snyder, Lois Wilkie, 75–76
"Soldiers Without Guns" (poster), *12*
Sondey, Meg, 203n3
Special Agent, Training Women, 3, 33, 179
Spokane, Washington, 57–59
Spokane Daily Chronicle (newspaper), 56
Spokesman-Review (newspaper), 57, 135
Star of Oregon, SS (Liberty ship), 39, *41*
Statesman Journal, 5–6, 145, 158
Stellar, Robert Woodley, 108–9
sterility, of welders, 107–8
Stolz, Lois Meek, 78
Streep, Meryl, 27
Strmiska, Edward, 162
Strmiska, Hermina "Billie," 161–63, 203n4; Anderson and, *165*, *166*; at Ingalls Shipbuilding Corporation, *165*
Stroman, Sarah, 79
St. Vincent Hospital, 116
suckers, 98
Sunday Oregonian (newspaper), 162–63
Swan Island Boys, 156, 157
Swan Island Municipal Airport, 41
Swan Island Shipyard, 6, 7, 17, 40, *42*, *43*; asbestos exposure on, 112–13; assignment ending at, 169–70; barracks on, 66, 70; certificate of availability for, 81; childcare at, 78–79, 80, 196n12; Clawson, Augusta, at, *52*; dormitories at, 69–70; housing for, 66; Nieman, and, 46, 192n12; *Oregon Trail* at, 49; production in, 42–44, 158; "Report on Welding Training and Shipyard Employment," 35–36; Roosevelt, F., visiting, 47; routine at, 2; SS *Schenectady* and, *154*, 155–58; T2 tankers at, 47, 153; training at, 2, 11, 34, 178–79, 203n1; welding school for, 85–86. *See also* women welders

T2 tankers, at Swan Island Shipyard, 47, 153

Taylor, Frank J., 44
teacher, at Girls' Vocational School, 1, 27, 29
Terminal Island shipyard, 17
Terrell, John Upton, 107, 110, 197n5
Texas (friend), 128
Theus, Gladys, 150
Thomas, Kathleen, 17
Thomas A. Edison Vocational School, 29, 32
Thompson, James G., 150
Thornbury, Zita L., 33
"The Time is Now!" (Clawson, Augusta), 34–35
Tin Hatters (swing band), *136*
toastmistress, for Altrusa International Service Club, 174, 185
Tojo, Hideki, 157, 202n14
toolbox accident, 101
Tote. *See* Shaw, James A.
Towell, Georgie, *133*
toxic fumes, 3, 92–93, *94*, 96–103, 111, 116
Trade and Industrial Education for Girls and Women, FSA, 32
trailer park, for shipyard workers, 70, *71*, *72*
Training Women for War Production, 3, 19, 33, 34
Truman, Harry, 174
turnover rate, of women welders, 19, 33, 87–88, 175

ultraviolet radiation injury, 100
unions: auxiliary, 145; boilermakers, 144–45; hiring hall, 81–82
United States (U.S.): Department of Labor, 93, 150, 179, 184; Employment Services, 61, 194n19; Office of Education in, 3, 33, 34, 36, 72, 183, 185. *See also* Maritime Commission
University of Oregon Medical School, 93
U.S. *See* United States

Index

vacuum cleaners, 98, 101
Vancouver, Washington, 189n5; Blood Center in, 120–21; Columbia River, 7, 38, 49, 60, 67–68, 117, 157; Kaiser Vancouver Shipyard in, 7, 40, 47, *48*, 75, 147
Vanport City (housing project), 67–69, 79–80, 194n2, 194n6
Vassar Alumnae Magazine, 34–35, 191n16
Vassar Alumnae Register, 177, 179
Vassar College, 28, 181, 182; Associate Alumnae, 29; graduate of, 1; Johnson, B., and, 25–26, 190n3; reunion forms, 23, 26–27, 184–86; senior portrait at, *26*; Vocational Bureau of, 33
Vassar Quarterly (newspaper), 28, 181
venereal disease, 119–20
ventilation, 88, 92–93, 98, 101
Vickery, Howard L., 42, 155–56, 158, 202n8
Victory Center, 137
The Victory Fleet (Maritime Commission publication), 76, 124, *125*
Virginia Chronicle (newspaper), 176
Virginia Gazette (newspaper), 182, 186
V-mail (Army Micro Photographic Mail Service), 8
Vocational Bureau, Vassar College, 33
Vocational Division, of Office of Education, U.S., 3, 34
Vocational Education, 36, 169–70, 176
vocational work, for women, 1, 2, 4, 32, 146, 176. *See also* Girls' Vocational School
Vodra, Bettie, 22–23
Vogelzang Law, 112
voltages, 85, 107–8
volunteer work, 185
Voshell, Les, 162, *163*

Wallace, Anne, 90, 102
Wanda the Welder, 3, 12
War Bonds, 82, 84, 136–37, 164, 166

war effort: OWI and, 7; posters for, 8–10, *9*, *12*; progress of, 6; support of, 2–3, 32
War Jobs for Women (informative booklet), 76
"War Jobs for Women" (OWI booklet), 6–7
War Manpower Commission, 9, 76, 123, 148, 149, 172–73
war production, 148, 169, 171, 172–73, 174; Kaiser, H., influence on, 61–63; NYA training and, 150; in Pacific Northwest, 141; repair and, 38–40; Training Women for, 3, 19, 33, 34; women workers and, 2–3, 6–8, 11, 18–19, 35
War Production Board, 19
"War Shifts the Emphasis" (Clawson, Augusta), 32
Washington, DC, 32, 47, 166, 176; agencies in, 19; Altrusa Club, 174; Federal Club Toastmistress in, 185; March on, 142; Metropolitan Chapter of the Arthritis Foundation in, 181; Office of Education in, 3, 33
"Washington Day Book" (Blads), 176
Waterman, Isaiah, 108–9
"We Can Do It" (poster), 10, 151
welderettes, 3, 163, 164
"Welders Assured," 107
welders booth, 31, 85, 92
Welder's Wheeze, 92
welding arcs, 107, 108
welding cart, *87*
welding helmet, *187*
welding instructors, 85–86
welding process, 85, 88–90, 100
welding rods, 85, 86, 88, 132, 166
welding school, 16, 84–86, 164
welding textbooks, 86
welding trainees, 85–90, 148, 183
welfare, of women workers, 76
Wendy the Welder, 3, 12

whirley, 101, 119
White House, 142, 166, 174
White's Biographical Bulletin, 56
"Who Is the Champion Woman Shipyard Welder?" (newspaper article), *167*, 203n11
Wiley, Bonnie, 163, 164
Willamette River, 7, 17, 36, 39, 49
Winfree, Flora Ann, 190n5
Winnie the Welder, 3, 12
Winston-Salem Journal (newspaper), 174–75
Wolff and Phillips architects, 76, 195n5
womanpower, 6, 123, 180
"Women at Work" (Bradley), 8, 15
Women in Action, rally, 34
Women Ordnance Workers (WOW), 11
"Women's Work and the War" (Pidgeon), 124
women welders, *13*, 18, 123–25, *138*, 139; camaraderie of, 3–4, 132–33; competition for, 161–62, *163*, 164, *165*, *166*, *167*; cultural influence of, 151; *Dear Laughing Motorbyke* about, 170; depicted in *The Life and Times of Rosie the Riveter*, 127–28; Earle on, 170; equipment for, 82–85; Furnold as first, 14; gynecologist for, 119; health hazards of, 99–100; hull assembly, *127*; Kaiser Company employed, 15; nerve strain of, 131; in Pacific Northwest, 3, 11; poster of, *126*; Strmiska, H., as, 162–64; Theus as, 150; training for, 2, 3, 5, 11, 81–90, 203n1; turnover rate of, 19, 33, 87–88, 175; Wallace on, 90; welding school for, 16, 84–86, 164; "Who Is the Champion Woman Shipyard Welder?," *167*, 203n11; working conditions for, 50–51

women workers, 131, 183; *Bomb-Bomb Girls*, 175; cancer in, 120; childcare for, 75–76, 77, 78–80, 171; disadvantages of, 180–81; discrimination against, 4, 35; dogmas about, 175; *Good Work, Sister!* on, 18; in industrial environments, 91–92, 107–8, 135, 139, 170; as inventory of industry itself, 14–15; Native Americans as, 148, *149*, 150; "Percentage of Women in Maritime Shipyards," 37–38; safety clothing for, 33, 91–92; vocational work for, 1, 2, 4, 32, 146; war production and, 2–3, 6–8, 11, 18–19, 35; welfare of, 76. *See also* women welders
Woodhouse, Chase Going, 179
working conditions, 50–51
workmen's compensation, 96, 110, 111
Works Progress Administration (WPA), 11, 16, 149
World War I, 25, 39
World War II, 1, 2–3, 25, 29, 121; asbestos and, 111–12; *Facing the Mountain* on, 137; La Du on, 17; NYA and, 149
WOW. *See* Women Ordnance Workers
WPA. *See* Works Progress Administration

X-ray burns, 111
X-rays, 107, 108, *109*, 111–12, 117, 197n3. *See also* fluoroscope machine

Yank (weekly publication), 10

Zimmerman, Hazel, *133*

ABOUT THE AUTHOR

MARK J. ANTHONY, ANTHONY PRODUCTIONS

Beverly Lionberger Hodgins was born in Portland, Oregon, and for many years enjoyed the surrounding rivers, lakes, mountains, and forests before moving to equally lovely Washington State. As the great-granddaughter of Oregon pioneers, Lionberger Hodgins has a distinct interest in all things regarding the settling, development, and history of the Pacific and Inland Northwest, and enjoys writing about fascinating people who lived before—particularly women who lived life on their own terms.

Lionberger Hodgins's screenplay *Wayward Warrior*, based on her husband's Vietnam service, was a semi-finalist for the Film*Makers* International Screenwriting Awards. She once served as a personal interest story reporter for the Washington State Employee Intranet. She is the author of *Mercy and Madness: Dr. Mary Archard Latham's Tragic Fall from Female Physician to Felon*, the essay "A New Dawn" published in the anthology *Chocolate for a Woman's Courage*, and poems published in college literary reviews. She lives in Spokane, Washington, with her husband, Tom.

www.ingramcontent.com/pod-product-compliance
Lightning Source LLC
Chambersburg PA
CBHW020405080526
44584CB00014B/1177